WOMEN'S HEALTH

Psychological and Social Perspectives

Christina Lee

SAGE Publications
London • Thousand Oaks • New Delhi

First published 1998

SAGE Publications Ltd
6 Bonhill Street
London EC2A 4PU

SAGE Publications Inc
2455 Teller Road
Thousand Oaks, California 91320

SAGE Publications India Pvt Ltd
32, M-Block Market
Greater Kailash – I
New Delhi 110 048

British Library Cataloguing in Publication data

A catalogue record for this book is available from the British Library

ISBN 0 7619 5728 6
ISBN 0 7619 5729 4 (pbk)

Library of Congress catalog card number 98-060526

Typeset by Photoprint, Torquay, Devon
Printed in Great Britain by Redwood Books, Trowbridge, Wiltshire

Women's Health

BEHAVIOUR AND HEALTH

EDITORS:

Christine Eiser
Reader in Psychology
University of Exeter, England

Jan Wallander
Professor of Psychology and Nursing
Civitan International Research Center, Alabama, USA

The application of psychological principles to health and illness is a rapidly developing field. Health psychology represents a synthesis of psychology, behavioural medicine, health behaviour, medical sociology and public health, and there has been an explosion in the numbers of students both at undergraduate and postgraduate level, with backgrounds ranging from psychology through sociology, nursing and public health.

Sage's series, *Behaviour and Health*, is a forum for introductory but scholarly volumes covering major topics and issues of interest in health and psychology.

For Harry

CONTENTS

ACKNOWLEDGEMENTS

The University of Newcastle, Australia, funded the twelve-month sabbatical which made it possible for me to write this book, and many people provided very generous support during this time. I am particularly grateful to Kerry Chamberlain and John Spicer of the Department of Psychology, Massey University, New Zealand; Keith Petrie of the Department of Psychiatry and Behavioural Science, University of Auckland, New Zealand; and Jane Ussher of the Department of Psychology, University College London, for arranging for me to spend some very productive time in each of those institutions, as well as to Christine Eiser and Jan Wallander, series editors, who accepted the proposal for this book and encouraged me in its preparation.

I am also appreciative of the many other colleagues, students and friends who gave me inspiration, discussed ideas, provided practical support, shared resources, and drank coffee with me during the writing of this book. These people include Felicity Allen, Kylie Ball, Wendy Brown, Claire Budge, Tarnya Davis, Joy Ellem, Kate France, Myra Hunter, Tannis Laidlaw, Janice Langan-Fox, Antonia Lyons, Rona Moss-Morris, Janice Muir, Margot Schofield, Lorraine Slaven, Christine Stephens and Trecia Wouldes. In particular I would like to thank the Women's Health Australia research team, and my family, for their support.

Most of all, I would like to thank Harry for his unfailing practical and emotional support.

1

THE SOCIAL CONTEXT OF WOMEN'S HEALTH

A central characteristic of male-dominated societies is that they implicitly define men as the norm, as standard human beings, and women as 'other'. Almost universally, human cultures are basically patriarchal in structure; they construct men's interests and concerns as more legitimate and more central than women's, and position men and men's lives as worthy in themselves, while regarding women as valuable chiefly in terms of their value to men, their relationships with men, and their differences from men (Millett, 1970). This cultural perspective has meant that theory, research and application in most academic fields have focused primarily on men, and health research has been no exception (Stanton, 1995). This, together with linguistic traditions that equate 'man' with 'adult human' and regard 'woman' as a special case, has meant that the study of 'women's health' has until recently been restricted to obstetric and gynaecological issues, and has tended to assume that the only interesting thing about women's health is reproductive capacity (Ussher, 1992b).

This traditional, patriarchal perspective has been challenged by feminist researchers who take a woman-centred perspective on health, one which starts from a perception that women's perspectives, women's subjectivity, are as legitimate as are men's. 'Women's health', from this perspective, is much more than obstetrics and gynaecology. Several health psychologists have argued that 'women's health' must be defined as broadly as possible, including all those diseases and physical processes which occur in women, and emphasizing those which occur frequently in women, those which are unique to women, and those which are more common among women than among men (Chesney & Ozer, 1995; Rodin & Ickovics, 1990). Arguments are made for the importance of understanding women and heart disease, women and stress, women and autoimmune diseases, women and smoking (e.g. Stanton & Gallant, 1995b).

However, if one argues that the psychology of women's health must encompass absolutely everything which is relevant to the health of women, then the study of women's health risks becoming a fairly random selection from an endless series of discrete topics, related only trivially to each other. While such an approach can cover important topics in women's health it lacks a conceptual focus.

The central issue for this book is the social construction of gender. From a psychological point of view, the unique aspects of women's health are those which are affected by women's social roles, and not purely by their biology. This book explores the ways in which social myths and stereotypes about appropriate or 'natural' behaviour for women impact on their well-being. An emphasis on social contexts and their impact on women's lives also means that a focus on specific illnesses and risk factors is seen as less important than an analysis which deals primarily with the essentially social nature of gender and of sex roles. This means that the book omits a number of topics which are central to women's physical health, most importantly heart disease and cancer. While these are the major causes of death and ill-health among women, it is not clear that women's social roles play a major part in women's experiences of these conditions.

WOMEN, MEN, AND MAJOR CAUSES OF DEATH

Recent volumes on the psychology of women's health (e.g. Adesso, Reddy & Fleming, 1994; Niven & Carroll, 1993; Stanton & Gallant, 1995b) have focused on the two major contributors to death and ill-health among Western women, cancer and heart disease. While these are clearly topics of major importance for women's health, as indeed they are for men's health, they are peripheral to a psychology of women's health which focuses on the social construction of gender. There are differences between men and women in the aetiology and prognosis of cardio-vascular diseases, in the commonest sites of cancers, and in reactions to treatment (e.g. Lerner & Kannel, 1986; Meyerowitz & Hart, 1995). However, these differences are to a large extent biological rather than social or psychological, and there is little evidence for major psychological differences between women and men in how they deal with the crisis of life-threatening illness. Thus, in a book which aims to explore aspects of society which make women's health-related experiences different from those of men, these medically important topics are of limited relevance.

Of course, both heart disease and cancer can be approached from a social perspective. Although coronary heart disease is less common in women than in men, rates of mortality and of long-term disability are higher for women (Wenger, Speroff & Packard, 1993), and there is some evidence to suggest that this is because women are likely to receive less effective treatment than are men (e.g. Young & Kahana, 1993). In general, however, research seems to suggest that the major risk factors of smoking, sedentariness, stress and social isolation are broadly the same for women and for men (e.g. Shumaker & Smith, 1995), and that the central experiences associated with heart disease, such as pain, anxiety, intrusive medical procedures, and major life changes, are also much the same for women as they are for men. What is needed is not so much a search for women's unique psychological experiences of heart diseases as a less biased programme of biomedical research and intervention.

A similar argument may be raised for cancer. Men and women tend to develop different types of cancer, with breast cancer being the most commonly diagnosed cancer in women, and prostate cancer in men, although lung cancer is the next most common for both sexes (American Cancer Society, 1994). It is argued (e.g. Meyerowitz & Hart, 1995; Wilkinson & Kitzinger, 1994) that research on cancer in women has tended to focus on cancer of the breast and reproductive organs, and to emphasize physical appearance and sexuality rather than other aspects of women's experiences of cancer and its treatment. But again it would seem that the experiences of pain, intrusive and noxious treatment, physical decline and incipient death may show more similarities than differences between the genders.

WOMEN'S HEALTH OR WOMEN'S ILLNESS

To a large extent, the study of 'women's health' has in fact been the study of women's illness, with an emphasis on specific risk factors and health-related behaviours. Major texts on women's health emphasize heart disease, cancer, menstrual and reproductive disorders, and behaviours such as smoking, drug use and medical screening. These are important topics, but they reflect a particular perspective on the psychology of women's health, with an emphasis on specific illnesses, specific causes of death, and intra-individual factors, rather than on the woman in a complex social and cultural context.

This perspective arises from the empiricist and reductionist approach which psychology has traditionally taken to its subject matter. The empiricist position emphasizes experimental control and the study of individual phenomena independently of their contexts, and this leads naturally to a reductionist focus on intra-individual factors. The primary aim of this book is to present an alternative perspective, to examine the psychology of women's health by examining the contexts within which women live.

Further, the book examines issues which are relevant to the everyday lives of all women throughout their lifespans, rather than focusing on illness and death, and on specific 'health behaviours'. While the experiences of women undergoing treatment for cancer, substance abuse or HIV/AIDS are important topics, the emphasis here is on everyday life

rather than on major health crises. The book explores women's experiences as parents, as family members, as employees and as members of
society, demonstrating the ways in which social inequities and social
assumptions about womanhood influence every aspect of women's lives,
and thus their physical and emotional health.

The primarily social and integrative perspective of this book is
supported by the fact that it adopts an explicitly feminist approach.
Psychology has traditionally taken the view that researchers should aim
to be value-free and should endeavour, as much as possible, to leave
social and political perspectives out of research. Clearly, however, all
research has a political dimension. Mainstream psychological research
on cigarette smoking, for example, which focuses on the individual
and ignores the social and economic context within which individual
decisions are made, is just as political as is research which focuses on the
economic environment that supports individuals' decisions to smoke
(Biglan, Glasgow & Singer, 1990).

Despite psychology's aspirations to the value-neutral methods and
models of classical physics, individual human beings cannot be understood without an appreciation of their sociocultural contexts (Sarason,
1981). Prilleltensky (1989) has argued that psychological research is
always political. Research which ignores the social context, which treats
it as a neutral background or as an inevitable aspect of an immutable
reality, is politically conservative rather than neutral, seeking solutions to
human problems in individual adaptation rather than in social change
(Bailey & Eastman, 1994; Kipnis, 1994; Spence, 1985). Conversely, a
psychology of women's health which starts from the perspective of the
social construction of womanhood is inevitably oriented towards social
explanations and social solutions.

FEMINISM, SCIENCE AND THE PSYCHOLOGY OF
WOMEN'S HEALTH

Feminism and social issues

While the psychology of women's health does not inevitably require
a feminist approach, the sociocultural perspective does lend itself to a
more political analysis than is usual in psychological work, and thus it
is useful to discuss the range of views, encompassed by the term
'feminism', which underlie the research and scholarship reviewed in
later chapters.

Three major types of feminism are usually distinguished (e.g. Riger,
1992), although these perspectives often overlap in practice. *Liberal
feminism*, firstly, is based on the assumption that sexism and inequity are
not inherent in the structure of society, but arise incidentally from
individuals' socialization experiences and expectations. Sexism is self-

perpetuating, because each successive generation is exposed to the same socialization processes. Yet at the same time it is readily changeable through strategies which raise people's awareness of social inequities. Change, according to this perspective, requires the promotion at an individual level of liberal values such as tolerance and respect for diversity, and the identification and modification of legislation, socialization practices and social institutions which cause specific inequities. This perspective sees social institutions as essentially benign and egalitarian, and sexism as accidental and readily eradicable through fairly minor changes to the detail of cultural institutions and customs.

Radical feminism, by contrast, takes as its foundation the view that power inequities between men and women are not accidental, but inherent in the structure of human society. This position holds that the dominant cultural discourses of patriarchal societies position men as 'naturally' superior to women. Social institutions, including law, government, education, employment and childcare systems, militate against women's freedom to live as they choose and to participate in society as the equals of men. By extension, radical feminism holds that changes to sex-based inequities will not result from the promotion of liberal or tolerant attitudes or from changes to the detail of our social lives, but only from fundamental change to the structure of society and the assumptions which underlie social organization.

A third perspective, *socialist* or *Marxist feminism*, extends the radical argument by proposing that capitalism and patriarchy are intrinsically connected and that the creation of a non-sexist society would require the dismantling of capitalism and its replacement with a radically different social system which acknowledged the role of women's unpaid labour in the maintenance of society.

These three approaches all identify fundamental inequalities between men and women, and regard these inequalities as unjustifiable. They differ radically, however, in their perspectives on the source of the inequity and thus in their views of the action required to change the situation. For example, despite equal-pay legislation in the majority of Western societies, women still earn significantly less than men (e.g. Australian Bureau of Statistics, 1995; Social Trends, 1995; US Bureau of Labor Statistics, 1991). From a liberal feminist perspective, this difference may be explained by socialization and education practices which discourage girls from entering high-paying and high-status occupations. Therefore, efforts to increase women's financial power should focus on raising girls' academic self-confidence and encouraging girls to consider taking the 'hard' options at school.

A radical feminist perspective, by contrast, would see this difference as arising from a social structure which values and rewards traditionally male occupations, such as the building trades, more highly than traditionally female occupations, such as nursing, and from a structure which places the unpaid burden of childcare and domestic labour inequitably on individual women. From this point of view, individual women's attitudes and choices are less important than the social forces which maintain an inequitable structure. Finally, a socialist feminist perspective would argue that the capitalist system relies on the exploitation of male workers, who in turn can only survive and raise families by exploiting their female partners, and that the balance can be redressed only by a revolutionary political change in the relationship between labour and capital.

Feminism and science

The idea of feminist science may seem alien to the psychologist who adopts a traditional, empiricist approach to knowledge, with its assumption of the unbiased, value-neutral observer. Feminist approaches to scientific epistemology, however, are based on the assumption that human observers are never unbiased. The social sciences in particular cannot be conducted from a position of neutrality, so it is important to acknowledge and explore the nature of the observer's bias.

Again, three main perspectives can be identified (Harding, 1986). *Feminist empiricism* adopts traditional scientific methods, with their emphasis on objectivity, replicability and experimental control, but aims to develop hypotheses, and interpret findings, with a conscious avoidance of sexist assumptions. This is perhaps the most common approach to research in the psychology of women's health, and the one which is most compatible with research traditions in psychology more generally. From this perspective, feminism in research means avoiding sexism through attention to women's perspectives, including such strategies as the inclusion of female subjects and of topics of particular relevance to women, avoidance of inappropriate over-generalization from male research samples, and avoidance of the interpretation of gender differences as evidence of the inferiority of women (Denmark, Russo, Frieze & Sechzer, 1988; McHugh, Koeske & Frieze, 1986).

A second perspective, *feminist standpoint* epistemology, rejects the notion of a single universal truth, holding instead that what is true depends on the point of view of the observer. Feminist standpoint approaches do not attempt to achieve experimental control by removing the event under investigation from its context. Rather, they take the individual-in-context as the basic unit of analysis and examine the role of social structures, social expectations and social constructions in the development of individual patterns of behaviour (Striegel-Moore, 1994). This perspective tends to be associated with the use of a broader range of scientific methods. Qualitative and exploratory methods, such as focus groups, semi-structured interviews and participant observation, are seen as having a role in the acquisition of knowledge which is equal to, although different from, that of more traditional empirical approaches. This research perspective is also associated with a different relationship between researcher and participants. Participants are viewed as collaborators in the research process, rather than as objects to be observed, and participants' perspectives on the topic and the research process are viewed as legitimate sources of hypotheses, methods and interpretations (Riger, 1992).

A third perspective on research, *feminist postmodernism*, takes a more radical perspective. Postmodernism regards all knowledge as socially constructed through language. Since we can have no other access to reality than through language, it is possible to regard reality itself as existing only as a social construction. The main tool of postmodernism, discourse analysis, seeks to analyse and to deconstruct this socially created reality, in order to demonstrate its arbitrariness (Gavey, 1989).

To an empirical scientist, the differences between standpoint epistemology and postmodernism may seem quite minor. Both reject the concept which is central to empirical science, that of an absolute external truth, in favour of the acceptance of multiple perspectives and multiple realities. There is, however, an essential difference in that standpoint epistemology requires the researchers to make an explicit judgement about the value of a particular standpoint for specific political or social aims, while postmodernism takes as its central assumption the arbitrariness of all standpoints, including feminism.

These three perspectives are very different, and thus the styles of research which arise from them are very different. For example, research on eating disorders which uses traditional psychological methods tends to emphasize the personal characteristics of women who develop eating disorders, and to assume that these characteristics are the major cause of disordered eating and should be the major focus of interventions. Standpoint-based research is more likely to examine social stereotypes of an attractive female body, media images of women, social pressures which make appearance salient for women, and broader social structures which lead to women being seen as objects for men's gaze rather than people in their own right, implying that these social factors are the major cause of disordered eating. A postmodern perspective might focus, not on the individual nor on the social structure which constrains that individual's choices, but on the way in which society constructs the concept of attractiveness and the role of body weight in that construction.

The three broad categories of feminist research, like the three broad categories of feminism, have in common an assumption that women's lives cannot be understood independently of their social context, whether that context is seen as essentially benign but in need of slight rearrangement, as fundamentally inequitable, or as totally arbitrary. Any approach to the psychology of women's health which emphasizes social context, then, will demonstrate considerable overlaps with these feminist perspectives.

GENDER, HEALTH AND SOCIAL CONTEXT

So what is the social context in which women lead their lives? One of the paradoxes of research in gender and health is the consistent finding that women are sicker than men but live longer (Doyal, 1995). In Australia, for example, life expectancy at birth is 79.9 years for women, 73.4 for men, but in the 1989–1990 National Health Survey 75 per cent of women reported a recent illness, compared with 60 per cent of men (Australian Bureau of Statistics, 1995). In the US, women are 25 per cent more likely to report that their activities are restricted by health problems, and are bedridden for an average 35 per cent more days per year, than are men (US National Institutes of Health, 1992). Further, women report twice as much anxiety and depression as do men (Paykel, 1991). Living longer does not necessarily mean a healthier old age either; older women have higher rates of arthritis, Alzheimer's disease, osteoporosis and diabetes than do older men (Heikkinen, Waters & Brzezinski, 1993). And health inequalities are even greater in developing countries, where the limited health services, in common with other scarce resources, tend to be used by men rather than women (Doyal, 1995).

A feminist approach argues that women's poorer health is explained by the fact that women are socially disadvantaged in terms of education, income and political influence. Although gender-equality laws have been enacted in the majority of developed countries over the past few decades, these have had little effect on women's status, quality of life, or access to traditionally male privileges. Consistent evidence from many countries supports the view that in most aspects of social life women continue to be seriously disadvantaged by comparison with men. Much of this research is summarized in later chapters, but national surveys (e.g. Australian Bureau of Statistics, 1995; Social Trends, 1995) are consistent in showing that women have less money than men, less financial security, less desirable employment, and less political and social power.

In Australia, for example, only 64 per cent of adult women are in paid employment of any kind, compared with 84 per cent of adult men. Women are concentrated in a small number of poorly paid occupations, with over half of female workers in clerical and sales positions, and are much more likely to be employed on a part-time or casual basis, with an associated reduction in security and work-related benefits (Australian Bureau of Statistics, 1995). Very similar patterns of employment are observable in the USA (US Bureau of the Census, 1992a), Sweden (Rosenthal, 1994), and the UK (Social Trends, 1995).

Traditionally, women have received less education than men. In the UK, 49 per cent of adult women have completed high school, compared with 55 per cent of men (Social Trends, 1995). The comparable figures in Australia are 53 per cent of women and 60 per cent of men, while 6 per cent of women and 10 per cent of men have university qualifications (Australian Bureau of Statistics, 1995). It is notable that this trend is changing. Among Australians aged under twenty-five, women are more likely than men to have completed high school and to have a post-secondary qualification, while among British school leavers, girls are more likely than boys to succeed in completing university entrance qualifications (Social Trends, 1995). However, educational qualifications remain gender segregated. Only 13 per cent of engineering students are women, compared with 85 per cent of nursing students (Australian Bureau of Statistics, 1995). Female graduates continue to earn less than male graduates, a difference which is explicable mainly by their field of study. Thus, women have less money and fewer earning opportunities than men, even before the inequitable impact of child rearing and unpaid domestic labour have an effect on career progression.

Socioeconomic status, however it is measured, is a strong predictor of longevity and of health (Adler et al., 1994; Carroll, Bennett & Davey Smith, 1993), and women are over-represented in the lower socio-economic levels. In the USA, 64.2 per cent of the adult poor are women (Gimenez, 1989). In Australia, 57 per cent of adults living on government benefits are women. Averaged across all adults and all sources of income, Australian women's incomes are 55 per cent of men's. Even when full-time paid workers only are considered, Australian women earn only 82 per cent of the earnings of men (Australian Bureau of Statistics, 1995). Similarly, US women earn 72 per cent of US men's income (US Bureau of Labor Statistics, 1991), while in the UK the median income for women is 75 per cent of that for men (Social Trends, 1995). The differential remains even when men and women are matched for occupational classification, and when men's greater likelihood of paid overtime is taken into account (Australian Bureau of Statistics, 1995).

SOCIAL MYTHS AND THE PSYCHOLOGY OF WOMEN'S HEALTH

A small number of pervasive myths about women and women's behaviour may explain a large proportion of this inequity. This book deals specifically with four myths which cover many of the aspects of women's social position that relate directly to their health. These include the 'raging hormones' myth, the hypothesis that women's normal hormonal function renders them inherently unstable, while men's does not; the 'motherhood' myth which positions women as naturally better fitted than men to care for children and which has the effect of restricting women's value as people to their reproductive capacities; the 'angel in the house' myth, which promotes the view that housework, childcare and family care are naturally the work of women, and thus prevents them from reaching their potential in other fields; and the 'woman as object' myth which positions women as objects for the male gaze, valuable according to the extent to which they are physically attractive and potentially sexually available to men.

Naturally, there are many other topics in which women's health is clearly embedded in a relevant social context but which I am unable, for reasons of space and time, to include.

One of the most important topics which has had to be omitted is that of the health of minority women, including indigenous women, women of colour, immigrant women, and women members of ethnic, religious and cultural minorities. Indigenous people, particularly those who have been colonized by members of dominant and powerful Western cultures, experience very poor health. Although mortality statistics do not necessarily reflect the whole experience of women's health, the difference in life expectancy for indigenous and non-indigenous women in Australia – 63.8 and 79.9 years respectively – is so large that it cannot be ignored (Australian Bureau of Statistics, 1995). The social impact of racism, which means that members of ethnic minorities have reduced educational, vocational and developmental opportunities and thus poorer health, is well documented (e.g. Funkhouser & Moser, 1990). Racism combines with sexism to make the position of minority women, both in terms of their social opportunities and in terms of their physical and emotional health, doubly disadvantaged (Reid & Comas-Diaz, 1990). This is an enormous topic, which must be dealt with in a way which sympathetically describes the different positions of indigenous minorities, indigenous majorities, immigrants, descendants of immigrants and of slaves, and members of religious or cultural minorities, and which really necessitates another, different, book.

Other specific groups of women could be the subjects of analyses within the framework of this book. I have included a chapter on lesbian women, because these are a group of women who are uniquely challenged by patriarchal structures, but several other non-ethnic minorities have had to be omitted. Disabled women, for example, are argued to be doubly affected, firstly by their disability and secondly by sexist assumptions that their value as people is diminished because they are unable to fulfil some aspects of a traditional female role (Solomon, 1993).

Another important topic which has been omitted is that of abuse, both physical and sexual, particularly that occurring within families. Patriarchal family structures and men's greater physical strength and sense of entitlement mean that men tend to be the perpetrators, women and children the victims, of abuse (Browne, 1993). There is extensive evidence linking a history of abuse with a wide range of negative physical and psychological outcomes, as well as with increased risk of self-harm and substance abuse (e.g. Koss, 1990). However, the patriarchal notion that men have the right to control and dominate members of their families tends to render sexual and physical violence within families invisible.

It is worth noting that men, like women, live in a social context and that their health is also constrained by social myths and expectations. A focus on women's health should not be taken as an indication that men have a straightforward and uncomplicated relationship with society, with social constructions of masculinity, and with their bodies. The fundamentally gendered nature of society does affect and restrict men (August, 1985), although in different ways and perhaps to a lesser extent than it does women. Research which considers the effect of socially constructed gender roles on men's health is growing steadily in quality and quantity. Liberation from restrictive gender-based roles, for example through a more nurturing approach to fatherhood, has the capacity to enhance men's well-being and social responsiveness, and such changes can only be beneficial, not only to men but to the women and children with whom they live (Silverstein, 1996).

While this book, then, is by no means comprehensive in its coverage of topics which are important to the psychology of women's health, the aim is to focus on selected topics in a way that illuminates the central social myths that limit and constrain women's lives and thus their physical and emotional well-being.

OUTLINE OF THE BOOK

Part I deals with the 'raging hormones' hypothesis. The concept that women are more constrained by their animal nature than are men, less able to transcend their biology, has a long history in the Graeco-Roman and Judaeo-Christian traditions (Wooley, 1994). In particular, the assumed role of women's reproductive organs as the source of disturbed and antisocial behaviour has an extensive and well-documented history. In modern times, this concept is expressed in the assumption that women's behaviours, thoughts and emotions are uncontrollably determined by their hormonal systems, while men's are not (Ussher, 1992b). The reason why normal healthy endocrine function is seen as sinister among women but not among men may be traced back to the notion of man as the standard, normal human being and the assumption that any variation from this 'standard' must be problematic or at least inferior. This myth is explored through reviews of evidence in three areas menstrually related distress, postpartum depression, and menopausally related distress. In all three areas, the research evidence indicates that: hormones actually have very little impact on behaviour or emotion, and are considerably less relevant than are social constructions of menstruation, of motherhood and of women's ageing.

Part II examines another myth which is based on the traditional medical view of women as essentially a set of reproductive organs with a body attached: the 'motherhood' myth. This myth positions motherhood as easy, natural and wonderful, the peak of women's achievements and the only reason for their existence. Combined with a social structure which places the considerable burden of childcare overwhelmingly on individual, often isolated, women and provides few financial or social rewards for this work, this myth serves to restrict women's personal, social, economic and vocational choices. This second myth is approached through chapters which review the evidence on childlessness, on fertility control, and on the experience of motherhood. Sociocultural views of motherhood create a perception of the infertile woman as necessarily unhappy and inferior, yet the evidence suggests that infertile women generally cope well with their circumstances, and women who remain childless by choice are as happy with their decision as are those who choose motherhood. The assumption that all normal women must want children also makes it difficult for society to deal with the universal practice of fertility control through contraception and abortion. Access to effective contraception and safe abortion contributes to the health of women and children, and religious or cultural proscription of fertility control is best understood as arising from a perception that women should not be free to choose in matters of sexuality and reproduction. The reality of motherhood in contemporary society is addressed in the final chapter of this part, which addresses the challenges of adjusting to parenthood and the social constructions that place this challenge on mothers while marginalizing fathers.

Part III explores work, both paid and unpaid, by focusing on the myth that women, whatever their other roles and responsibilities, are always available to care for children, to manage a household, and to provide care for dependent relatives. The view that domestic labour is not 'work' if it is carried out by a female member of the household, and that women will 'naturally' place other people's needs before their own, serves to limit women's opportunities to develop other aspects of their lives. The first chapter in this part explores the relationship between paid and unpaid labour, the assumption that women in paid employment will also carry out the majority of unpaid labour while men in similar circumstances will have someone else to do it for them, and the effects of these assumptions on the well-being of women and their children. The second chapter examines the gendered nature of caregiving for frail or disabled family members, and the way in which the rhetoric of deinstitutionalization and community care is used to exploit individual women.

Part IV explores a myth which is perhaps most central to the maintenance of patriarchy and to the continuation of gender inequity: the view that women are valuable only to the extent to which they are useful, attractive and sexually available to men. This view arises out of a male-centred perspective of human society, which sees men and their experiences as central, and women primarily as objects of the male gaze. Chapters on weight and eating, on ageing, and on the special position of lesbian women, show how narrow and restrictive notions of physical attractiveness for women, together with the view that women's value depends entirely on the extent to which they are attractive and available to men, serve to restrict the lives of all women.

The psychology of women's health must be broader than the study of individual women and must address and reflect on social circumstances. A focus on the individual can describe women's experiences within each of these domains but it cannot provide directions for change, or explain why the health experiences of women and men are so different. A genuine psychology of women's health cannot avoid a political perspective, but must acknowledge the political, social and cultural context within which we all live.

Part I
IT'S YOUR HORMONES, DEAR
INTRODUCTION

The three chapters in this part critically evaluate the myth that women's behaviour and emotions are controlled by their hormones, and thus the view that women are less able than men to behave rationally. There exists a widespread perception that the normal, healthy fluctuations in women's hormonal levels associated with the menstrual cycle, with childbirth and with menopause are necessarily problematic and, further, that there is something innately mysterious and sinister about these normal biological processes. In its most extreme form, this perception leads to a belief that women are incapable of truly rational thought, that women are inherently unpredictable and unreliable, and that as a consequence they are less capable than men of participating fully in adult life. Invocation of hormonally related instability has been used to restrict women's access to education, to employment, and to political power.

These chapters present evidence dealing with premenstrual syndrome, with postnatal depression, and with the menopause. In all three cases, there is little evidence for high levels of distress or of abnormal behaviour among women; where distress does arise, there is little evidence relating this to hormonal fluctuations. Rather, the majority of research supports a social-construction view of this distress. While many people accept the existence of menstrually related psychological distress as a fact, controlled research finds little evidence for any cyclic changes in mood or emotion in normal women. Postnatal depression, also widely assumed to be hormonally caused, is not reliably related to any specific hormonal changes, although it is strongly correlated with lack of social support and with practical difficulties with a baby or child. And contrary to popular belief, rates of psychological distress are low both during and after menopause; where distress arises, it is better explained by social and familial stress than by hormonal changes.

The 'raging hormones' myth can be seen to arise from a traditionally male-centred view of the body which interprets female difference as pathology. This myth serves to belittle women and to deny them full adult status. While women may experience genuine distress in association with the early years of motherhood or with the midlife period, this distress is most usefully understood as a reaction to difficult social circumstances. These chapters review evidence in order to de-mythologize a series of issues for women's health and well-being which are conventionally couched in biomedical terms, but which may be better understood, and better dealt with, from a psychological perspective.

2

PREMENSTRUAL SYNDROME: IS ANATOMY DESTINY AFTER ALL?

An almost universal assumption exists, within both the scientific and the lay community, that a large proportion of pre-menopausal women experience a disorder, involving substantial and unpleasant physical and psychological symptoms, on a cyclic basis, and that this condition is the direct result of the hormonal fluctuations of the menstrual cycle. Many people, both scientists and lay people, accept this as a simple, inalienable biological fact. However, this chapter examines evidence which casts doubt on the usefulness of this concept. The research demonstrates that most women do not experience menstrually related changes which interfere with their lives to any appreciable extent, and that where such changes are identifiable, they do not have a simple biological basis but are embedded in a complex social and cultural context.

Historical analyses suggest that menstruation has always been viewed as a mystery and a problem. While most Western people would probably reject the view that it is a curse which must be surrounded by taboos and superstitions, a considerable degree of secrecy and shame is still associated with menstruation, and it is generally regarded as a troublesome, messy and dirty process, an embarrassing reminder of women's animal nature (Delaney, Lupton & Toth, 1988).

Ussher (1992b) has argued that the traditional male domination of science and medicine has led to a tendency to view the natural processes of the female body as abnormal, and thus to pathologize those biological processes which occur normally in women but not in men. Even when the normality of menstruation is acknowledged, it is still assumed to be a problem, with the implication that it is normal for women to have, and to be, problems (Nicolson, 1992). Further, in both historical and contemporary discourse, menstruation is overwhelmingly described in terms of failure to conceive and, by implication, in terms of failure as a woman, rather than as a normal, healthy bodily process which, for most women most of the time, signals success in avoiding an unwanted pregnancy (Martin, 1988). The concept of the premenstrual syndrome serves to influence and maintain societal definitions of appropriate behaviour for women, by denying the reality of women's emotions, particularly anger, and providing an apparent biological explanation which can become a rationale for ignoring or discounting the existence of distressing personal and social circumstances (Caplan, McCurdy-Myers & Gans, 1992).

As Lovering (1995) has argued, negative perspectives on women's bodies may serve to maintain menstrually related distress, as well as to deny the subjective reality of women's unhappiness by explaining it away as 'just your hormones'. Further, by implicitly endorsing the view that women are biologically destined to have as many pregnancies as they possibly can, negative views of menstruation serve to reinforce the concept that women exist for the sole purpose of procreation (Martin, 1988).

MENSTRUALLY RELATED DISTRESS?

A recent review (Klebanov & Ruble, 1994) indicated very little consensus on the definition of this condition, its symptoms, prevalence, relationship with physical and psychological well-being, effect on social and occupational skills, or the component of the menstrual cycle with which it is associated. This lack of consensus on such fundamental issues must lead the reader to consider critically whether such a condition actually exists; a number of reviewers (e.g. Bancroft, 1993; Brown, 1993; Caplan et al., 1992) have concluded that 'menstrually related distress' or the 'premenstrual syndrome' is not a useful construct, as there is no evidence for the existence of a consistent syndrome, or for a single underlying cause of apparently menstrually related distress. After reviewing the evidence on the existence of menstrually related distress, this chapter considers more broadly the sociocultural meaning of menstruation and the way in which both women and men develop a view of menstruation as negative, mysterious and shameful (e.g. Lovering, 1995).

If an argument against the concept of 'premenstrual syndrome' is to be sustained, it is necessary to consider why it is that it has such currency, not only among the medical and scientific community, but also among the many women whose genuine experiences of distress should not be minimized or denied. Many women are affected by their beliefs about menstruation and about its effects on their behaviour, and for many of them the effects are negative (Ussher, 1992a).

Do cyclic changes actually exist?

Variables which are said to demonstrate menstrually related cyclicity include mood, physical symptoms such as cramps and water retention, and ability to cope with normal personal, social and occupational activities (American Psychiatric Association, 1994). Klebanov and Ruble, however, have argued that research findings on the existence of cyclic changes in any of these variables are mixed and inconclusive. Reports of pain, water retention and weight gain show some consistency, but cyclic changes in water retention and weight gain are found only with self-report, and these effects disappear if objective measures are taken (Klebanov & Ruble, 1994).

There is no evidence for any cyclic changes in cognitive functioning (e.g. Gordon & Lee, 1993), short- or long-term memory (Richardson, 1992a) or motor performance (e.g. Black & Koulis-Chitwood, 1990), despite suggestions from biological determinists such as Dalton (1969) that women have a reduced capacity for carrying out complex tasks, operating machinery or making decisions during the premenstrual and menstrual phases of their cycles, and that they should therefore be restricted to occupations and activities in which important decisions or dangerous activities are not involved.

An extensive review (Sommer, 1992) concluded that there was no evidence for menstrually related changes in examination performance, or in a comprehensive range of experimental tasks testing cognitive abilities, including abstraction, disembedding from distracting contexts, short-term memory performance, arithmetic, verbal skills, visuospatial ability, rote tasks, simple decision-making, tolerance of frustration, or time-interval estimation, although some evidence did suggest a slight premenstrual decrement in fine motor co-ordination. The proposal that women should be barred from complex, challenging and rewarding tasks, or given 'light duties' to perform during the premenstrual period (Dalton, 1969), thus seems unsupportable and may be better under-stood as arising from negative social myths about women and about menstruation than as having any basis in fact (Richardson, 1992b).

Approximately half the published research identifies cyclic changes in mood, while the other half finds none (Klebanov & Ruble, 1994). Prospective studies of Australian (Jarvis & McCabe, 1991) and German (Laessle, Tuschl, Schweiger & Pirke, 1990) women have found no evi-dence for any cyclic changes in depression or general well-being, and the overall conclusion of the review by Klebanov and Ruble was that 'actual support for the existence of perimenstrual symptoms is weak' (1994: 186). Given the general bias towards the publication of positive findings, together with the cultural expectation that cyclic changes do occur and thus that well-conducted research should find at least some evidence for them (Ussher, 1992a), this suggests that if most women actually experi-ence any cyclic effect at all, it may generally be negligible.

To confuse the issue further, some researchers (e.g. Ussher & Wilding, 1992) have found improvements in performance during the pre-menstruum. Asso (1992) has argued that biological fluctuations do affect women's functioning, but in a positive, not a negative, way, while Stewart (1989) found that two-thirds of her sample reported at least one positive change during the week before menstruation. These positive changes included increased sexual interest and enjoyment, more energy, a tendency to clean, tidy and get things done, increased creativity, and a perception of increased attractiveness.

Defining menstrually related distress

A central problem in interpreting the literature in this field is the wide range of definitions, and associated wide range of prevalence estimates. Estimates of the prevalence of menstrually related distress range from 95 per cent (Corney & Stanton, 1991) to 5 per cent (Brooks-Gunn, 1986), demonstrating that different researchers must be studying quite different phenomena. Even standardized self-report surveys such as the Menstrual Distress Questionnaire (Moos, 1968) produce conflictual findings. A series of standardized surveys across several countries (Logue & Moos, 1986) concluded that between 55 and 70 per cent of women reported some physical discomfort and between 23 and 70 per cent some negative affect, estimates which are too broad to be of any actual use. Further, Klebanov and Ruble (1994) have argued that figures such as these give a quite false impression of a pandemic of menstrually related distress. The majority of women describe any symptoms as extremely mild and causing negligible distress. The demand characteristics of self-report surveys based on the assumption that unpleasant cyclic changes are an unquestionable fact need to be considered in interpreting widespread reports of mild and negligible levels of symptoms. Further, several researchers (e.g. Ainscough, 1990; McFarlane & Williams, 1994; Ussher & Wilding, 1992) have found no differences between those women who consider that they have premenstrual problems and those who do not, although others (e.g. Christensen, Board & Oei, 1992; Keenan, Lindamer & Jong, 1992) have found that women who report premenstrual difficulties do appear to experience a higher level of symptoms than those who do not. These conflicting findings, together with the wide range of prevalence estimates obtained by Logue and Moos (1986), provide additional support for the argument that there may be a strong social or cultural basis to women's reports of symptoms during the premenstrual phase.

Recently, the American Psychiatric Association has attempted to bring some standardization to research and clinical work by including preliminary definitions of menstrually related distress in DSM–III–R and DSM–IV. These two definitions are almost identical, although the name was changed from late luteal phase dysphoric disorder (LLPDD) in DSM–III–R to premenstrual dysphoric disorder (PDD) in DSM–IV, because the original name suggested some link between the condition and endocrine activity, a hypothesized link for which there is no evidence. DSM–IV (American Psychiatric Association, 1994) defines PDD as involving 'symptoms such as markedly depressed mood, marked anxiety, marked affective lability, and decreased interest in activity . . .

during the last week of the luteal phase in most menstrual cycles during the last year. The symptoms begin to remit within a few days of the onset of menses and are always absent in the week following menses' (p. 715). It specifies that PDD is only diagnosed if the condition is comparable in severity to a major depressive episode, and if it involves obvious and marked impairment in either social or occupational functioning, and notes that many women who report some level of menstrually related distress will not meet these criteria.

DSM–IV also specifies that PDD should be confirmed with prospective daily ratings over at least two cycles. This is an important point, as research has reliably shown that retrospective reports produce inflated rates by comparison with daily ratings (e.g. Boyle & Grant, 1992). Further, there is little consistency in women's experience of symptoms across consecutive cycles, and many women who report that they suffer from menstrually related distress will actually have no symptoms at all in a proportion of cycles (Walker, 1994; Watkins, Williamson & Falkowski, 1989). Prospective verification is essential in research. Vanselow, Dennerstein, Greenwood and de Lignieres (1996), recruiting women with self-reported premenstrual distress for an intervention trial, found that fewer than 20 per cent of volunteers actually met DSM criteria. The phenomenon of recall bias appears particularly problematic in this area, as it may combine with powerful sociocultural expectations of what one is supposed to experience, to produce inflated retrospective reports of symptoms.

While the development of a definition of PDD may help to standardize research, the DSM–III–R and DSM–IV provisional criteria still require subjective interpretation. Hurt et al. (1992) applied these criteria with a sample of women seeking help for menstrually related distress, and found that anywhere between 14 and 45 per cent of the group could be classified as meeting DSM–III–R criteria, depending on one's inter-pretation.

One of the most carefully designed studies of prevalence in a normal population (Rivera-Tovar & Frank, 1990), using a prospective, blind, study over ninety days, found that 5 per cent of a sample of US students met criteria for LLPDD. This suggests that some women do experience menstrually related distress, but that it is by no means the norm, and it should be noted that experiencing distress on a cyclic basis does not necessarily mean that that distress is hormonally mediated.

The vast majority of women do not experience significant levels of distress on a cyclic basis. Interestingly, though, there is a dearth of information on the normal, non-problematic experience of menstruation, and both the scientific and the lay literature present an unrelievedly negative picture of all women (Chrisler & Levy, 1990; Laws, 1992; Lupton, 1994). It is this bias which has been identified as a major source of misattribution and reporting bias among women (Rittenhouse, 1991).

A further argument against the existence of a unitary, biologically determined syndrome is another fundamental disagreement, this one over the phase of the menstrual cycle during which symptoms are supposed to occur. Dalton's (1969) pioneering work in this area identified the two weeks prior to menstruation, as well as the menstrual period itself, as a time when most women suffered major disruption to their mood, competence and general behaviour (incidentally, assuming a twenty-eight-day cycle and five days of menses, this leaves a total of nine days in each cycle when women were not at the mercy of their hormones and could be considered capable of rational action). Most contemporary American work focuses on the three or four days before menstruation, and DSM–IV specifies that symptoms will usually (although not always) remit by the second day of menstruation. However, surveys from Spain (Herrera, Gomez-Amor, Martinez-Selva & Ato, 1990) and the Netherlands (Van der Ploeg & Lodder, 1993) have found that distressing symptoms peaked during, rather than before, menstruation. Again, this inconsistency supports a sociocultural, rather than a biological, explanation of the symptoms.

Menstrually related madness?

It is traditionally assumed that women are at increased risk of madness during the immediate premenstrual period; Dalton (1969) claimed that half of all female psychiatric admissions occurred in the few days before menstruation. More recent research, however, suggests that if there is any such effect, it is better explained by the occurrence of major emotional stresses which precipitate both the psychiatric admission and the onset of menstruation (Klebanov & Ruble, 1994). It does appear that a subgroup of women with psychological disorders, including depression (Endicott, 1993) and panic disorders (Kaspi, Otto, Pollack, Eppinger & Rosenbaum, 1994), will show exacerbation of symptoms in the premenstrual period, although again the question of the direction of causality has not been resolved. DSM–IV stresses the need to distinguish between PDD and the premenstrual exacerbation of other conditions, although it is not clear why other conditions might be expected to undergo menstrually related changes in severity, and it has been argued (e.g. Ussher, 1992b) that this assumption is another example of a prevalent and unexamined attitude that ascribes women's emotional distress to their hormones. A recent review of the literature on cyclically recurring psychoses found no evidence linking these to LLPDD or PDD (Severino & Yonkers, 1993). Prospective studies (Eckerd, Hurt & Severino, 1989; Ziv, Russ, Moline, Hurt & Zendell, 1995) have found no objective evidence for menstrually related problems among women with personality disorders, even though all of Ziv et al.'s (1995) subjects claimed that they suffered from premenstrual syndrome. While women with previously diagnosed depression appear to be more likely to receive a diagnosis of premenstrual syndrome (Bancroft, Rennie & Warner, 1994), it is arguable that the premenstrual symptoms reported in these women are an expression of continuing depression. Again, findings in this area suggest that the reporting of premenstrual symptoms may be culturally determined, a reaction to a need to understand undifferentiated psychological distress by seeking a socially sanctioned explanation.

Biological factors

A further fundamental question, on which there is again little consensus, is whether, if cyclic changes do exist among some women, they can be explained by hormonal or other physiological factors. Klebanov and Ruble (1994) concluded that this question remains unanswered, despite decades of research. Physiological variables which have been related to menstrual symptoms include oestrogen, progesterone, luteinizing hormone, follicle stimulating hormone, aldosterone, prolactin, cortisol, melatonin, monoamine oxidase, and endogenous opiates; however, the evidence relating any of these variables to symptoms is either negative or inconsistent.

Although biological determinists such as Dalton (1984) have continued to ascribe premenstrual distress to insufficient levels of progesterone, research has consistently found no differences in the hormonal profiles of women with and without menstrually related distress (e.g. Dennerstein, Brown, Gotts, Morse, Farley & Pinol, 1993; Rubinow et al., 1988), and no relationship between hormonal levels and levels of reported symptoms (e.g. Hammarback, Damber & Backstrom, 1989). Further, controlled clinical trials (e.g. Freeman, Rickels, Sondheimer & Polansky, 1990; Maddocks, Hahn & Moller, 1986) have failed to show any effect of progesterone treatment on premenstrual symptoms. Vanselow et al. (1996), in a randomized controlled trial, found no difference between treatment and placebo groups, but all groups improved significantly on depression, anger, anxiety, menstrual distress, pain, and water retention, suggesting that progesterone has no specific effect, but also that expectations play a major role in response to treatment. Richardson (1992b) has reported that very large placebo effects are the norm in research on treatment for premenstrual symptoms, and that this reflects the psychosocial nature of the problem.

It would appear, overall, that there is little evidence for the existence of a unitary syndrome afflicting large numbers of women on a regular basis, although it is important to acknowledge that 'these findings do not negate the possibility that a subset of women experience clinically significant symptoms that are hormone related' (Klebanov & Ruble, 1994: 192).

There is some evidence (e.g. Giannini, Melemis, Martin & Folts, 1994; Redei & Freeman, 1995) to suggest that, at least in a small proportion of those women who are diagnosed with menstrually related distress, there may be some relevant biological factors which distinguish them from other women. However, the direction of causality has not been established, and it is possible that identified physiological differences are a result of high levels of psychosocial stress or depression, and thus that a biological explanation does not identify the primary cause of this distress (Klebanov & Ruble, 1994).

The majority of research, in fact, seems to indicate that biological factors play an extremely minor role, and that a combination of expectations (Lovering, 1995; Richardson, 1992b), misattributions (Rittenhouse, 1991) and a sociocultural tendency to understand women's distress in general as explicable in terms of hormones rather than in more complex and socially constructed ways (Ussher, 1992b) may be the best explanation.

As well as the definitional problems, this area is plagued by methodological difficulties which make even well-conducted and rigorous research very difficult to interpret; these include the identification of phases of the menstrual cycle by self-report, differences between researchers in the number of days premenstrually which are regarded as 'premenstrual' or 'late luteal', the problem of identifying adequate controls, and strong demand characteristics, which are even stronger in research that makes use of retrospective self-reports or in which women are informed of the purpose of the research (Klebanov & Ruble, 1994; Ussher, 1992a).

Expectations and attributions

Several researchers (e.g. Gallant, Popiel, Hoffman, Chakraborty & Hamilton, 1992) have found that cyclicity of self-reports is greater among women who are aware of a study's focus on premenstrual symptoms than among women who are blind to the purpose of the study. Two studies (Klebanov & Jemmott, 1992; Ruble, 1977) have manipulated women's perception of their menstrual phase using bogus test results. In both cases, women who were persuaded that they were in the last few days before menstruation reported more pain, more water retention, and more negative symptoms than women who believed themselves to be in the intermenstrual phase. While retrospective reports of previous premenstrual symptoms were also a significant predictor of symptoms in the Klebanov and Jemmott (1992) study, the use of self-reports means that this effect may also be explained by expectancies, and by a socially constructed tendency to value consistency in self-report. A further study (Fradkin & Firestone, 1986) approached these expectations in a different way; the provision of information which convinced women that pre-menstrual syndrome was the result of social myths rather than of biological factors had the effect of reducing those women's subsequent reports of symptoms and of mood disturbance.

There is also evidence for the existence of stereotyped expectations about menstruation in the broader community. Clarke and Ruble (1978) found that adolescent boys and pre-menarcheal girls, asked to complete the Menstrual Distress Questionnaire according to their beliefs about the normal experience of menstruation, demonstrated strong negative stereotypes of the range and severity of symptoms. Adult men, too, have been shown to have strongly negative perspectives on menstruation, far more negative than those of women (Brooks-Gunn & Ruble, 1986). Martin (1988) has analysed the seemingly objective discourses of medical textbooks, showing that their description of menstrual processes is overwhelmingly couched in terms of regression, decline and failure.

There is surprisingly little research which compares women's moods and symptoms with those experienced by men; the scientific community seems to take for granted that women must show greater lability and more negative affect and symptomatology than men, but what evidence there is does not support this assumption. McFarlane, Martin and Williams (1988), and McFarlane and Williams (1994), have shown that women's reports of symptoms are not greater than or different from those experienced by men, and that the degree of change in mood and functioning is much the same for men as it is for women over a similar length of time. Fluctuations which could be attributed to the menstrual cycle were shown to be considerably less than those associated with stressful life events or, indeed, days of the week.

Stress (Gallant & Hamilton, 1992; Heilbrun & Frank, 1989) and in-effective coping styles (Choi & Salmon, 1995) have been shown to be associated with self-reports of premenstrual distress; Abidoye and Agbabiaka (1994) found in a survey of Nigerian students that pre-menstrual distress was highest when the premenstruum coincided with examinations, suggesting that environmental stressors play a role in the experience of symptoms. Women who do experience PPD appear to use different coping strategies at different times of their menstrual cycles (Burrage & Schomer, 1993; Fontana & Palfai, 1994). This suggests that expectations of menstrual distress, and perhaps assumptions that any problems which arise during the premenstruum must be biological rather than social in origin, may interfere with some women's ability to deal appropriately with more genuine causes of their distress. Women's attribution of depression or anger to 'hormones' may be more socially acceptable than is the expression of anger over inequitable social or personal arrangements, but it also diminishes the probability of effective coping action being taken.

The perception that menstrually related distress is biologically caused has led investigators to a focus on pharmacological interventions, despite the lack of evidence that any drug treatment is superior to placebo (Klebanov & Ruble, 1994). The deeply held cultural view of women's bodies as inevitably inferior and problematic (Nicolson, 1992; Ussher, 1992b), and of women's passivity and helplessness in the face of their 'raging hormones' (Ussher, 1992c) might explain the lack of research which focuses on taking positive action to reduce subjective feelings of distress.

There is, however, some preliminary research which indicates that exercise may play a role in promoting menstrually related well-being. A correlational study that assessed symptoms retrospectively (Gannon, Luchetta, Pardie & Rhodes, 1989), a prospective study that assessed symptoms at three stages of the menstrual cycle (Aganoff & Boyle, 1994), and a randomized experiment conducted over twelve weeks (Steege & Blumenthal, 1993) all reported that women who exercise regularly score lower than non-exercisers on symptoms of menstrual distress. More well-designed interventions, incorporating random assignment, prospective assessments, and blinding of participants to the focus of the research, are required to elucidate the impact of exercise on premenstrual and menstrual symptoms. However, these pilot studies do suggest that a more positive approach, one which seeks to determine active strategies which women might use, may produce some valuable and potentially empowering strategies in place of the largely ineffective pharmacological interventions.

SOCIOCULTURAL INFLUENCES ON PERCEPTIONS OF MENSTRUATION

Any attempt to understand the experience of menstrually related disorders, and the gap between assumptions about menstrually related distress on the one hand and the findings of empirical research on the other, must address the issue of the cultural interpretation of menstruation. Our culture is characterized by strongly negative attitudes to menstruation (Klebanov & Ruble, 1994; Treneman, 1988), which begin well before puberty in both boys and girls (Clarke & Ruble, 1978; Lovering, 1995), continue among adult men (Brooks-Gunn & Ruble, 1986; Laws, 1992) and women (Koff, Rierdan & Stubbs, 1990), and are reinforced by the professional discourse of medical texts (Martin, 1988) and the lay discourses of advertisements and popular culture (Treneman, 1988). Such attitudes may explain the persistence of beliefs that menstruation causes major physical and psychological distress in a majority of women, as well as why premenstrual symptoms seem to be less common in some non-Western cultures (e.g. Chandra & Chaturvedi,

1989) and among migrant women of non-Western ethnicity (Van den Akker, Eves, Service & Lennon, 1995) than among women of European background.

Media images of menstruation both promote and reflect a negative stereotype of women (Treneman, 1988). Advertisements for menstrually related products are the major context in which menstruation is mentioned in the media, and analysis of these advertisements reveals an unremittingly negative view of femaleness. The female body is seen as unclean, menstruation as necessarily a problem which should be surrounded by secrecy and shame. In particular, the knowledge that one is menstruating, and any evidence of that menstruation, is disgusting and must be kept secret from men (Berg & Coutts, 1994; Delaney et al., 1988; Treneman, 1988). In order to sell their product, advertisements promote a view that the use of menstrually related products at all phases of the cycle ('just in case') is necessary in order for women to feel confident and physically clean (Berg & Coutts, 1994).

Content analysis of articles in women's magazines (Chrisler & Levy, 1990) has also identified an unremittingly negative approach to menstruation and premenstrual symptoms, together with a great deal of incorrect information about what can be attributed to menstruation (including cold sores and tinnitus as well as the more commonly described depression, feelings of worthlessness, and suicidal thoughts). Such articles promote the concept that most women experience negative symptoms; implicit in the message is that not experiencing such symptoms is somehow unfeminine, and that there is very little that women can do to relieve or avoid this curse of womanhood. With such representation in the media, it is unsurprising that even educated women's knowledge of menstruation has been found to be incomplete and negatively biased (Koff et al., 1990).

Ussher (1992b) has argued that the female body has historically been constructed as problematic and dangerous, demonstrating that the interlinked concepts of premenstrual symptoms, postnatal depression and the menopausal syndrome have been used to pathologize the whole of adult women's experience, and to promote the idea that all women are always biologically disordered. The view that women are helplessly dependent on the fluctuations of their hormones leads to a denial of full adult status to women. Women are defined as erratic and unreliable, and a belief in women's inescapable, biologically determined tendency to irrational mood swings and unpredictable changes of mind is one factor underlying the systemic discrimination against women which is still apparent in Western society (Delaney et al., 1988). Ussher's (1992b) conclusion that 'PMS as a concept is not valid. PMS is a political, not a medical, category. It controls women. It ties women to their biology. It dismisses women's anger. It provides reductionist and reactionary explanations for women's discontent or distress' (pp. 46–47) is a powerful feminist reaction to a history of unrelieved negativity.

Blood is an obvious symbol of life which transcends cultures, and menstruation is simultaneously a symbol of life and fertility, of death through the shedding of blood, and of the failure of fecundity. Formal menstrual taboos and rituals still exist in many countries, including parts of southern Italy (Scalise, 1989) as well as in African (Rasmussen, 1991; Strassman, 1992) and Indian (Ullrich, 1992) cultures. These taboos, which are based on the 'unclean' status of menstruating women, appear to be maintained by the role they play in promoting female fidelity and increasing men's confidence in their paternity. Waldeck (1988) has argued that menstrual taboos serve to reinforce a view that defines women exclusively in terms of sexual and reproductive activities, and Lupton (1994) points to Western men's negative views of menstruation as centring on its role in restricting men's sexual access to women.

There is considerable variation in the ways in which non-Western cultures conceptualize menstruation, and this means that Westernization has affected women's experiences of menstruation in various ways. Ullrich (1992) described a relaxation of menstrual taboos among Havik Brahmins in southern India, associated with a gradual Westernization of the society and a change in women's primary role within marriage from that of childbearer to that of equal adult partner, which was associated with a reduction in menstrually related distress. On the other hand, Fitzgerald (1990) found that increasing Westernization was associated with more symptoms in Samoan and Hawaiian women, whose traditional cultures promote respect for women.

Although Western societies do not in general seclude women during menstruation, and formal taboos on handling food or engaging in sexual activities are generally restricted to religious and cultural minorities, menstruation continues to be surrounded by taboos in contemporary society. It is usually considered improper to discuss menstruation in mixed-sex groups, or to make it known that one is menstruating; even advertisements for menstrually related products avoid any mention of the purpose of their products, or use of the colour red, while surveys indicate that the majority of Western people regard sexual activity during menstruation as improper (Delaney et al., 1988; Treneman, 1988). Several feminist writers (e.g. Delaney et al., 1988) have highlighted the strength of our culture's negative perspective on menstruation by proposing alternative cultural norms, such as a practice of celebrating when girls reach menarche, or of wearing a red item of clothing as a public signal that one is menstruating. The foreignness of these ideas merely serves to emphasize the continued existence of attitudes which surround menstruation with secrecy and shame.

Lovering (1995) conducted an ethnographic analysis of adolescents' discourses about menstruation, demonstrating that both boys and girls found menstruation embarrassing and shameful in a way which had no parallel in aspects of male sexual development. This shame continues into adult life, and while there is little research on men's views of menstruation, Laws (1992) has shown that adult men also treat menstruation as a shameful secret, Brooks-Gunn and Ruble (1986) have demonstrated that men's attitudes to menstruation are considerably more negative than are women's, and Lupton (1994) has described men's primary reaction to menstruation as one of disgust. Lovering (1995) has argued that this pervasive disgust leads to a cultural perception that women's bodies, and particularly anything associated with sexuality or reproduction, are problematic, inferior, and not open to public discussion. Menstruation appears to be an embarrassing reminder that we are animals, and because it occurs only among women, it supports the view that women are somehow closer to our animal nature, less able to transcend the physical reality of blood and flesh, than are men.

POSITIVE PERSPECTIVES ON MENSTRUATION

A number of feminist writers (e.g. Delaney et al., 1988; Ussher, 1992b) have also suggested that the ascription of negative moods among women to their hormones, and thus the effective denial of their subjective experience of reality, has served to deny women the ability to express anger and discontent, and therefore has served to maintain the social inequities which might veridically lead to legitimate feelings of anger and disquiet.

In response to the unremittingly negative view of menstruation in both scientific and everyday discourse, these writers have called for a more positive understanding of women's bodies, both by providing a more balanced perspective on menstruation and by considering women as more than just their reproductive systems. Klebanov and Ruble (1994) have also pointed to the need for research that examines the experiences of the non-distressed majority of women. Chaturvedi and Chandra (1990), who found that 95 per cent of a sample of Indian nursing students reported some positive emotions during the premenstrual phase, felt the need to explain this in terms of the unique Indian culture, since there is almost no Western research on positive aspects of the menstrual cycle. Delaney et al. (1988) argued that the traditional research focus on negative aspects of menstruation leads inevitably to negatively biased findings; they suggested that even the name of the most commonly used assessment instrument, the Menstrual Distress Questionnaire (Moos, 1968), produced a negative set in the minds of researchers and participants. Somewhat facetiously, they went on to develop the Menstrual Joy Questionnaire, a scale which asked women to rate, for different stages of their menstrual cycle, the extent to which they had experienced each of ten positive states. Chrisler, Johnston, Champagne and Preston (1994) were unable to resist administering this scale to female students, and assessing their reactions to it. Retrospective reports of positive symptoms did show a small degree of cyclicity, with highest ratings for the intermenstrual phase and lowest for menstruation itself, and Chrisler et al. (1994) interpreted this as further evidence for the strength of women's belief that cyclic changes were an inevitable aspect of their lives. Sixty-five per cent of respondents reported that they had never previously thought of menstruation as positive in any way, although a small number reported positive aspects of menstruation, including assurances that they were not pregnant, that they were in good health, that they were able to have children, or that they were adult women. Most students reacted to the scale with surprise and disbelief, but 30 per cent felt that completing the questionnaire had been a catalyst for them to reassess their reactions to menstruation, suggesting the existence of an overwhelmingly negative bias which had previously prevented them from ever considering it in a positive light.

This small project suggests that research, interventions and educational programmes which aimed to redress the negative bias of our popular and scientific culture might go a long way to reducing women's expectations that to be truly feminine means experiencing sorrow and pain on a regular basis. It remains to be seen whether a change in women's expectations about menstruation would affect the extent to which they experience menstrual and premenstrual distress, but future research which operates from the perspective of women as actively coping with their social lives and with natural biological processes, and focuses on what women can do to enhance their lives rather than on the inevitability of feminine distress, may change our understanding of normal menstruation.

3

POSTPARTUM DEPRESSION:
THE SORROWS OF MOTHERHOOD

In most societies, childbirth is seen as a potential crisis, one which puts women at risk of mental illness. Postpartum depression, in particular, has entered the popular imagination as a disease, a distinct and bio-logically caused entity which strikes women without warning at a time of emotional and physical vulnerability.

The use of the term *postpartum* or *postnatal* implies a causal relation-ship between childbirth and depressive disorders, and it is widely assumed that depression in the postpartum period results directly from hormonal changes associated with childbirth. The tangible realities of fatigue, responsibility and hard work are ignored, and women's genuine struggles to cope with the challenging reality of caring for a new baby are explained away as a result of the ubiquitous 'hormones'. This assumption persists despite the lack of any good evidence relating post-partum depression consistently to any physiological variable (Whiffen, 1992). Hormones, and reproductive processes in particular, are assumed to be a major determinant of women's behaviour. There is, of course, no doubt that levels of hormones and electrolytes fluctuate dramatically throughout pregnancy, childbirth and the immediate postpartum period (Glover, 1992; O'Hara, Schlechte, Lewis & Varner, 1991), but it is less clear that there is any relationship between these biological events and post-partum depression (Albright, 1993; Hopkins, Marcus & Campbell, 1984).

It does appear that the 'baby blues', a mild and transient condition of tearfulness and depression in the few days immediately following birth, may be related to changes in hormone levels, but this is quickly resolved and has little long-term impact on the woman, her baby or her family. It is also the case that a very small proportion of women develop major psychoses following childbirth. But postpartum depression of more than a few days' duration, depression which has a major impact on the new mother's life, has not been shown to be related to any physiological variables, either transient childbirth-related changes or longer-term char-acteristics of individual women's physiology.

Psychiatric admission rates are higher for new mothers than for other groups of women (Kendell, Chalmers & Platz, 1987), but it is not clear that actual rates of depression are higher than at other times (Stanton & Danoff-Burg, 1995). The excess admissions appear to result from women's greater contact with medical services at this time, combined with the possibility that moderate levels of distress, which might not normally be considered in need of professional intervention, are complicated by the need to care for a new baby.

The consensus of a substantial body of research is that postpartum depression is best explained by psychosocial factors (Kumar, 1994), including life events, lack of appropriate social support, and unrealistic expectations of motherhood, as well as inaccurate cultural stereotypes of motherhood as easy, natural and fulfilling, and of the mother–child relationship as immediately and unambiguously positive.

There exists a widespread assumption that any association between childbirth and depression must be explained by hormones, and progesterone is widely prescribed for postpartum depression. However, as for menstrually related distress, there is no evidence for a causal link, and hormonal fluctuations do not differ between women who do and do not develop postpartum depression (Harris, 1994).

Yet the myths remain. These myths have a socially conservative impact, encouraging mothers to internalize their problems and to blame their own inadequacies, rather than to recognize the difficulties of motherhood. More generally, these myths, together with myths about menstruation and menopause, promote a view of women as inherently unstable, erratic and incapable of truly autonomous decision-making, helplessly driven by seething hormones to behave in irrational ways (Ussher, 1992b). What, after all, could be more irrational than reacting with depression to an event as natural and joyous as the birth of a baby?

This implicit view, and its obverse, that men are not affected by their hormones, and are therefore more rational, more consistent and more in control of their own behaviour than are women, pervades most human societies. Thus, while it is important to acknowledge that psychiatric disorders do arise in the postpartum period among vulnerable women, it is equally important to emphasize that, for the majority of women who have difficulty coping emotionally with the demands of caring for a new baby, the problems lie in the social demands of motherhood and not in any physiological or personal inadequacy of those women.

POSTPARTUM DISORDERS: DEFINITIONS AND PREVALENCE

In any discussion of postpartum depression, it is important to distinguish it from other postpartum conditions, which may be more closely related to physiological variables.

Postpartum psychosis

Postpartum psychosis, characterized by hallucinations, delusions and other schizophrenia-like symptoms, is the most dramatic but the rarest psychological event in the immediate postpartum period and must be distinguished from postpartum depression. It is identical to other psychotic conditions, with the minor variations that the content of delusions and hallucinations is likely to be associated with childbirth or the baby, infanticidal intentions and behaviours may be present, and it has a somewhat more positive prognosis than other psychoses (Harding, 1989). Postpartum psychosis occurs in all human societies, at a relatively consistent rate of 0.01 to 0.02 per cent of all births, and there is evidence dating back 150 years to show that this rate has been constant over time (Kumar, 1994). A recent comparison of the characteristics of Saudi Arabian and Scottish women with postpartum psychosis (Rahim & Al-Sabiae, 1991) illustrated the strong similarities in onset, course and presentation in very different societies.

A previous history of psychotic illness is the strongest risk factor for postpartum psychosis, and the consensus is that postpartum psychosis, in common with non-postpartum psychoses, results from an interaction between a pre-existing biological vulnerability to psychosis and a stressful experience, in this case childbirth.

An English study of pregnant women with a history of non-postpartum psychotic illness (Marks, Wieck, Checkley & Kumar, 1991) found that 28 per cent developed psychotic episodes and a further 23 per cent severe non-psychotic depression during the postpartum period, suggesting that childbirth is an event of high risk for women with an existing propensity to psychotic disorders. Women who experience postpartum psychosis are also at elevated risk for later episodes, both postpartum and non-postpartum: a long-term study of Swiss women with a history of postpartum psychosis (Schopf & Rust, 1994) found that 66 per cent had later non-postpartum psychotic episodes, and 33 per cent had recurrences of postpartum psychosis following subsequent births. Childbirth seems to play a crucial role in the development of psychosis in women with a biological predisposition to psychotic disorders, although a definitive physiological trigger has not yet been clearly identified (Harris, 1994). In general, research finds no link between postpartum psychosis and previous life events (Marks et al., 1991), stress (Brockington, Martin, Brown, Goldberg & Margison, 1990), social support or marital difficulties (Dowlatshahi & Paykel, 1990), providing further support for a biological, rather than a social, explanation.

Baby blues

Postpartum depression must also be distinguished from postpartum dysphoria, or 'baby blues', a condition of tearfulness, mood swings and irritability which occurs in a high proportion of mothers in the first few days following childbirth, and normally resolves itself within ten days of the birth (O'Hara et al., 1991). It is frequently regarded as a normal reaction to the birth of a child, and Kumar (1994) concluded that it also occurs at a relatively constant rate across cultures and is not related to any environmental, social or cultural factor. Prevalence estimates vary, depending on the assessment technique used, from 26 to 85 per cent of all mothers (O'Hara et al., 1991), indicating that, in common with premenstrual syndrome, it is a condition which is yet to be clearly defined and distinguished from normal experience. While there is a strong bias towards the assessment of negative outcomes of childbirth, research which has assessed positive mood as well has found that, for the majority of women, positive feelings coexist with depression and tiredness (O'Hara, Zekoski, Philipps & Wright, 1990).

There is some evidence linking the 'baby blues' with changes in oestrogen levels (O'Hara et al., 1991; Harris, 1994). However, transient depression and tearfulness also appear to be a relatively common reaction to medical procedures. Iles, Gath and Kennerley (1989) found that symptoms after childbirth were actually lower than in a group of comparison women undergoing elective gynaecological surgery, suggesting that the reaction may not be specific to childbirth. Whether hormonal fluctuations play a role or not, it takes most women several days to recover from the physical strain of childbirth, and transient emotional distress during this time appears normal.

Postpartum depression

Postpartum depression is considerably more serious than 'baby blues' and the symptoms are more persistent. Barnett and Gotlib (1988) have suggested that the difference is one of degree rather than kind, and that postpartum depression is diagnosed when the mild dysphoria fails to resolve itself or becomes more serious over time. Although the rate of postpartum depression is also relatively constant across cultures, its development seems mainly influenced by psychosocial rather than biological factors. There is no convincing evidence for hormonal causation (Kumar, 1994), and Dalton (1984) is one of the few who have continued to ascribe postpartum depression to hormones rather than to psychosocial influences.

Whiffen (1991, 1992) and Albright (1993) have both concluded that no obstetric or hormonal variable has been shown unequivocally to be related to non-psychotic postpartum depression. While there are marked physiological changes in the days immediately following childbirth (O'Hara et al., 1991; Robinson & Stewart, 1993), there are also major psychological and social changes, which may be most dramatic with the birth of the first child. Proponents of social and sociocultural views of the aetiology of postpartum depression point to the lack of physiological difference between women who do and do not experience postpartum depression, and argue that acceptance of a biological model of postpartum depression is likely to lead to inappropriate biomedical treatment, while neglecting interventions that address the psychosocial aspects of the condition (Nicolson, 1990).

Depressed mothers do report more problems and less satisfaction with their babies, but it is not clear whether this is a cause or a consequence of their depressed state (Whiffen, 1992). Variables which predict the onset of postpartum depression include relationship difficulties, low perceived social support, previous depressive illness, and life stress, all of which are also important predictors of non-childbirth-related depression (Whiffen, 1991, 1992). In fact, previous, non-postpartum, episodes of depression are the strongest predictor of postpartum depression (Gotlib, Whiffen, Mount, Milne & Cordy, 1989). Further evidence for the continuity between postpartum and non-postpartum depression comes from research showing that those postnatally depressed women who have a history of previous, non-postpartum, depression tend to be more depressed, slower to recover, and more likely to relapse than those with no previous depressive history (Bell, Land, Milne & Hassanyeh, 1994).

Evidence such as this has led many researchers (e.g. Purdy & Frank, 1993; Ussher, 1992b, 1992c; Whiffen, 1991, 1992) to question the usefulness of distinguishing postpartum from any other sort of depression. Extensive empirical research finds no difference in presentation between postpartum depression and other major depression (Whiffen & Gotlib, 1993), and qualitative studies of depressed mothers' experiences (Mauthner, 1993; Nicolson, 1989) lead to similar conclusions. DSM–IV (American Psychiatric Association, 1994) allows the specifier 'with postpartum onset' to be applied to most categories of depression if they occur within four weeks of the delivery of a child, but does not provide a separate diagnostic category for postpartum depression, because of the lack of evidence that it is in any way distinct.

Life events, particularly those involving the partner or close family, have been shown consistently to increase the risk of postpartum depression in several different cultures (Aderibigbe, Gureje & Omigbodun, 1993; Robinson & Stewart, 1993). Childbirth itself is a life event which requires major readjustments (Ruchala & Halstead, 1994). While these vary with circumstances, many new mothers face a change in role, a change in financial status, and a change in marital relationship simultaneously. Depression in the postpartum period may be seen as a problem of adjustment to new social and personal circumstances, and not essentially different from other adjustment disorders.

Interestingly, Pfost, Lum and Stephens (1989) found two groups of mothers to be at lowest risk of depression: those with high traditional femininity scores and those who had definite plans to return to work. It may be that these two different groups of women, those who feel positively towards the adoption of a traditional mothering role, and those on the other hand who have clear plans on how they will avoid such a role, are the women who experience the least divergence between their personal preferences and their new lifestyles, and thus those who adjust best to the change.

Rates of postpartum depression are relatively consistent across countries, although the use of a range of assessment techniques has produced a variety of prevalence estimates. Most recent research uses the Edinburgh Postnatal Depression Scale (Cox, Holden & Sagovsky, 1987), and community-based surveys in Canada (Zelkowitz & Milet, 1995), Sweden (Lundh & Gyllang, 1993) and New Zealand (Webster, Thompson, Mitchell & Werry, 1994) have found prevalence rates of between 6 and 10 per cent, although one American survey (Roy, Gang, Cole, Rutsky, Reese & Weisbord, 1993) found a higher prevalence of 17.4 per cent. Research which uses clinical interviews (e.g. Ballard, Davis, Cullen, Mohan & Dean, 1994; Hobfoll, Ritter, Lavin, Hulsizer & Cameron, 1995) tends to obtain slightly higher rates, as does research which uses other standard questionnaires (e.g. Aderibigbe et al., 1993; Spangenberg & Pieters, 1991). Standard scales such as the Beck Depression Inventory, however, may not be appropriate because they confound the effects of depression with normal consequences of childbirth such as changes in weight, eating patterns, sleeping patterns and sexual activity (Huffman, Lamour, Bryan & Pederson, 1990).

Problematically for those who continue to adhere to the biomedical view of postpartum depression, the symptoms may have their onset at any time up to twelve months after the birth of the baby and may be preceded by a period of normal adaptation. Only about half of diagnosed cases have their onset in the first two weeks after childbirth (Glover, 1992), and the condition is quite heterogeneous in nature by comparison with postpartum psychosis. Further, postpartum depression persists much longer than the physiological changes associated with childbirth. A follow-up of women who had experienced postpartum depression (Philipps & O'Hara, 1991) found high rates of depression to persist four and a half years later, while the rate of depression among mothers of toddlers is the same as that among new mothers (Cox, Murray & Chapman, 1993); being a mother of a young child involves considerable ongoing psychosocial stress, and this makes it particularly difficult for mothers to recover from depression.

Most damning for the hormonal account is the finding that fathers, too, experience postpartum depression. Richman, Raskin and Gaines (1991) found that fathers were as likely as mothers to be clinically depressed two months after the birth of a child. A British study (Ballard et al., 1994) found that fathers were less likely than mothers to be depressed, but 9 per cent of fathers were depressed six weeks after the birth, and 5.4 per cent were depressed at six months. Further, both mothers and fathers of children aged three to five had similar levels of depression to mothers and fathers of newborns, again suggesting that explanations of postpartum depression are more likely to be found in the continuing stresses of caring for a small child than in any hormonal change associated with childbirth. Fathers are at greatest risk of depression if mothers are depressed (Ballard et al., 1994; Lovestone & Kumar, 1993), possibly because the mothers' depression means that more of the stressful and tiring tasks of new parenthood are taken on by the fathers.

POSTPARTUM DEPRESSION AND PSYCHOLOGICAL ADJUSTMENT TO MOTHERHOOD

Personal factors

The consistent absence of any evidence for a biological cause of postpartum depression has led to research examining the impact of psychological variables on mothers' postpartum adjustment. The assumption behind this research is that women with certain psychological characteristics will show poor adaptation to the demands of their changed role, and that these difficulties will lead to a sense of personal failure and thus to depression. Empirical research has indicated that postpartum depression is more common among women who have high levels of anxiety, low self-esteem, or insecure emotional attachments, and also among obsessive, over-controlled and perfectionist women whose expectations of motherhood may be unrealistic (Albright, 1993).

Research on intrapersonal precursors and correlates of postpartum depression has been criticized, however, for its focus on the individual. Implicit in these models is the view that there is some deficit intrinsic to a particular subgroup of women, which causes them to fail as mothers (Mauthner, 1993; Ussher, 1992b, 1992c). When this attitude is combined with a sociocultural perspective that motherhood is easy, natural, and the most important thing a woman can do in her life (Ussher, 1992b), it is unsurprising that depressed mothers experience high levels of guilt and self-blame (Beck, 1992). It is arguable that the characteristics which have been identified – anxiety, insecurity and low self-esteem – may arise from women's socialization experiences rather than from intrinsic inadequacies of individual women. The social nature of postpartum depression is further supported by research which has shown that aspects of the woman's social and family environment have an important impact on coping in the postpartum period.

Social support

Social relationships, and in particular social support, play an important role in buffering the effects of life events and other stressors, so it is not surprising that social support and, particularly, support from the partner both during and after the pregnancy have been negatively associated with depression (Collins, Dunkel-Schetter, Lobel & Scrimshaw, 1993; Demyttenaere, Lenaerts, Nijs & Van Assche, 1995; O'Hara, 1986). Women's perceptions of the appropriateness or adequacy of the support received have predicted depression in many studies, including research with Australian (Boyce, Hickie & Parker, 1991), Belgian (Demyttenaere et al., 1995), and Canadian (Gottlieb & Mendelson, 1995) samples.

Research which shows demographic differences in rates of postpartum depression may also be explicable in terms of social support. A Canadian study (Zelkowitz & Milet, 1995), for example, found the highest rates of depression among unemployed women, those with low occupational status, and recent immigrants. Unemployed immigrants who were having their second or subsequent child were at highest risk, and it is likely that these women are also characterized by high demands and low social support. Lack of social support may also explain the higher rates of postpartum depression among women without partners which have been found both in the USA (Hobfoll et al., 1995) and in New Zealand (Webster et al., 1994).

New mothers need practical help as well as emotional support, as caring for a small child is demanding and exhausting. Two American studies, one with low-income mothers (Collins et al., 1993) and one with couples expecting their second child (Jordan, 1989) found that practical help was perceived as more important than social support in maintaining well-being, lending support to the notion that the additional workload of caring for a baby may be a major source of stress for parents.

It is worth noting, however, that a focus on the importance of social support for mothers can lead to the blaming of fathers, which is no more helpful than the blaming of individual mothers for their depression. While some fathers do fail to provide adequate support to their partners and their children, the social and financial context must be acknowledged here as elsewhere. Although births outside formal marriage have increased in recent years, it is still the case that over 95 per cent of new mothers have a male partner (Australian Bureau of Statistics, 1995), and that, despite rhetoric about absent fathers, the majority of men are willing to support their partner and child.

Fathers of new babies may feel pressured to work longer hours to provide financially. Like new mothers, new fathers may lack the skills to care practically for their babies, and unlike new mothers, fathers may not feel the same necessity to learn. Fathers may react to the reality of a crying or difficult baby with avoidance and a culturally mediated view that the day-to-day care of the baby is 'naturally' the responsibility of the mother. Cultural stereotypes may make it more difficult for a father who wishes to be actively involved in the care of his child to find time and to feel comfortable with activities which are traditionally seen as gender-inappropriate. Cultural stereotypes, too, view fathers as taking a secondary role in the care of babies and make it easier for men to choose to avoid personal responsibility than it is for women.

SOCIOCULTURAL INFLUENCES ON POSTPARTUM DEPRESSION

Media images of pregnancy and childbirth reflect a view that women should experience unalloyed happiness and love at the arrival of their baby. Rarely do the popular media acknowledge the physical and emotional challenges that accompany the birth of a new baby. These one-sided images, coupled with smaller family sizes and a breakdown of traditional multi-generational families, mean that many new mothers (and fathers) have had little experience with babies, and lack the necessary practical skills and the confidence to develop them. They may find that the experience of having a baby is very different from their expectations, and thus may face strong feelings of guilt and failure when their experiences are not entirely blissful (Albright, 1993; Ussher, 1992b).

Research on normal adaptation to motherhood indicates clearly that looking after a baby is difficult and stressful. Ruchala and Halstead (1994) interviewed fifty healthy non-depressed mothers in the first two weeks after a child was born; women described their experiences as 'hectic' and 86 per cent reported extreme fatigue. They considered that they had had to make major adjustments and that the arrival of the baby had interfered with other responsibilities and relationships; most were also worried about their ability to provide appropriate care. Thus, even for the non-depressed mother, the workload is high, anxiety about whether one is doing the right thing is considerable, and fatigue and disturbed sleep add to the difficulty of adjustment (Brown, Lumley, Small & Astbury, 1994).

Research which identifies a group of women as suffering from postpartum depression may create a false dichotomy between normal and abnormal adjustment and imply that women will either be completely happy in their new role or will suffer from an 'illness'. The reality of mixed, and often negative, feelings among normal, healthy new mothers is not often acknowledged (Brown et al., 1994). It is interesting to note that one study of new mothers (Small, Brown, Lumley & Astbury, 1994) found that one-third of those who met criteria for depression did not want to label it 'postpartum depression'. Their interpretation of their experiences was that they were not suffering an illness, but were dealing as best they could with lack of support, isolation, fatigue, and physical strain. These women said that what they needed was not a diagnosis but practical assistance with very real responsibilities and difficulties.

Glover, Liddle, Tayler, Adams and Sandler (1994) have argued that negative moods are so normal and natural among new mothers that not feeling depressed, or experiencing euphoria or hypomania (the 'baby pinks'), in the early postpartum period may be a sign of abnormal adjustment and may be associated with an increased risk of major depression in later weeks. Dunnewold and Sanford (1992) have pointed out that many women who are not diagnosed with depression feel anxious, unhappy or disappointed after the birth of their child, and have suggested that the normal reactions and responses of new mothers need to be examined further. Antenatal classes and self-help materials for pregnant women and their partners frequently restrict themselves to the physical side of pregnancy and birth, and with few exceptions (e.g. Kitzinger, 1982) are silent about the arguably more difficult personal and relationship adjustments which are necessary after the birth of the baby. More realistic education, and more realistic role models in the mass media, might help women feel less abnormal, and less guilty, when they encounter the inevitable difficulties.

There is little research that explores women's experiences of the often dramatic changes in role which mothers of new babies undergo. It may not be socially acceptable for women to admit to experiencing grief over their loss of independence, or loss of a culturally defined 'attractive' body, or over the perception that they must now put their own needs after those of their children, but this does not mean that many women do not experience such feelings, even if they are simultaneously very positive about many aspects of their new role.

Depression in new mothers seems antithetical to the joy and celebration which surrounds the arrival of a new baby in all human cultures. The cultural assumption that the natural physiological process of childbirth gives way to a natural and confident ability to care for a child comes up sharply against the incontrovertible fact that women have no innate biological knowledge of how to change a nappy, soothe a crying baby, or tell the difference between heat rash and scarlet fever (Kitzinger, 1982).

With parenthood comes responsibility, and with responsibility comes both anxiety and an additional workload. This workload is disproportionately felt by women rather than men (Bittman, 1992). The special status accorded pregnant women frequently disappears when the child is born (Cox, 1988); fathers of babies disappear to the safe, familiar world of paid employment; and increasingly mothers have to juggle the needs of the baby with a need to earn money as well as their own needs for adequate food and sleep and a need to maintain a relationship with their partner (Brown et al., 1994). Kitzinger (1982) has described the way in which both women and men internalize the cultural notion that childcare is women's business, and that women are, or should be, experts while the role of men is, or should be, primarily to provide financial support to the mother so that she is able to care for the baby. In searching for psychosocial factors which are consistent across the wide range of cultures in which postpartum depression is reported, the key may be related to the internalizing of cultural expectations such as these, and the pressures that this puts on women.

Ussher (1992b) has described a long-standing cultural discourse which positions women as deficient, and unstable, because of their biology. Women are defined as ill or abnormal at practically every stage of their life cycle, as the ubiquitous 'hormones' rule their behaviour. Premenstrual symptoms give way to postnatal depression, which in turn gives way to menopause. The next chapter extends the discussion of this view of women as abnormal as a result of their hormones, by examining what happens when hormonal fluctuations cease.

4

MENOPAUSE: 'WHAT CAN YOU EXPECT, AT YOUR AGE?'

Recent years have seen a considerable increase in research interest in the menopause, accompanied by a shift away from an earlier, biomedically oriented emphasis on pathology which had much in common with research on premenstrual syndrome and postnatal problems, and towards an understanding of normal menopause in its social context (Ballinger, 1990). Initial research in this area (e.g. Wilson, 1966) focused on women who sought medical treatment and concluded that the menopause was a medical condition, inevitably associated with psychological distress and physical deterioration, a view which was consistent with strongly negative cultural stereotypes of menopause and ageing (Hunt, 1994; Matthews, 1992). While the biomedical perspective continues to dominate the literature (Rostosky & Travis, 1996), such views are now challenged by the findings of research which examines the midlife experiences of normal women (e.g. Avis & McKinlay, 1991; Matthews et al., 1990).

Increasing research interest in the menopause is frequently attributed to increases in life expectancy and the fact that women in developed countries now live an average of thirty years after the menopause. However, assumptions about women and about the relationship between women's hormones and their physical and emotional well-being have played a role here as in the topics discussed in the two previous chapters (Carolan, 1994). Menopause is still widely viewed as a purely biological process, 'an endocrine deficiency disease' (MacLennan, 1988: 158) and the universal prescription of exogenous hormones to restore 'normal' functioning is still commonly advocated (e.g. Barnes, 1991; Wilson, 1966). More recently, however, the emphasis of at least some research has shifted to an examination of the experience of normal menopause within the social context of women's lives.

This chapter presents evidence which challenges the traditional assumptions that midlife problems among women are primarily caused by hormonal changes, that menopause is inevitably accompanied by unpleasant symptoms and depression, and that it signifies the 'beginning of the end' (Hunt, 1994: 148), the advent of an emotionally empty old age bereft of a meaningful social role. The majority of women in fact appear to suffer few negative consequences during the menopause and post-menopausal years (Matthews et al., 1990), and personal problems arising during this life stage may be better explained by life events and by negative stereotypes associated with ageing for women, than by hormone levels (Ballinger, 1990).

In recent years, an assumption has arisen that hormone replacement therapy (HRT) is appropriate for all menopausal and post-menopausal women. This view is based on a hormone-centred view of women's health, and persists despite evidence showing a lack of association between hormone levels and well-being (Ussher, 1992c), as well as the arguments of non-interventionist feminist writers (e.g. Carolan, 1994; Coney, 1993; Dickson, 1990; Greer, 1991; Jones, 1994), who critique the widespread medicalization of what they regard as a normal and healthy stage in women's lives.

MENOPAUSE: SHORT- AND LONG-TERM CHANGES

Menopause is a natural physiological process resulting from ageing of the ovaries, leading to cessation of ovulation and of oestrogen production (Strickland, 1988). Natural menopause occurs gradually over a number of years; during this peri-menopausal period, oestrogen levels decrease and menstrual periods become irregular and then cease. The post-menopause, which is defined retrospectively after twelve months without menstruation, is reached at an average age of 50.4 years (World Health Organization, 1981).

Most research focuses on 'menopausal symptoms', although Cole and Rothblum (1990) have criticized the use of the term 'symptom' as implying that menopause is a disease, and suggest the word 'sign' instead. Short-term menopausal signs, which occur during the peri-menopause and disappear once hormone levels stabilize, are generally divided into three categories: vasomotor (e.g. hot flushes, night sweats); psychosomatic (e.g. headaches, palpitations, dizziness) and psychological (e.g. tiredness, forgetfulness, irritability, nervousness, loss of concentration) (Dennerstein, Smith, Morse, Burger, Green, Hopper & Ryan, 1993).

Epidemiological evidence suggests that, contrary to popular stereotypes, these 'symptoms' are not common during normal menopause. The most commonly experienced signs of menopause, and the only ones which are reported across most cultures (Beyene, 1986), are hot flushes and night sweats, and these have been unequivocally linked to changes in circulating oestrogen (Gannon, 1993; World Health Organization, 1981). However, the prevalence of indicators of menopause, even those with strong links to endocrine status, varies markedly between countries, suggesting that sociocultural factors play a role (Hunt, 1994).

An Australian survey of women in their fifties (France, Lee & Schofield, 1996) found that 81 per cent reported having experienced at least one hot flush and over half had experienced night sweats or vaginal dryness, although the majority of these women did not find the experience particularly distressing. By contrast, only 18 per cent of a sample of Chinese women in their forties and fifties (Tang, 1994) reported hot flushes, with 74 per cent of the sample regarding the menopause as a benign and natural process which gave no cause for concern. A larger survey of women from several South East Asian countries (Boulet, Oddens, Lehert, Vemer & Visser, 1994) also found lower levels of symptomatology and less distress than is reported in Western surveys. Even in a sample of Hong Kong Chinese women who had undergone complete hysterectomy and oophorectomy (Haines, Chung & Leung, 1994), vasomotor and other menopausal signs were less common than among Western women. Hot flushes were reported rarely in a survey of 500 middle-aged Filipino women (Ramoso-Jalbuena, 1994). They most frequently reported headaches and irritability, which are relatively uncommon in Western societies. Such variation suggests that socio-cultural factors play a central part in women's experience of the menopause.

Since Kraepelin introduced the concept of involutional melancholia, an assumption has existed that depression is prevalent during menopause, but in fact there is little evidence to suggest that peri- and post-menopausal women are particularly prone to depression or to other negative psychological states. An Australian cross-sectional study (Slaven & Lee, 1998) found that, although signs (particularly hot flushes and night sweats) did vary across groups defined by menopausal status, peri- and post-menopausal women did not show elevated levels of depression, anxiety or negative moods, by comparison with pre-menopausal women.

Several large-scale longitudinal surveys from the USA demonstrate the lack of a relationship between menopause and depression. Matthews et al. (1990), who followed a community sample of healthy women for several years, concluded that natural menopause led to few changes in normal women's psychological well-being. Indeed, two other large-scale longitudinal studies, the Massachusetts Women's Health Study (Avis & McKinlay, 1991) and the National Health Examination Follow-up Study (Busch, Zonderman & Costa, 1994), indicated that subjective well-being actually improved slightly among American women as the climacteric progressed.

In another longitudinal American study (Kaufert, Gilbert & Tate, 1992), participants were interviewed five times over several years; on each occasion, about 10 per cent of women scored in the depressed range of the Center for Epidemiological Studies Depression Scale (CES–D), but there was little consistency across time. Of those women who scored highly on the CES–D at any time, over half did so only once, illustrating the relative transience of depressive symptoms.

By contrast, one smaller study of English women (Hunter, 1990) did show a small but significant increase in depression during menopause. However, this sample was drawn from women attending menopause clinics, and treatment-seekers do tend to have higher levels of distress than most women (Morse, Smith, Dennerstein, Green, Hopper & Burger, 1994). In this sample, depression was best predicted by pre-menopausal depression, suggesting that it may be ongoing distress, rather than the biology of menopause, that leads to depression among women in this age group. Avis, Brambilla, McKinlay and Vass (1994), in an American survey, also found the strongest predictor of depressed mood during the peri-menopause to be a history of depressive illness, rather than any variable related to menopause itself.

While American research (Kaufert et al., 1992; McKinlay, McKinlay & Brambilla, 1987) has shown rates of depression to be significantly higher among women who have had a hysterectomy, it cannot be concluded that hysterectomy causes depression. Ballinger (1977) found high levels of depression among women attending a medical clinic before under-going hysterectomy, and it has been argued that 'depression . . . may even be a cause rather than a consequence of this surgery' (McKinlay et al., 1987: 345), since depressed women may actively seek out medical and gynaecological reasons for their distress. Further, two Australian surveys (France et al., 1996; Slaven & Lee, 1998) have failed to find any relationship between hysterectomy and various measures of mood, symptomatology and psychological distress, and a prospective American study (Everson, Matthews, Guzick, Wing & Kuller, 1995) found that women undergoing hysterectomy or oophorectomy did not experience negative psychological outcomes. Thus, the apparent relationship between hysterectomy and depression in some studies from the USA may be an artifact of culturally specific factors which influence the provision of hysterectomy in that country.

There are well-documented longer-term physical effects of menopause. Low levels of circulating oestrogen affect lipid metabolism, increasing post-menopausal women's risk of coronary heart disease to a level similar to that of men (Strickland, 1988). Low levels of oestrogen also affect the rate of calcium resorption from bone, leading to reductions in bone mineral density and to an increased risk of osteoporosis (Riggs & Melton, 1986). Coronary heart disease is the primary cause of death in women in Western countries (Lerner & Kannel, 1986), while osteoporosis is responsible for considerable morbidity and mortality, particularly through fractures to the hip, wrist and spine (Smith, Smith & Gilligan,

1990). These long-term effects have a major impact on women's life expectancy, their quality of life and their ability to live independently.

OESTROGEN DEFICIENCY: THE BIOLOGICAL HYPOTHESIS

Following the development of artificial oestrogen in the 1960s, the view that menopause was an oestrogen-deficiency disease led to the treatment of a wide range of experiences among midlife women with exogenous oestrogen (Wilson, 1966) and the suggestion that all women should use exogenous oestrogen from menopause until death (e.g. Barnes, 1991). Contemporary prescribing practice generally follows the recommendation of combined (oestrogen and progestogen) HRT for all women whose uteruses are intact (Writing Group for the PEPI Trial, 1995), since unopposed oestrogen has been shown to increase the risk of endometrial cancer (Ziel & Finkle, 1975), while the addition of progestogen virtually eliminates this risk (Whitehead et al., 1978).

Only the classic vasomotor signs of hot flushes and night sweats are clearly relieved by HRT (Gannon, 1993). Thus, HRT may relieve psychological distress in those instances where it results from the discomfort associated with vasomotor signs, which in extreme cases may interfere significantly with quality of life (Daly, Gray, Barlow, McPherson, Roche & Vessey, 1993). However, placebo-controlled research (e.g. Strickler, Borth & Cecutti, 1977; Thomson & Oswald, 1977) has found no effect of oestrogen on depressive or anxious symptoms. Life stressors, previous history of depression, and attitude towards the menopause are stronger predictors of a woman's psychological well-being than is her endocrine status (Gath et al., 1987; Hunter, 1990).

The value of the long-term use of combined HRT to reduce the risk of cardiovascular disease is not yet clearly established. There is good evidence that oestrogen, either alone or in combined HRT, will reduce low density lipoprotein cholesterol and increase high density lipoprotein cholesterol (Udoff, Langenberg & Adashi, 1995) and thus reduce a significant risk factor. However, there is as yet no evidence from clinical trials regarding the effect of HRT on actual mortality or morbidity from cardiovascular disease (Barrett-Connor, 1994).

HRT is also potentially useful in the prevention of osteoporosis for those women at high risk. It increases bone mass in women with osteoporosis (Christiansen & Riis, 1990; Lindsay & Tohme, 1990), and a recent large-scale prospective survey (Cauley, Seeley, Ensrud, Ettinger, Black & Cummings, 1995) has shown that use of HRT is associated with a reduced risk of osteoporotic fractures. At least six years of HRT is needed to achieve maximum benefit (Ravnikar, 1992; Stevenson, 1990), and rapid bone loss occurs after discontinuation of HRT (Hammond,

1989). When menopause is regarded as an oestrogen deficiency syndrome, such evidence seems to provide a rationale for indefinite oestrogen supplementation for all women, as recommended by Cauley et al. (1995), but non-pharmacological interventions, such as weight-bearing exercise and adequate calcium intake, both before and after menopause, have also been shown to reduce the risk (Smith et al., 1990), and may obviate the need for medical treatment.

Possible side effects must also be considered when any individual woman is making a decision about HRT. In the short term these include breast tenderness, weight gain, nausea, backache, abdominal cramps, rise in blood pressure, dizziness, depression, anxiety, and the return of menstruation (Marsh & Whitehead, 1992). Side effects may be reduced through individual adjustments to dosage (MacLennan, MacLennan, O'Neill, Kirkgard, Wenzel & Chambers, 1992), but surveys conducted in Australia (France et al., 1996) and Scotland (Garton, Reid & Rennie, 1995) found that between 31 and 43 per cent of previous users of HRT specified side effects as their main reason for stopping, suggesting that these symptoms are not uncommon.

More seriously, some recent research suggests that there may be an increased risk of cancer of the breast (Colditz et al., 1995) and of the ovary and endometrium, even from combined low-dose HRT (Barrett-Connor, 1992; Goddard, 1992), although other research (e.g. Stanford, Weiss, Voigt, Daling, Habel & Rossing, 1995) has failed to find any relationship between combined HRT and cancer.

The biomedical evidence suggests that HRT will be useful for a minority of women, those who experience oestrogen-deficiency-related symptoms or are at elevated risk of heart disease or osteoporosis. However, there have been dramatic increases in usage rates in recent years. A Finnish study (Topo, Klaukka, Hemminki & Uutela, 1991) demonstrated a five-fold increase between 1976 and 1989 among women aged forty-five to sixty-four, and there is some debate as to the appropriateness of this increase. Comparisons of randomized surveys across countries and over time do suggest the existence of differences in usage which are unlikely to be attributable simply to differences in health and risk-factor status. Methodologically consistent surveys of European women aged over forty (Oddens, Boulet, Lehert & Visser, 1992, 1994) demonstrate this, with rates ranging from 3 per cent in Italy, through 4 per cent in the Netherlands, 8 per cent in France, 12 per cent in Denmark, to 25 per cent in the former West Germany. In Australia, two surveys in different regions produced quite different figures: 31 per cent among Perth women aged forty-seven to sixty-two (Williams, Ming & Vyse, 1992), and 20 per cent among Melbourne women aged forty-five to fifty-five (Shelley & Smith, 1992). Usage is even higher in the USA, with a Californian survey (Harris, Laws, Roddy, King & Haskell, 1990) finding over 32 per cent of women aged fifty to sixty-five reporting current use.

It would appear that the decision to prescribe or to request HRT is not solely based on the experience of physiological symptoms (Oddens et al., 1994). While the structure of health care and medical practice in indi- vidual countries may play an important role, research has also identified differences among individuals, with European surveys consistent in showing that HRT users are more highly educated (Hemminki, Malin & Topo, 1993; Oddens et al., 1992; Sinclair, Bond & Taylor, 1993), and other surveys indicating that they are more likely to seek medical advice and to perceive menopause as a medical condition (Ferguson, Hoegh & Johnson, 1989).

LIFE EVENTS AND SOCIAL STEREOTYPES: THE SOCIOCULTURAL HYPOTHESIS

Alternatives to the oestrogen-deficiency hypothesis generally take the view that distress associated with the menopause is better explained by the increased probability of major life events occurring during the menopausal years, combined with the impact of social expectations and of negative sociocultural constructions of ageing for women.

Feminist scholars (e.g. Greer, 1991) have also pointed to the way in which normal women's experiences have been medicalized and the reality of personal distress and social rejection has been denied, by an assumption that women's behaviour is primarily caused by hormonal changes. This stereotype, which has been discussed in the previous chapters with reference to premenstrual and postpartum experiences, may be even stronger for ageing women, as ageism and sexism combine to make them a particularly stigmatized segment of the population (Mantecon, 1993); negative stereotypes of ageing are further discussed in Chapter 11, which deals with women's experiences of ageing and old age.

Women in their middle years typically experience substantial changes in their personal lives (McKinlay et al., 1987), and these changes may provide explanations for psychological distress. Menopausal women are disproportionately likely to experience major life events such as divorce, illness or death of a spouse, death or disability of a parent, or children leaving home (McKinlay et al., 1987), and Ballinger has argued that 'events such as changes in family structure, problems with parents, involvement in outside work and reappraisal of future role may have more impact on mental health at this time than the physiological changes of menopause' (Ballinger, 1990: 784).

France et al. (1996), with a sample of Australian women in their fifties, found that 16 per cent of respondents scored within the clinical range of the GHQ; however, only 2 per cent of the sample were unable to identify a recent major life event which they believed had precipitated their distress. Evidence such as this fails to support assumptions that distress among midlife women is explicable by endocrine changes and should be treated with HRT. A tendency to attribute women's distress to biological events may result in reduced recognition of distressing personal circumstances, both by health professionals and by the women themselves, and thus a reduced probability that appropriate interventions will be used (Carolan, 1994). The figure of 16 per cent may also be contrasted with findings from pilot surveys of the Women's Health Australia study, which reported a rate of 44 per cent among women aged eighteen to twenty-three (Lee, 1997), suggesting that very high rates of distress can occur among women who are not experiencing menopausal changes.

Many feminist writers have argued that cultural expectations of menopause, and of ageing, strongly influence women's experiences of menopause. Martin (1988) pointed to the way in which menopause, like menstruation, is overwhelmingly described in medical texts in terms of atrophy, decline and loss. Jones (1994) has argued more generally that society as a whole has constructed menopause as a biomedical event representing deterioration and decline, and has contrasted this with the actual experiences of menopausal women, which do not revolve purely around medical and biological issues but include concerns about changes to appearance and sexuality, and worry about the broader social and personal impact of ageing. Attitudes towards menopause and expectations of menopause are more negative in men and in young women than in middle-aged and older women (Gannon & Ekstrom, 1993), suggesting the existence of a stereotype which is strongest in those who are least involved.

The emphasis that Western societies place on youth, especially among women, is well documented, and Lennon (1987) has argued that menopausal distress may be related to the negative cultural meaning of menopause and ageing in Western societies. While it is difficult to compare women's experiences cross-culturally, some research does suggest that in non-Western cultures, in which older women have a clearly defined and respected social role, women report considerably less menopausal distress (Beyene, 1986). Tang's (1994) finding of low levels of symptoms and few concerns about menopause among Chinese women supports this argument. The lower levels of symptoms and distress experienced by women in other Asian countries (Boulet et al., 1994; Ramoso-Jalbuena, 1994) also support the view that the experience of menopause is culturally determined, although these comparisons may be confounded by cultural differences in willingness to discuss signs of menopause.

The sociocultural perspective would suggest that menopause, as a symbol of the end of a woman's youth and fertility, will be most distressing for women who occupy traditional gender roles and who have internalized a cultural view that values youth and physical attractiveness over maturity and wisdom in women (Lennon, 1987). While there is no empirical research which directly addresses this hypothesis, there is considerable evidence for the existence of a powerful negative stereotype of ageing, particularly for women (Mantecon, 1993). The view that post-menopausal women are substantially diminished as women by their inability to bear children, that they are past their useful life, was commonplace until recently in Western cultures (Siegal, 1990). While this view might not be stated explicitly by contemporary commentators, it is still implicit in social views of ageing women as unattractive and unnecessary members of society (Hunt, 1994). Qualitative research with working-class Italian immigrant women in Australia demonstrates the existence of a discourse which conceptualizes menopause as a symbol of the devalued status of old women and the participants' uncertainty and reluctance about the social role they would fill as older women in their adopted country (Gifford, 1994).

American research (e.g. Mansfield, Theisen & Boyer, 1992) indicates that women draw their information about the menopause largely from their friends and from the mass media; since there are strong negative ageist and sexist biases in contemporary American culture (Mansfield & Voda, 1993), this means that women are not exposed to a range of positive role models in the older age groups, and this may serve to increase women's distress about ageing and about menopause as a symbol of that process.

A particularly distressing aspect for some women may be the assumption that the menopause means the end of an active sexual life. Western cultural stereotypes of women equate sexual interest and activity with youth and deny the sexuality of older women (Carolan, 1994). While some (e.g. Sourander, 1994) have argued that oestrogen is essential for women's sexuality, as well, incidentally, as for the preservation of their personalities, it is evident that sexual interest continues during and after menopause. The relationship between oestrogen levels, physiological indicators of sexual arousal, and subjective sexual desire is not particularly close, and sexual response seems influenced more by psychological and social context than by physiological changes (Leiblum, 1990). Hawton, Gath and Day (1994) surveyed pre- and post-menopausal English women and found that sexual behaviour, attitudes and satisfaction were not related to age or menopausal status, but were most closely associated with the quality of the respondent's marital relationship. Koster and Garde (1993), in a longitudinal study of Danish women, found that 70 per cent showed no change in sexual activity or desire between the ages of forty and fifty-one years. Sexual activity and desire were best predicted by subjective health and by partner availability, and did not relate to menopausal status or symptoms, although those who had expected a reduction in sexual desire were the ones most likely to experience it. Expectations were also an important predictor of sexual activity and desire in a survey of post-menopausal Central American women (Bonilla-Becerra, Quintero-Zurek & Vela-Ortega, 1991); this group did show an overall reduction in sexual interest, though it was greatest for less educated women and for those with negative expectations. Cole and Rothblum (1990), pointing to heterosexist assumptions and biases in research on the menopause, surveyed lesbian women and found no evidence for any reduction in sexual desire or activity during the menopause; many women reported enhancement of their sexual experiences and of relationship quality. Such research suggests that sexuality is not necessarily diminished among post-menopausal women, and that expectations are more important than hormonal changes in any reduction of sexual interest (Leiblum, 1990).

IMPROVING QUALITY OF LIFE DURING THE MENOPAUSE

If distress among midlife women cannot be explained by endocrine changes, and will not necessarily be relieved through pharmacological intervention, there are likely to be more appropriate ways for individual women to deal with symptoms and with distress which arises during this life stage.

France et al. (1996) asked Australian women whether they used any strategies, other than HRT, to help them cope during the peri-menopausal years. Twenty-eight per cent had made changes to their diets which they felt had been beneficial, while 14 per cent felt that keeping active and busy helped to distract them from their symptoms, but the most frequent coping response, spontaneously reported by 68 per cent of the sample interviewed, was regular physical activity.

Empirical research has clearly established the positive effects of exercise on general physical and psychological health (Blumenthal et al., 1989), and there are several reasons for assuming that exercise may be particularly beneficial for menopausal women. Firstly, the health benefits of exercise have a number of important overlaps with the benefits of HRT: in particular, exercise has beneficial effects on coronary heart disease (Blair, Kohl, Paffenbarger, Clark, Cooper & Gibbons, 1989), bone mineral density (Smith et al., 1990), and vasomotor signs (Gannon, 1988). Secondly, exercise positively affects depression, anxiety, self-esteem, and general mood (Leith & Taylor, 1990). Thirdly, older women have the lowest rates of exercise of any community group in developed countries (C. Lee, 1993), and thus promotion of moderate regular exercise may have great potential to alleviate distress in this group.

Slaven and Lee (1994, 1997) found that women who chose to exercise scored significantly lower on measures of mood disturbance and on menstrual and menopause-related symptoms than women who did not exercise. This effect was found for pre-menopausal, peri-menopausal and post-menopausal women both with and without HRT; differences between exercisers and non-exercisers were considerably larger than those between groups defined by menopausal status. Wilbur, Dan, Hedricks and Holm (1990) obtained similar results with an American sample, showing that both recreational activity and work-related activity were associated with better general health and fewer symptoms among pre-, peri-, and post-menopausal women; however, Guthrie, Smith, Dennerstein and Morse (1994) found differences in physical health, but not menopausal symptoms or psychological health, between meno-pausal Australian women who exercised and those who did not.

Slaven and Lee (1997) also found an acute effect of exercise among regular exercisers; regardless of menopausal status, regular exercisers showed significant decreases in negative mood, increases in perceived vigour, and decreases in menopause-related signs, including hot flushes, immediately after a session of aerobic exercise. This is consistent with the findings of Hammer, Berg and Lindgren (1990), who found that aerobic activity reduced the frequency of hot flushes among a Scandinavian sample. Although there is a need for prospective studies with women systematically assigned to exercise and attention-control groups, such research suggests a possible role for exercise, and perhaps for other lifestyle interventions, in alleviating negative experiences among mid-aged women. Further, it suggests the possibility that lifelong medication may be avoided by many women who adopt or maintain positive health habits during the middle years.

The evidence presented in this chapter suggests that menopause is generally a benign process, not associated with major symptoms or changes to quality of life. Those women who do experience negative psychological states during the pre- and post-menopausal years are usually characterized by ongoing psychological distress which precedes the menopause, or experience major life events which are coincident with the physiological changes.

However, there are strongly negative sociocultural perspectives on menopause and on women's ageing, with menopause seen as a symbol of an older woman's diminished social value. Loss of reproductive function comes to symbolize loss of social worth, and the internaliza-tion of these cultural values may underlie many women's negative experiences.

Research has focused on the medical aspects of menopause, and clinic-based samples still predominate in the literature. This leads to a negative picture of menopause and an assumption that it is a condition in need of treatment, rather than a normal life stage. Future research might usefully

examine the role of expectations and sociocultural stereotypes in determining women's experience of menopause and the role of lifestyle and
educational interventions in the prevention of negative experiences
during midlife.

Feminist analyses of the menopause also suggest that structural
inequities in contemporary society mean that midlife is more of a crisis
for women than it is for men. Since women are traditionally valued more
for their attractiveness to men than they are for their personal and
intellectual development, ageing is associated with a reduction in social
power and perceived value for women (Hunt, 1994). Broader cultural
change which supports an acknowledgement of women as valuable
members of society at all ages might remove many of the negative myths
and stereotypes which surround menopause.

Part II
EVERY WOMAN'S DESTINY
INTRODUCTION

A second myth that serves to undermine women's health and well-being is the myth of motherhood: the notion that motherhood is easy, natural and wonderful, that it is the peak of fulfilment and the achievement of women's main purpose for existence, and that women who do not have children are either tragically unfulfilled or deeply flawed.

The idea that motherhood is women's destiny, combined with the fanciful notion that women have some innate knowledge of how to care for babies and bring up children, serves to restrict women's life choices and their capacity to participate fully in adult life. Regardless of individual preferences, it seems that social forces pressure women into taking on the majority of the work of caring for children and putting their own personal, educational, financial and developmental pursuits to one side; at the same time, fathers find it difficult to resist pressures to work longer and harder outside the home, regardless of their own preferences.

The first chapter in this part deals with childlessness, discussing infertile couples and those who choose to remain childless. Sociocultural views of motherhood create an artificial dichotomy between the happy, fulfilled mother and the tragically infertile woman. The research evidence, by contrast, suggests that there is a continuum in degree of interest in having children as well as in ability to conceive. Involuntarily infertile women generally cope well with their circumstances, and women who remain childless by choice are as happy with their decision as are those who choose motherhood. Through contrasting mothers with those women who present for infertility treatment, however, the research literature serves to maintain the myth that all women desire motherhood, that every woman has the right to as many babies as she wants, and that the only thing that stops women from having children exactly when and how they choose is their biology. There is little research which examines the full spectrum of women's attitudes and choices regarding motherhood. Infertile women who choose not to seek medical intervention, women who are forced by economic or other factors to remain childless or to have fewer children than they would have preferred, and women who choose to pursue other life goals, are not well represented in the psychological literature. Thus, the assumption is maintained that all women want babies and that those who cannot have them naturally should be supremely grateful for the existence of modern reproductive technologies. This is also contradicted by the evidence, that *in vitro* and other artificial reproductive technologies are generally unsuccessful and tend to increase, rather than alleviate, infertile women's distress.

Societies which assume that all women want children have difficulty in dealing with the universal practice of fertility control through contraception and abortion, which is discussed in the following chapter. There is ample evidence that women will seek to control their fertility, through illegal and dangerous means if legal and safe methods are denied them, and that access to effective contraception and safe abortion contributes to women's health and longevity, as well as reducing infant mortality by providing the means for women to space their children optimally. Religious and cultural proscriptions of fertility control are based on a desire to limit women's freedom of choice rather than on any actual concern for the well-being of women and their families or the presumed sanctity of tissue which might perhaps, under other circumstances, have grown into an infant.

Chapter 7 examines the reality of motherhood in contemporary society. Although most women have children, and most mothers express great satisfaction with motherhood, bringing up children is a task which falls inequitably on women in all societies, and serves to reduce their ability to involve themselves with other life goals. Thus, this part aims to demythologize motherhood, by presenting evidence that it is not always desirable for all women, not worth undergoing painful and usually unsuccessful medical intervention, and a limiting life choice with far-reaching consequences, in a society which sees the care of children both as something other than genuine work, and as inherently the duty of women.

5

CHILDLESSNESS BY CHANCE OR CHOICE: PERSONAL TRAGEDY OR SOCIAL DEVIANCE

This chapter examines the impact of infertility on both women and men, as well as discussing the impact of assisted conception and the experiences of the voluntarily childless. It is argued that a culturally mediated view, that women must give birth to babies in order to achieve full adult status, combines with a more recent perspective, arising in part from the development of assisted reproduction technologies, that all couples should be able to have as many babies as they want whenever they want. This combination, it is argued, produces a considerable amount of unnecessary distress and social stigmatization.

While parenthood is considered an important life goal for both men and women, our culture views parenthood as more central to women's lives than it is to men's. 'The socialization process to which women are exposed through formative and adolescent years carries with it a compelling message that motherhood and womanhood are synonymous. Despite pursuit of a career, a woman's real destiny and achievement appears to be motherhood' (NHMRC, 1995, p. 19). Women who do not have children experience considerable social stigmatization, although the experiences of the voluntarily childless demonstrate that personal fulfilment and psychological health are quite possible without motherhood (Connidis & McMullin, 1993; Veevers, 1980).

Social pressures on women to bear children, if necessary by going to extraordinary lengths to conceive their own child, are just one part of the 'motherhood imperative' which serves to restrict women's life choices, their control over their bodies, and their ability to act as fully independent members of society. In a culture in which the care of children remains overwhelmingly women's work, unpaid and largely unsupported by the state (Bittman, 1992), and in which women are expected to compromise their education, their careers and their leisure time in order to care for family members (Smith, 1991), motherhood involves restrictions of choice which are not paralleled in fatherhood. The culturally mediated view that women – at least married women – must go to extraordinary lengths, if required, in order to become mothers (Oakley, 1993; Whiteford & Gonzalez, 1995), and that women who are not mothers are of little value, pressures women to make decisions which will limit their personal, intellectual and social development and prevent them from reaching their economic and political potential. While the joys of mother-hood cannot be denied, and the raising of children has enormous value to society, women must make a difficult choice.

INVOLUNTARY CHILDLESSNESS

Childlessness is construed very differently in our society depending on whether it is perceived as voluntary or involuntary (Lampman & Dowling-Guyer, 1995). However, this distinction is not nearly as clear as it appears. Infertility is generally defined as the failure to achieve a pregnancy after twelve months of unprotected sexual intercourse (e.g. Daniluk, 1991), but this definition is less simple than it might seem, and infertility, in the sense it is generally used in the psychological literature, might be better defined as the inability to have a baby when it is wanted.

It is worth emphasizing that people will only discover that they have fertility problems if they decide to have a baby, and that in general they will only be included in research on fertility problems if they decide to seek treatment or advice about conception. Many women or couples choose to remain childless, to delay childbearing, or to have fewer children than they might otherwise have had, for a wide variety of individual reasons. These include, but are by no means limited to, because they are not in a stable relationship; do not have the social or economic resources to cope with a baby; are busy pursuing personal, educational or career goals; or have chronic medical or health conditions which might interfere with their capacity to care for a child in the longer term. Some of these people may define themselves as childless by choice, some as childless by circumstance. Most would not be aware of whether or not they are biologically able to conceive, and many childless women have not made a definite commitment, either to remain childless or to seek to have children. Thus, the distinction between voluntary and involuntary childlessness is not always clear cut.

Further, many couples who seek treatment for infertility do later conceive naturally (Slade, Raval, Buck & Lieberman, 1992); Oakley (1993) estimates that 5 per cent of couples seeking *in vitro* fertilization conceive while on waiting lists for treatment. Naturally fertile couples have approximately one chance in three of conceiving with each ovarian cycle, but 20 per cent will take between one and two years to conceive (Valentine, 1986).

While a number of authors (e.g. Daniluk, 1991; Morrow, Thoreson & Penney, 1995) cite the figure of one in six couples as infertile, the actual proportion of couples who are unable to conceive is not known. Australian statistics indicate that just over 90 per cent of women do have children at some stage in their lives (Australian Bureau of Statistics, 1995), and international comparisons suggest that this figure is fairly consistent across cultures (Poston & Trent, 1982). However, an unknown proportion of women who do become mothers may have been in an infertile partnership for at least some of their lives, may have sought assisted conception, or may have taken several years to become pregnant, and an unknown proportion of women who do not become mothers might be potentially fertile, under different circumstances or with a different partner.

Involuntary childlessness, thus, is better viewed as a biopsychosocial phenomenon than as a disease or biological condition, as it arises only when there is a relative or absolute inability to conceive, in combination with a psychologically, socially or culturally driven wish to have a child, and the existence of personal, social and financial circumstances which mean that childbearing is seen as an appropriate choice by the individual or couple involved.

A complicating issue with research into involuntary childlessness is the wide range of causes of failure to conceive, and the fact that some of these causes (e.g. ovarian failure, absence of sperm) may be seen as absolute barriers to conception while others (e.g. occasional anovulatory cycles, low sperm count) reduce the probability of conception but do not completely exclude the possibility. Because many 'infertile' individuals are in fact subfertile, infertility is generally considered a property of a couple rather than of an individual: a woman who has frequent anovulatory cycles, for example, may fail to conceive with a male partner who has low sperm motility but may conceive with a different partner.

Despite this, and despite research which indicates that only around 40 per cent of cases of infertility arise mainly or entirely from characteristics of the woman, with 40 per cent resulting from characteristics of the man and 20 per cent from the interaction of problems in both partners (Valentine, 1986), research on failure to conceive has focused almost exclusively on women (Rowland, 1992).

Ussher (1992b) has discussed the cultural pressure on women to become mothers, and the assumption that a woman without a baby must be unhappy and unfulfilled, no matter how successful and creative her life may be in other ways; in a similar vein, Rowland (1992) and Whiteford and Gonzalez (1995) have described how reproductive technologies reduce a woman's personal value to her ability to conceive, and result in a neglect of other aspects of her as a human being. While men do in general grow up with the expectation that they will be fathers, there appears to be less pressure and less stigma attached to childless men than to childless women.

The 'biological clock' myth, the myth that all women are overwhelmed by an irrational desire to have a baby once they reach a certain vaguely defined age, and the patronizing view that a woman should have a baby while she can, regardless of her preferences, because she will certainly change her mind and regret it when it's too late, is a myth which, like the raging hormones myth, implies that women are less rational than men, less able to plan their lives, and less able to make sensible and consistent decisions. Resistance of this myth by choosing to remain childless is stigmatized as unfeminine and unnatural, and thus women are pressured into making choices which will limit their lives in important ways. Interestingly, though, women who are not in conventional heterosexual relationships – lesbian women and women without partners – are subjected to quite different social pressures. These women, as Alldred (1996) has argued, are viewed as already deviant, and choosing motherhood under these circumstances is not seen as a natural and positive thing to do, but as evidence of further deviance, of selfishness and perversion.

Role of psychology and behaviour in infertility

Traditionally, psychoanalysts have blamed infertility on the woman's inability to resolve her childhood conflicts; somehow a woman's psychosocial immaturity prevented her from conceiving (Deutsch, 1947), and thus failure to become a mother was proof of failure to become an adult woman. A better understanding of the range of biological causes of fertility in both women and men has served to dilute, but not completely remove, the tendency to blame infertility on women's psychological inadequacies (Kikendall, 1994). Psychosocial stress and anxiety may also play a role in reduced fertility in at least some instances, perhaps by affecting immune functioning (e.g. Kedem, Bartoov, Mikulincer & Shkolnik, 1992). However, further research is needed to develop an understanding of the interaction of psychological and biological processes in problems of conception (Edelman & Golombok, 1989; O'Moore & Harrison, 1991). Wasser (1994) has argued, on evolutionary grounds, that it would make sense for rates of fertility to drop when adults were stressed; however, the majority of evidence relating infertility and stress is cross-sectional in nature, comparing naturally fertile couples with those who choose to seek treatment for infertility, and thus is open to a range of interpretations.

Lifestyle factors such as smoking and drinking may affect fertility, though these factors appear to have a stronger influence on male infertility (e.g. reducing sperm count and motility) than on female infertility (Florack, Zielhuis & Rolland, 1994). This suggests that lifestyle interventions might affect fertility particularly in men, but there is no systematic research which explores this possibility. In fact, there is little research in general on the prevention, or the non-medical treatment, of infertility (Oakley, 1993).

Psychological consequences of infertility

All cultures place a strong positive value on parenthood, and Western cultures place strong pressures on women to expect and wish to become mothers (Ussher, 1992b). The view that failure to have children is a major tragedy is reflected in the titles of research articles such as 'Infertility: A crisis with no resolution' (Butler & Koraleski, 1990) and 'Infertility: An unanticipated and prolonged life crisis' (Forrest & Gilbert, 1992). Couples who seek treatment for infertility do report distress, and at the time of seeking treatment 50 per cent of women and 15 per cent of men describe it as the most upsetting thing that has ever happened in their lives (NHMRC, 1995). However, there is no evidence that people entering fertility treatment programmes are experiencing major or unresolved psychological disturbance, or indeed are any more distressed than are naturally fertile couples.

Research from Australia, Finland, Hong Kong, the UK and the USA, using a wide range of assessment strategies (e.g. Callan & Hennessey, 1989; Chan, O'Hoy, Wong & So, 1989; Connolly, Edelmann, Cooke & Robson, 1992; Cook, Parsons, Mason & Golombok, 1989; Downey & McKinney, 1992; Edelmann, Connolly & Bartlett, 1994; Vartiainen, 1992), has shown consistently that people attending fertility clinics, both male and female, are generally well-adjusted and stable, with no evidence of clinical levels of anxiety and depression, or of poor sexual and personal relationships.

Where distress has been identified, this seems to be related to self-blame or guilt (e.g. Morrow et al., 1995; Stanton, Tennen, Affleck & Mendola, 1992) or with the use of avoidant coping strategies (e.g. Cook et al., 1989; Morrow et al., 1995; Stanton et al., 1992), rather than resulting directly from the infertility. Striving to conceive can have a negative effect on sexual and emotional relationships, as sex can come to be seen as a task or homework, or as a reminder of continuing failure (Andrews, Abbey & Halman, 1991; Burns, 1995; Greil, Porter & Leitko, 1989). Thus, it is the way in which a person interprets or reacts to infertility which leads to distress, not the simple fact of infertility itself.

Obviously, reproductive failure will be interpreted differently by different individuals, and a number of authors have stressed the hetero-geneity of circumstances and reactions which may be involved (Lupton, 1994). Kikendall (1994), for example, showed that women's distress was related to the degree to which they viewed motherhood as part of their ideal self. At least some couples have reported that their relationships

have improved as a result of working through the issues associated
with infertility (Greil et al., 1989; Mendola, Tennen, Affleck, McCann
& Fitzgerald, 1990), and Callan and Hennessey (1989) found that
infertile couples had a better relationship quality than did couples with
children.

It might be expected that women, socialized to view motherhood as
the peak of their achievements, would be more distressed than men,
but this is not generally the case, although women and men do seem
to experience infertility somewhat differently (e.g. Berg, Wilson &
Weingartner, 1991; Stanton et al., 1992; Ulbrich, Coyle & Llabre, 1990).
Abbey, Andrews and Halman (1991) found that, while women were
more stressed and felt more responsible for the infertility than did their
husbands, women in comparison couples were also more depressed and
rated their marital relationship more poorly than did their husbands.
This illustrates the importance of adequate controls and of avoiding the
trap of attributing any problems in infertile couples or individuals to
the infertility itself.

Given the stress which our culture places on bearing children, and the
fact that only those who are sufficiently concerned about their failure to
conceive to seek treatment are included in research on infertility, it is
surprising how little evidence there is for high levels of distress. It
should be emphasized that infertility research focuses exclusively on
people who have chosen to seek treatment, and it is reasonable to
assume that these people may be more distressed by their infertility than
people who do not seek treatment. Even with this potential bias, though,
there is little evidence that infertility is a major stressor.

There is no evidence on what proportion of people who are unable to
conceive will seek treatment, nor is there any evidence on whether
treatment-seekers are more or less distressed by their fertility problems,
or otherwise psychologically different, by comparison with people who
choose not to seek treatment. It is possible, for example, that a proportion
of people who do not conceive naturally will simply accept that they are
not going to be parents, and experience little or no distress over the
matter. The exclusive emphasis on people who seek treatment may create
an artificial dichotomy between the happily fertile and the discontented
infertile, bearing with it the implicit view that only people with children
can be happy, and that becoming pregnant is the answer to women's
distress. In reality, there may be a range of attitudes to childbearing
among both the fertile and the infertile, and there may be a proportion of
infertile people who are quite content with that state.

Overall, the admittedly limited literature certainly does not support a
view of involuntary childlessness as a tragedy of major proportions for
most people who seek treatment. It does, however, appear that treatment
for infertility can cause considerable distress, and it is arguable (e.g.
Lupton, 1994; Scritchfield, 1995) that the emphasis on high-technology

'cure', rather than on an acceptance that some women do not conceive in some partnerships, is responsible for the majority of the distress surrounding infertility.

REPRODUCTIVE TECHNOLOGIES

The increased range and availability of technological methods for assisting conception has brought with it a range of moral, legal, social and psychological questions. The two main forms of reproductive technology are artificial insemination (AI) and an ever-increasing range of variants on *in vitro* fertilization (IVF). AI is used when the male partner is infertile or has insufficient sperm for natural fertilization, while the female partner has no conception-related problems. It involves the introduction of a donor's sperm, or a concentrated sample of the partner's sperm, into the woman's vagina. Conception and implantation then occur naturally. IVF refers to a range of techniques which involve the removal of an ovum from the woman's body, or the use of a donor ovum, its fertilization in the laboratory using either the male partner's or a donor's sperm, and the later implantation of the resultant embryo in the woman's uterus.

While lay discourses present reproductive technologies as the source of miraculous happiness for unfulfilled women whose lives would otherwise be tragically empty (Lupton, 1994; Rowland, 1992), the evidence suggests that this is not the case. It is worth noting that the long-term outcomes of successful IVF are positive, with marital and family quality being high and the children showing healthy physical and psychological development (Abbey, Andrews & Halman, 1994; McMahon, Ungerer, Beaurepaire & Tennant, 1995), but outcomes for the majority of couples are less benign.

Involvement in an IVF programme is enormously disruptive to normal life, particularly for the woman. The cost in time, money and emotional stress is extremely high and the probability of bearing a healthy child is relatively low (Rowland, 1992). The National Perinatal Statistics Unit, which collates data from IVF and related programmes in Australia and New Zealand, estimates that the probability of a live birth resulting from any one treatment cycle is around 10 per cent (NHMRC, 1995), although evidence from other countries would suggest that this may be a little higher than the success rates elsewhere, and the distress associated with the treatment is considerable.

Couples frequently enter treatment with high levels of optimism, and there may be little distress associated with the first cycle of treatment. Reading, Chang and Kerin (1989), for example, followed thirty-seven US women through one treatment cycle, and found that general psychological adjustment was fairly positive throughout; however, only two women became pregnant. Repeated cycles of treatment are associated with increasing levels of depression (Beaurepaire, Jones, Thiering, Saunders & Tennant, 1994), although much of the research on the effects of continued treatment is cross-sectional in nature and thus raises interpretation problems. For example, a cross-sectional comparison of 104 couples who had been in treatment for infertility for one, two or three or more years (Berg & Wilson, 1991) showed that emotional strain was higher in the first year, but that relationship quality and sexual functioning were lower in the second and subsequent years. However, couples who choose to remain in highly invasive, expensive and un-successful treatment for infertility for three or more years may be unusual in a number of ways, and poor relationship quality may be a precursor, rather than a result, of these couples' continued search for conception.

Assessment of Australian women before and after a failed IVF cycle showed increases in depression and reductions in self-confidence (Hynes, Callan, Terry & Gallois, 1992), while similar American research (Litt, Tennen, Affleck & Klock, 1992) found that six out of thirty-six women who failed to conceive during an IVF cycle developed clinical levels of depression. These findings would suggest that the normal outcome of treatment, failure to conceive, has negative effects on women's well-being, although there is a need for appropriate controls; other research has shown that couples who do conceive may also experience decreases in marital adjustment and other related variables (e.g. Slade et al., 1992).

A Canadian project (Benazon, Wright, & Sabourin, 1992) which fol-lowed 165 couples through eighteen months of fertility treatment found significant increases in stress and reductions in marital quality. While 29 per cent of couples did conceive over this time period, and conception was associated with less marital distress, this relatively large-scale study demonstrates that the majority of couples will not conceive, and their relationships are likely to deteriorate. Of course, adequate controls are as necessary here as in other areas, as it appears that marital satisfaction also trends downwards in couples who are not seeking fertility treatment (Belsky & Pensky, 1988).

For the majority of patients, treatment for infertility involves dealing with distress, grief and a sense of failure when they do not conceive (Hurwitz, 1989). It has been argued that the production of a baby is not necessarily the only positive outcome of assisted conception (NHMRC, 1995), and that coming to terms with childlessness may also be regarded as a successful conclusion to treatment. However, the actual procedures involved in assisted conception are themselves unpleasant and highly intrusive, and women must also deal with shame, embarrassment and physical pain during the procedures, as well as a more generalized sensation of loss of control and alienation from their own bodies

(Hurwitz, 1989; Rowland, 1992). If the most frequently occurring 'positive outcome' is an acceptance of childlessness, there are considerably less intrusive, upsetting and expensive ways of achieving this goal.

There is also a real risk of negative health effects from reproductive technology, with a recent Australian review (NHMRC, 1995) describing ovarian hyperstimulation syndrome, ovarian cysts, and pelvic infections as relatively common, and noting that perinatal difficulties, including prematurity, malformations, multiple births and Caesarian deliveries, are more common in technologically assisted than in normal pregnancies. Oakley (1993) estimates that multiple births, with their attendant physical, emotional and financial strains and vastly increased risk of foetal abnormality, miscarriage and neonatal death, are twenty-seven times as likely following IVF as they are for normal conception. There appear to be few longer-term health effects on the mother, however, except for the increased risk of Creutzfeldt-Jakob Disease among women who have taken human pituitary gonadotrophin, a treatment which was discontinued in the 1980s because of this risk (NHMRC, 1995).

Another important issue is that of who should benefit from reproductive technologies. The costs of IVF are prohibitive, and only the wealthy are able to persist with treatment, despite the rhetoric that reproductive technologies give every woman the chance to have her own baby (Rowland, 1992). Most treatment clinics have a policy of accepting only women who are married, while some have additional irrelevant criteria, which include being within certain arbitrary age limits, having an 'ideal' level of body fat, and being exclusively heterosexual (Campion, 1995). A few insist that the woman must not be employed outside the home and that she must have a male partner with a full-time paid job (Campion, 1995), and some (e.g. Humphrey, Humphrey & Ainsworth-Smith, 1991) have suggested that candidates should undergo thorough screening for marital quality, physical health and social adjustment.

It is notable that very similar, indeed more stringent, restrictions are placed on people who wish to adopt or foster children (Campion, 1995). Although it would be completely unacceptable on social and political grounds to attempt to apply any such criteria to natural motherhood, it appears that the rhetoric of babies for all through the miracles of modern technology actually means fertilization attempts for the chosen few, and babies for even fewer. Movements to restrict access to reproductive technologies (or indeed to contraception or abortion) need to be considered in conjunction with other movements which aim to restrict women's reproductive choices in other ways. Arguments for restriction of the availability of reproductive technologies to women who meet arbitrary criteria of suitability are difficult to justify, but appear to be grounded in the same discourse which holds that women are either not entitled to contraception and abortion services, or that this decision rests with the medical profession rather than with those actually concerned with the consequences of the decision. This perspective is grounded in a socially conservative view which would replace individual decision-making with social control of fertility. Only those women who meet conservative criteria for fulfilling the traditional role of 'good mother', it is assumed, have the right to benefit from reproductive technology or from the misfortune of children in need of adoption (Campion, 1995).

A final concern with reproductive technologies is the culturally based assumption that, since the technology exists, women should undergo treatment rather than accepting their childlessness or seeking to adopt or foster a child in need of care (Lupton, 1994). Becker and Nachtigall (1994) have argued that the combination of a perception among women that they must try anything in the quest for their own baby, and the biomedical assumption that all undesired conditions can and should be 'cured' through the application of technology, has led to women undergoing high-risk interventions with little chance of success. Campion (1995) has argued on similar lines, that voluntary childlessness is so strongly stigmatized that women feel obliged to go to heroic lengths in order to prove that they really are infertile; she suggested that many women experience an enormous sense of relief when they finally stop treatment, feeling that they have proved their point and can now get on with their own lives.

CHILDLESS BY CHOICE

It is notable that there is very little research on the experiences and decisions of women who choose not to have babies. While the majority of women do have children, Australian statistics (Australian Bureau of Statistics, 1995) show that over 9 per cent of women have not had children by the age of fifty, while slightly older American figures indicate that 17 per cent of women aged between thirty-five and thirty-nine are childless (US Bureau of the Census, 1987). Not all these women are childless by choice, but surveys in the USA have indicated that 19 per cent of women and 13 per cent of men do not want children (Seccombe, 1991). Morgan and Chen (1992) predicted that anything up to 25 per cent of the US population may remain childless by choice in the near future, although a more recent survey from Australia found that only 8 per cent of women aged eighteen to twenty-three said that they wanted to be childless at the age of thirty-five, with 64 per cent wanting one or two children and 28 per cent wanting more than two.

Reading and Amatea (1986) noted that voluntary childlessness is viewed within the psychological literature as a deviant lifestyle, and that the decision to remain childless is widely assumed to be a defensive one, arising from childhood trauma or a disturbed family life. Seccombe

(1991) and Somers (1993) demonstrated the existence of a stereotype of the childless, or 'childfree', as selfish, immature, lonely and unhappy, while Lampman and Dowling-Guyer (1995) found that students held a stereotype of the voluntarily childless as selfish, cold and excessively ambitious. Alldred (1996) has pointed out the contradictions in social stereotypes of motherhood: the argument that all heterosexual women with partners who choose not to have children, and all lesbians and single women who choose to become mothers, must be motivated by greed and selfishness, while, conversely, greed and selfishness are completely absent from married women's decisions to have children, makes no coherent sense but underlies many attitudes and decisions about the provision of health and social services to women.

Popenoe (1993), in an article bemoaning the decline of the American family, has explicitly excluded childless couples from his definition of the family, describing them as 'adults who merely have an intimate relationship of some kind' (p. 529), and implying that this state of affairs is somehow reprehensible, or at least a very poor second to parenthood.

However, empirical research does not support the negative stereotype of the childless woman. Reading and Amatea (1986), for example, compared female graduate students who had chosen not to have children, with female graduate students with children. They found that the childless women reported having had relationships with their own mothers which were actually better than those reported by the women with children; further, the childless women reported that their fathers had been more likely to encourage them to become independent and active than had the fathers of the women with children. Childless women and women with children had quite different views of motherhood; the mothers ascribed motherhood to altruistic motives while the childless women saw it as a selfish choice, and saw motherhood as a less salient role in adult life. Similarly, Callan (1986), in Australia, found that the voluntarily childless saw high costs and low satisfaction in parenthood, while parents' views were the opposite. Thus, it appears that both parents and non-parents make life choices which are largely congruent with their attitudes.

A Scottish survey of the voluntarily childless (Campbell, 1983) found that they held negative views of childbirth, of children, and of childcare tasks, and viewed parenthood as a loss of control over their lives, a financial burden, and a heavy responsibility. A large-scale Canadian survey (Veevers, 1980) found that, although the voluntarily childless perceived that they were discriminated against and rejected by some members of their families and social groups, the majority believed strongly that they had made the right choice and that their lives were happier and more fulfilled than they would have been with children. Further, another Canadian study (Connidis & McMullin, 1993), this time with couples aged fifty-five and over, found that those who were childless by choice were just as satisfied and happy with their lives as were those parents who had close relationships with their children, and both groups scored better than either the involuntarily childless or those who had distant relationships with their adult children.

In Australia, Callan (1987) found that mothers and the voluntarily childless scored similarly on measures of well-being and marital satisfaction; infertile women did report lower levels of well-being than the other groups, but they also reported satisfaction with the freedom and flexibility they experienced and the amount of love and social support they received. Voluntarily childless women spent more time with their husbands and had closer relationships with them, a phenomenon which was also found by Somers (1993) in a survey of childless American couples.

Thus, while our socialization might lead us to assume that parenthood is an essential feature of a normal adult role (Gerson, Posner & Morris, 1991), in fact there is a range of attitudes to parenthood. There is, however, very little research on these attitudes and the process of decision-making involved in deciding whether, when and how often to produce offspring. The research on infertility is based on the assumption that all women are, or should be, driven by a powerful internal urge to have babies. While it is clear that some women do report such an urge, it is also clear that other women have children because of social expectancies, because of contraceptive failure, or for a range of other personal, social or cultural reasons. Myths such as the existence of the 'biological clock' or 'maternal instincts' put pressure on women to procreate and to feel obliged to seek intervention if procreation does not occur naturally.

Motherhood is, of course, a positive choice for many women, but the problems faced by women who do not become mothers, for whatever reason, appear to arise more from a cultural construction of motherhood as the ultimate goal for all women than from any intrinsic biological need for parenthood. Women may be childless for a range of reasons, and the artificial dichotomy between tragic women who are unable to conceive, and selfish women who do not want to conceive, cannot be maintained. While many infertile women are involuntarily childless, other infertile women may be perfectly content with their lot. Conversely, some fertile women may choose not to have children because they feel this is a responsible choice (for example, because they lack a supportive partner, are involved in pursuing other life goals, or simply do not feel much interest in motherhood). Other fertile women may choose to have children, despite personal and financial difficulties, because they feel that motherhood is an experience they want, or because of perceived pressure from partners and families.

The research on infertility, with its assumption that motherhood is unequivocally desirable for all women, and that women should go to extraordinary lengths if necessary to conceive, disguises the cultural imperative of compulsory motherhood in the rhetoric of freedom of choice and of the achievement of happiness through technology. Given the enormous workload which falls inequitably on mothers in contemporary Western society (Bittman, 1992), true freedom for women is achieved not through technological intervention but through greater equity, greater social and financial support for the valuable role of parenting (Wasser, 1990), and genuine, uncoerced, freedom to choose.

6

FERTILITY CONTROL

Access to adequate contraception and to abortion, and conversely to adequate support for women who choose to have children, is essential for women's ability to determine the course of their lives and to avoid poverty and illness. In many countries, however, powerful social institutions attempt to restrict women's rights to make decisions about childbearing.

This chapter argues that the positive effects of free access to contraception and abortion far outweigh the negative effects, for women and for their families and, as a consequence, for the societies in which they live (Westhoff & Rosenfield, 1993). The medical risks associated with both contraception and legal abortion are low, and much lower than the risks to both mother and child of unintended pregnancy (Maine, Karkazis & Bolan, 1994; Westhoff & Rosenfield, 1993). The ability to choose whether and when to have children is essential to women for financial, social, medical and personal reasons, and because of this birth control is a social reality which, despite a long history of attempts to suppress it, cannot be legislated away (David, 1992a). Restricting legal access to fertility control methods does not reduce women's need for birth control, but rather puts pressure on women to make use of illegal or clandestine birth control methods, with potentially serious medical consequences. It is well established, for example, that placing legal restrictions on the availability of abortions has no impact whatsoever on abortion rates but does increase the risk of mortality and of serious medical complications (David, 1992a; Maine et al., 1994).

Abortion is a safe medical procedure when conducted in appropriate professional settings (Maine et al., 1994), but illegal abortions are often conducted by untrained individuals in unsanitary conditions. Estimates of the worldwide annual death rate from illegal abortions range from 100,000 (Kulczycki, Potts & Rosenfield, 1995) to 200,000 women (Dixon-Mueller, 1990); in sub-Saharan Africa, approximately 50 per cent of all maternal deaths result from unsafe illegal abortion (Rogo, 1993). Many of the women who die as a result of illegal abortions leave small children without adequate care. One-third of the world's women live in countries where legal abortion is virtually unobtainable (Dixon-Mueller, 1990). The relative safety of legal abortions is indicated by US figures which show a death rate of 0.5 per 100,000 legal abortions, a rate which is twenty-five times lower than for childbirth, and one hundred times lower than for major surgery (Stotland, 1991).

Maine et al. (1994) have argued that the provision of safe abortions and adequate contraception would have a major impact on women's well-being in developing countries, with Dixon-Mueller (1990) estimating that better abortion services could save up to 100,000 lives annually. Westhoff and Rosenfield (1993) suggested that adequate fertility control in developing countries could also reduce infant mortality by as much as 20 per cent, by enabling women to space their children appropriately and to provide adequate care for each child.

Restriction or denial of women's access to fertility control is frequently justified by appeals to moral arguments about the sanctity of life. However, attitudes and policies which promote involuntary motherhood or which prevent women from spacing their children optimally are better understood as arising from sexist and authoritarian views of women and of society. Efforts by cultural and religious organizations to limit women's access to fertility control arise from a perception that women's right to self-determination must inevitably conflict with the wider society's need for a steady supply of children. However, the view that women are incapable of making sensible decisions about their fertility, and the view that most Western women will decide against motherhood if they have the choice (e.g. Popenoe, 1993), are not supported by the evidence. A converse, though equally authoritarian, view, that certain sections of the world's population will produce children indiscriminately if they are not coerced into birth control, is also at odds with the available evidence.

Shepler (1991) and Timpson (1996), among others, have argued that the anti-abortion movement is grounded in the paternalistic assumption that women are incapable of making serious moral choices and that male-dominated social organizations must make them on their behalf. The greatest benefit to women and their children, however, is more likely to result from policies and practices which allow women the freedom to make informed decisions about childbearing and then to control their fertility safely and legally (Kulczycki et al., 1995; Westhoff & Rosenfield, 1993).

Control of fertility through contraception, abortion and infanticide has been part of all human societies for as long as recorded history (David, 1994). It is necessary in reviewing the literature to distinguish contraception from abortion, because the majority of Western people make this distinction and because there are relevant differences in social attitudes, but these are by no means distinct and coherent categories. The contraceptive pill and the intrauterine device, for example, are generally regarded as contraception, while mifepristone (RU–486) is generally regarded as an abortion method, even though all have a similar mode of action, allowing fertilization but creating a uterine environment which causes early miscarriage of the conceptus. Barrier methods of contraception (e.g. condoms and cervical caps), the 'rhythm method' of timing sexual activity to avoid the ovulatory phase, and sexual activities which avoid vaginal penetration, all work by preventing sperm and ovum from coming into physical contact; yet influential social organizations such as the Catholic Church find some of these to be acceptable methods of controlling fertility and others not.

Despite conservative views that abortion and contraception are necessarily unnatural and conflict with women's 'natural' wish to be mothers (Boyle, 1992), the majority of women in all human societies are motivated to control their family size and to space their children appropriately. However vague the distinction may be, survey respondents from many countries agree that contraception is preferable to abortion (e.g. Lindell & Olsson, 1993; Remmenick, Amir, Elimelich & Novikov, 1995). In order to avoid the need for abortion, however, it is necessary to have access to adequate contraception. Low abortion rates among teenagers in Denmark (Segest, 1994) and in the Netherlands (Ketting & Visser, 1994) have been explained as the result of widespread sex education, beginning before adolescents become sexually active, and the ready availability of contraception. When access to contraception improves, the rate of abortion tends to decrease, as demonstrated in a survey of the birth control practices of Russian migrants to Israel (Remmenick et al., 1995).

FERTILITY CONTROL IN INDUSTRIALIZED COUNTRIES

Effective fertility control is generally available to adult women in modern secular societies, although adolescents may have difficulty in accessing appropriate services. A large-scale survey of Australian women aged forty-five to fifty found that only 6 per cent of respondents were in a potentially fertile sexual relationship but not using contraception. Overall, 35 per cent of respondents reported not being in a potentially fertile sexual relationship, while 28 per cent had undergone tubal ligation and 17 per cent had partners who had undergone vasectomy. Although 88 per cent reported having used the contraceptive pill at some stage, only 6 per cent were using it at the time of the survey (Research Institute for Gender and Health, 1996). A Swedish survey of women in their twenties (Lindell, Olsson & Sjöden, 1995) found that 43 per cent used contraceptive pills and 22 per cent barrier methods, with only 12 per cent reporting no contraceptive use. While these surveys suggest that the majority of adult women in developed countries use contraception, demand for abortion is still high. Forrest (1994) found that 56 per cent of pregnancies in the USA were unintended and that half of these resulted in abortion, suggesting that even in developed countries many women are not able to make optimal use of contraceptive services.

US research has shown that inadequate contraceptive use is associated with younger age, poor knowledge of fertility and contraception, and with minority status (Radecki & Beckman, 1994). Zabin, Astone and Emerson (1993) found, with urban Black American teenage girls, that ambivalence about having a baby was as likely as positively wanting a baby to be associated with pregnancy. In underserved areas, women must make a positive decision to take steps to avoid pregnancy, and actively seek out contraceptive services if they are to be able to plan when or whether to become pregnant.

The majority of sexually active European adolescents do report using contraceptives (Choquet & Manfredi, 1992; Kraft & Rise, 1991), although Kang and Zador (1993) reported that only 43 per cent of their sample of sexually active Australian teenage girls used effective contraception and similarly low rates of contraceptive use were found among Brazilian adolescents (De Souza, de Almeida, Wagner, Zimmerman, de Almeida & Caleffi, 1993), 12 per cent of whom reported having had abortions.

Despite arguments that the family is the appropriate place for adolescents to learn about sexuality and contraception, and despite evidence from the USA that education from parents does lead to a decreased likelihood of teenage pregnancy (Baumeister, Flores & Marin, 1995), research from the USA (Baumeister et al., 1995) as well as from South Africa (Mayekiso & Twaise, 1993; Nicholas, 1993) indicates that parents generally provide little information about sexual matters, and even less specifically relevant to the avoidance of pregnancy. A recent review (Creatsas, 1993) concluded that countries which provided sexual education in schools had lower rates of teenage pregnancy and abortion than those which did not, providing support for the value of formal education in the adoption of appropriate fertility control methods.

Collection of accurate data on abortion rates is complicated by the existence of legal restrictions and social pressures which affect reporting rates to variable extents at different times and in different places (Barrieto et al., 1992). Some reasonably reliable data are, however, available. An international review of the use of induced abortion (Tietze & Henshaw, 1986) found rates between 200 and 400 abortions per 1,000 live births in developed countries. Of women aged between fifteen and forty-four, the percentage undergoing abortions during the study year ranged from around 1.5 per cent in France, 2 per cent in Scandinavia, to 2.2 per cent in Japan, to between 2.4 and 2.9 per cent in the USA. British statistics (Social Trends, 1995) suggest that 7 per cent of conceptions occurring within marriage, and 35 per cent of those in unmarried women, are terminated by abortion, including 50 per cent of all conceptions among unmarried girls under sixteen. More recently, in a large-scale Australian survey of women in three different age groups (Research Institute for Gender and Health, 1996), 17 per cent of respondents aged forty-five to fifty and 8 per cent of those aged eighteen to twenty-three reported having had at least one abortion. The Centers for Disease Control and Prevention (1995a) report that abortion rates in the USA have remained fairly stable since 1980; in 1992 there were 335 abortions per 1,000 live births, and 2.3 per cent of women aged fifteen to forty-four underwent abortions in that year. Almost 90 per cent of abortions were curettages occurring during the first trimester, a pattern which is also observed in the UK (Social Trends, 1995).

Characteristics of women seeking abortions vary as a result of regional and cultural differences. An Australian survey (Adelson, Frommer & Weisberg, 1995) found that only 17 per cent of abortion recipients were teenagers, with 54 per cent aged in their twenties and 9 per cent over thirty. Forty-four per cent of this sample were married, and the sample was generally well educated and came from a representative range of ethnic and religious backgrounds. In Britain, 69 per cent of abortion recipients are aged twenty to thirty-four (Social Trends, 1995). By contrast, US women having abortions are predominantly under twenty-five and unmarried, although 46 per cent have children already (Centers for Disease Control and Prevention, 1995a).

A survey of 596 US women who sought abortions in 1987 (Russo, Horn & Tromp, 1993) found that the majority had two or more children already, and most were single heads of households; over a quarter had a child under two years at the time of the abortion. These findings suggest that the reasons of women who seek abortions in the USA are not frivolous ones; women seeking abortions are frequently those without the resources to cope with another child, and these abortions may prevent serious medical and psychosocial consequences for these women and their existing children.

In the USA, Black women are three times as likely as White women to have abortions (Centers for Disease Control and Prevention, 1995b), despite evidence from other sources (e.g. Lynxweiler & Gay, 1994) that attitudes to abortion are generally more negative among Black than White Americans. This difference may be explained by differences in socioeconomic status, educational level, and access to adequate family planning services (Centers for Disease Control and Prevention, 1995a). The high rate of unwanted pregnancy among Black Americans is of concern, since the Centers for Disease Control and Prevention (1995b) report that maternal mortality is three times as high among Black Americans as it is among White Americans, and that this difference can be attributed to differences in access to appropriate health care. Further, Black women who have abortions tend to be less in favour of abortion and to perceive less social support for their decision than other groups of women (e.g. Lynxweiler & Wilson, 1994), suggesting that they may find the experience more distressing. Such evidence supports the importance of genuine freedom of choice, access to family planning services, and the need to examine the adequacy of government child support and other services for women who would prefer to have children despite difficult personal circumstances.

FERTILITY CONTROL IN DEVELOPING COUNTRIES

Contraceptive knowledge and availability are limited in many developing countries. Across the board, contraceptive use in developing countries has climbed from 9 per cent of all married couples of childbearing age in the 1960s to over 50 per cent in the 1990s, but there is enormous variation between countries and regions in knowledge, availability and use of appropriate contraception (Segal, 1993).

Education of women has been associated with increased used of contraception, smaller family sizes, better maternal and child health, and more satisfactory child spacing. There is evidence from Mexico (Tapia Uribe, LeVine & LeVine, 1993) and Chile (Herold, Thompson, Valenzuela & Morris, 1994) to indicate that both general and sexually specific education of women leads to increased use of contraception, which in turn allows women to control the size of their families and to space their children more advantageously. However, high levels of Western education are not essential. Kaur (1991) reported that 73.2 per cent of married Punjabi couples used some sort of contraception to prevent or limit fertility, even though 80 per cent of the women were illiterate, and it is clear that religious and social differences among and within non-Western countries mean that caution must be used in generalizing from one region to another.

Research from Africa (e.g. Oheneba-Sakyi, 1992; Terefe & Larson, 1993) suggests that contraceptive education will be most effective if husbands are included in the programme and encouraged to participate in decision-making about contraceptive use and child spacing. Sai (1993) has argued that women's relative powerlessness, both at a political and a family level, contributes significantly to low contraception use, and that power inequities between the genders are greater in developing than in Western countries. Social and political changes which enhance women's personal power and freedom of choice may also be important prerequisites to the development of health systems which provide access to fertility control.

FREEDOM OF CHOICE

Given the opportunity, women throughout the world will make sensible decisions about limiting the size of their families and spacing their children optimally. Segal (1993) has shown that increased access to contraception in developing countries has been associated with a reduction of the total fertility rate per woman from over six in 1960 to around four children per adult woman in the 1990s, with associated increases in the health and well-being of those children, and reductions in child mortality.

Opposition to fertility control comes to a large extent from churches and conservative social and political groups (Sai, 1993), although David (1994) argues that it is necessary to distinguish between public discourse and private beliefs and practice, and David, Dytrych, Matějček and Schüller (1988) have pointed out that official religious and government policies in many countries diverge from semi-official or unofficial advice and practice. For example, Welch, Leege and Cavendish (1995) found considerable variation in attitudes to abortion among registered Catholic parishioners in the USA, while Bryan and Freed (1993) found that the majority of college students, both Catholic and non-Catholic, engaged in premarital sexual activity, used contraception, and supported freedom of choice regarding abortion. On this point it is worth noting that the fertility rate in Italy, a country with strong official opposition to fertility control, is only 1.3 children per adult woman (Willén & Montgomery, 1993).

Objections to fertility control arise from three main arguments, none of which can be sustained in the face of evidence: the possibility of harm to the woman, views about the morality of destroying a non-viable foetus, and various vaguely described negative social consequences of women's freedom to control their fertility (Boyle, 1992).

Impact of abortion on the woman

Legal abortion is one of the safest of medical procedures; the risk of physical complications is much lower than the risks associated with childbirth (Maine et al., 1994). Emotional response to abortion will depend on a number of factors, including the woman's age, number and age of her existing children, her family situation, the extent to which the pregnancy was unplanned or unwanted, and the existence of medical reasons for abortion (Adler, 1992). The evidence is overwhelming that women do not choose abortion lightly, but that the majority experience no significant psychological distress (e.g. Adler, David, Major, Roth, Russo & Wyatt, 1992).

Russo, Horn and Schwartz (1992) examined records of abortion patients in the US and concluded that women sought abortions for a wide range of personal and familial reasons, and as a result of external circumstances such as material poverty, unemployment, and lack of support. Nearly half already had children, and the majority chose abortion out of a desire to maintain or increase the quality of life for themselves, their partners, and their existing and potential future children through the avoidance of physical, psychological, social and economic disadvantage.

The decision to abort for medical reasons, either because of major foetal abnormality or because of risk to the mother, is perceived quite differently from elective abortion for non-medical reasons. Even when the women and their partners have undergone counselling and assistance in the decision process, and have made a positive decision to abort rather than bear a disabled child or risk death, the event is interpreted more as a miscarriage than as an elective abortion (Kolker & Burke, 1993).

Miscarriages, or spontaneous abortions, are relatively common. Apgar and Churgay (1993) estimated that 20 per cent of pregnancies will spontaneously abort, although most of these are extremely early, and the rate is closer to 2 per cent for medically confirmed pregnancies. The Women's Health Australia survey (Research Institute for Gender and Health, 1996) found that over 30 per cent of women aged forty-five to fifty reported having had at least one miscarriage, suggesting that this is an extremely common event in women's lives. Reactions to spontaneous abortion of a wanted pregnancy will depend on the woman's individual circumstances (Madden, 1994; Moulder, 1994), but are generally characterized by short-term grief, anxiety and depression, which is normally resolved successfully within a few months (Iles & Gath, 1993; Prettyman, Cordle & Cook, 1993; Slade, 1994), especially if the woman has other children (Cecil, 1994; Neugebauer et al., 1992). Reactions to medical abortions follow a similar pattern, with short-term distress which may be severe but which resolves itself rapidly, especially if there are other children or a subsequent planned pregnancy (Zolese & Blacker, 1992). Serious negative consequences are rare, and associated with previous psychiatric illness and with membership of sociocultural groups which oppose elective abortions (Zolese & Blacker, 1992).

There are moral and ethical arguments about abortion on the grounds of foetal abnormality or medical risk to the woman (e.g. Blumberg, 1994), generally revolving around the questions of the quality of life of people with disabilities, and of parents', physicians', and the community's right to judge that value. However, people who support absolutist arguments against abortion on the grounds of disability frequently miss the point that individual decisions are always embedded in a personal and social context (e.g. Stotland, 1991). Lack of social support and lack of community and government services for the care of disabled children mean that raising a disabled child is an enormous financial and emotional burden for a family (Singhi, Goyal, Pershad, Singhi & Walia, 1990) which significantly limits other major life choices for parents and siblings (LeClere & Kowalewski, 1994).

The majority of abortions, however, are conducted for social or non-medical reasons. Most women who find themselves unexpectedly pregnant do not seem to have difficulty in deciding whether they want a baby. Cohan, Dunkel-Schetter and Lydon (1993) found that the majority of women had decided very early, usually before receiving the results of a pregnancy test, whether they wished to abort or continue with the pregnancy, and were unlikely to change their minds. Contrary to the notion that adolescents make decisions impulsively and poorly, Resnick, Bearinger, Stark and Blum (1994) found that every one of a sample of pregnant teenagers had discussed their decision with at least one person, usually their mother or male partner, before deciding on abortion.

An expert panel convened by the American Psychological Association (Adler et al., 1992) concluded on the basis of an extensive literature review that abortion is highly unlikely to be followed by any negative psychological consequences. Although some (e.g. Speckhard & Rue, 1993) have argued for the existence of a distressing 'post abortion syndrome', psychological distress following abortion is considerably lower than that associated with childbirth (Stotland, 1991). The majority of reviewers (e.g. Adler et al., 1992; Blumenthal, 1991; Clare & Tyrrell, 1994; Dagg, 1991; Posavac & Miller, 1990; Romans-Clarkson, 1989; Stotland, 1991; Wilmoth, deAlteriis & Bussell, 1992) have concluded that there is little evidence for significant levels of psychological distress, and that the better designed and more credible investigations are unanimous in demonstrating that the outcomes are generally benign and the psychological risks very low.

Negative psychological states associated with elective abortion are at their highest during decision-making and immediately before the abortion, and the most common reaction following abortion is a sense of relief (Adler et al., 1992) and a feeling of having undergone a significant developmental experience (Stotland, 1991). Partner conflicts are also highest during the decision-making period, and relationships generally return to normal shortly after the abortion (Barnett, Freudenberg & Wille, 1992).

Women who cope best with abortion are those who cope best with other life challenges, and are characterized by optimism, self-efficacy for coping, high self-esteem and a sense of personal control (Cozzarelli, 1993; Major & Cozzarelli, 1992; Major, Cozzarelli, Sciacchiatano, Cooper, Testa & Mueller, 1990). Social factors associated with poor coping include conservative religious beliefs or cultural views which oppose abortion (Congleton & Calhoun, 1993; Wilmoth et al., 1992), little social or partner support for the decision (Congleton & Calhoun, 1993; Major & Cozzarelli, 1992), low confidence that one has made the right decision, or a perception of having been pressured into the choice (Congleton & Calhoun, 1993; Romans-Clarkson, 1989). Women with a history of psychiatric disorder are also likely to react negatively (Dagg, 1991).

This evidence suggests that the best strategy is to provide adequate information, counselling and practical support, and to assist women to make up their own minds (Romans-Clarkson, 1989). Pressuring women into having abortions can have negative consequences, while there is good evidence that denial of abortion to women who wish to terminate their pregnancies is associated with long-term psychological and social problems, both among the unwilling mothers and among their children (Clare & Tyrrell, 1994). While denial of abortion is now quite rare in most parts of the developed world (Clare & Tyrrell, 1994), there is some long-term evidence on its impact (Dagg, 1991; David, 1992b; David et al., 1988), indicating that women who have been denied abortion experience anger and resentment which may last for years, and that children born under such circumstances experience social, interpersonal, intellectual and occupational difficulties that tend to become more severe with age.

Moral and social objections to fertility control

Given the strong evidence that adequate contraception and abortion will improve maternal and child health in the developed and the developing worlds, and that women are generally quite able to make up their own minds and to cope with the consequences of their fertility-related decisions, it is remarkable that the topic of abortion should continue to generate enormous controversy in some countries.

Although individuals' views on abortion are often polarized into the so-called 'pro-life' and 'pro-choice' camps, the issue is much more complex than a simple choice between conflicting rights, or an opinion on whether a non-viable foetus is a human being or not, and any particular decision is always made in a specific context in which other problems and the availability of alternatives will come into the decision (Stotland, 1991; Timpson, 1996). It is worth stressing that the term 'pro-life', used to refer to people who oppose abortions, is inaccurate, emotionally loaded, and deeply misleading (Stotland, 1991). Anti-abortionists are not generally in favour of movements which aim to protect life, such as movements against military spending or against capital punishment (Boyle, 1992). Rather, anti-abortion attitudes correlate most strongly with moral and political conservatism (Boyle, 1992; Truett, 1993), religiosity (Bryan & Freed, 1993), opposition to women's rights in general (Welch et al., 1995) and authoritarian, punitive and hostile opinions concerning homeless people, drug users, and AIDS sufferers (Peterson, Doty & Winter, 1993), rather than with any positive views about the value of life. Several authors (e.g. Boyle, 1992; Willis, 1984); have argued that the motivations of anti-abortionists are best understood as a wish to control women's sexuality and, by punishing those women who are sexually active, to restrict the behaviour of others. Thus, Boyle (1992) has suggested that the term 'pro-social-control' would be a more accurate label for anti-abortionists while Stotland (1991) suggests 'anti-choice'.

Shepler (1991) has argued that the discourse of the anti-abortion lobby disguises an assumption that women are incapable of making moral choices. Further, she has argued that an insistence on the need for external regulation of women's fertility derives from a paternalistic and controlling perspective on women's lives, which seeks to deny full adult status to women. Alternatively, though, it can be argued that many anti-abortionists are perhaps not primarily anti-women so much as primarily punitive in their attitudes to social problems, believing that people who find themselves in difficult situations are not entitled to social support in resolving their problems. Boyle (1992) has used the logical inconsistencies of the widely held argument that abortion should not be permitted except if the woman has been raped, to point out that this argument is not based on the presumed sanctity of a non-viable foetus but on a desire to punish women for expressing their sexuality. According to this view, women who are raped are not responsible for what has happened and therefore should be free to deal with the consequences of the event as they choose. Women who become pregnant through freely chosen sexual activity, however, should be prevented from exercising the freedom to make use of an existing strategy to deal with the pregnancy, because their actions deserve punishment.

Although some anti-abortionists argue that giving a child up for adoption is an appropriate response to an unwanted pregnancy, evidence suggests that this is frequently highly traumatic for the mother (Lauderdale & Boyle, 1994; Weinreib & Murphy, 1988), while an Australian survey (Sobol & Daly, 1992) showed that it was a very unpopular choice, with only 3 per cent of single adolescent mothers actually giving their babies up for adoption.

It is, however, clear that control of women's access to abortion has the effect of controlling and limiting their sexual behaviour (Willis, 1984). Wine (1985) has argued further, that control of women's sexuality in general and of their ability to control childbearing in particular serves to maintain the sex-based division of labour and other sex-based inequities in society. If women must deal constantly with the possibility or actuality of unintended motherhood in a society in which mothers are expected to put the interests of their children before their own personal development, this serves to limit their educational and occupational attainments, and to tie them to dependence on a wage-earning husband regardless of their own aspirations or interests. Timpson (1996) has interpreted women's right to control their fertility in terms of women's right to self-determination, and argued that groups which oppose abortion are motivated not by a desire to celebrate and protect human life but by a desire to limit women's choices and freedom.

Certainly if one wishes to keep women poor, unhealthy and dependent, then making them individually responsible for their children, denying them access to fertility control, and providing inadequate social services is an effective means of achieving this end. And if this denial can be wrapped in positive language, the discourse of life and of naturalness and fulfilment, then it will seem more acceptable than if it is shown for what it is: a denial of women's human rights. Women's ability to control their fertility is essential for their health and well-being and that of the next generation. Fertility control needs to encompass not only free access to contraceptive and abortion services, but also social and financial support for those women who make the choice to bear children.

7

CHOOSING MOTHERHOOD:
'I'M JUST A MUM'

While not all women desire children, and the ability to avoid, limit or delay childbearing has a significant positive impact on women's physical and psychological health, the majority of women do become mothers. Most human cultures view motherhood as both natural and easy; something that every woman desires, the achievement of which marks a woman's attainment of true adulthood, true fulfilment and true happiness. Media images overwhelmingly portray happy mothers, contented babies and helpful partners (Nicolson, 1990). The reality, however, is less unambiguously positive. This chapter reviews evidence on normal experiences of motherhood, particularly the major life transition which accompanies the birth of the first child. As Hopkins, Campbell and Marcus (1989) have pointed out, normal transition to motherhood and postpartum depression lie along a continuum of successful adjustment; thus, there are clear overlaps with the earlier chapter on postpartum depression, but the focus here is on the nature of the decision and of the transition to motherhood in the majority of women, who do not seek psychological or medical help.

The past decades have seen radical changes in Western women's expectations; the development of more effective contraception, readier availability of abortion, greater endorsement of egalitarianism in heterosexual relationships, and the existence of a wider range of personal options for women mean that the context within which decisions about childbearing is made might be expected to have changed radically (Ulvik, 1993). Family size in Western countries has decreased markedly during the twentieth century. Contemporary social norms indicate a preferred family size of two or perhaps three children, while a generation ago the preference was for four or more (Willén & Montgomery, 1993).

Fertility rates in many developed countries are now below replacement level, with Willén and Montgomery (1993) reporting that in Europe, only Sweden, Ireland and Iceland, with rates of 2.1, exceed the replacement rate of two children per woman. The rate in Britain is 1.7 (Social Trends, 1995), while in the USA it is 1.9, in Denmark 1.7, and in Italy, despite strongly pro-natalist religious and cultural traditions, 1.3

(Willén & Montgomery, 1993). Although the fertility rate is still well above replacement level in developing countries, Segal (1993) estimated that the overall fertility rate in those countries had fallen from 6.1 to just over 4 children per woman since 1960, largely as a result of improved access to contraception. Despite these reductions in family size, however, the vast majority of women do still become mothers (e.g. Australian Bureau of Statistics, 1995), and reports of the death of the family (e.g. Popenoe, 1993) have been greatly exaggerated.

Social and personal constructions of motherhood and womanhood do, however, seem to have lagged behind the reality of smaller family sizes and greater potential for choice. Childcare manuals seem to have remained embedded in the 1950s, with a focus on the 'good mother' as a self-denying woman with no other role or interests in life (Marshall, 1991), supported by a hard-working, income-earning, largely absent, necessarily male, partner. Phoenix and Woollett (1991) have argued that psychology has both reflected and supported an artificial and outdated view of 'good' and 'normal' motherhood which fails to take into account the realities of most women's lives, which frequently include paid work, whether for financial or personal reasons, the presence of other children, the absence of a male partner or other supportive relationships, and a potential range of social and financial problems.

'Good' motherhood, as contemporary society constructs it, places impossible and incompatible demands on women. Motherhood is characterized as requiring total selflessness on the part of the woman, who subordinates herself to the needs of her children and their father. Being a mother in contemporary society has been argued to be incompatible with a feminist approach to life (Nicolson, 1993) and indeed with full personhood (Davies & Welch, 1986). Contemporary discourse on motherhood is fundamentally contradictory. On the one hand, it is viewed as natural and easy, requiring no particular effort or skill, and thus the mothering role is accorded very low social status, and staying at home to care for children is regarded as 'not working'. At the same time, however, motherhood is regarded as the highest state to which a woman can aspire, and the fulfilment of her existence.

The myth of the magical mother–infant bond (Eyer, 1994), and the fanciful notion that women, by virtue of their biology, have special innate knowledge of how to care for babies, knowledge which men cannot achieve, contribute to continuing inequities in men's and women's levels of responsibility for the care of family members and, as a consequence, to women's lower social and economic status (Hooyman & Gonyea, 1995). Simultaneously, women who choose not to have children are regarded as having missed out on the greatest experience a woman can have. Thus, a life choice which has major pitfalls is represented as the only right and healthy decision for women to make, despite a social milieu in which alternative choices for women are quite possible. As

Willén (1994) put it, 'Women . . . are caught in a structural dilemma with no obvious right or wrong way to behave and no possibility of making an optimal decision. Every choice is a compromise, with the women as losers' (p. 6).

CHOOSING MOTHERHOOD

Given the changes, both social and technological, which allow women greater freedom of choice, and the strains and personal sacrifices associated with the motherhood role, one might expect women who have children to have undergone a protracted and careful decision process. But although it is clear that women and their partners do frequently plan the number and timing of their children, most people seem to engage in surprisingly little serious consideration of whether or not to have children (Grewal & Urschel, 1994). Indeed, respondents in a Swedish survey (Willén, 1994) regarded the entire concept of questioning whether or not to have children as 'absurd'.

Once Willén's (1994) respondents felt that crucial conditions, such as the completion of education, the establishment of a stable, financially secure, relationship, and a sense of personal maturity, had been met, these couples generally stopped using contraception or switched to a less effective method; most couples seemed to be allowing a pregnancy to happen, in a wait-and-see manner, rather than specifically planning a baby at a particular time.

Not all groups see parenthood in this way, and decisions about parenthood are clearly embedded in a sociocultural context. Gabriel and McAnarney (1983) compared low-income single Black Americans with White, middle-class couples; while the middle-class couples, like their Swedish counterparts, saw parenthood as something that one should delay until after achieving economic independence and a stable relationship, the single Black women saw motherhood as one of the steps towards adult maturity, rather than something that should necessarily be delayed until after they had finished school or formed a long-term relationship.

Willén (1994) found that her respondents identified both external and internal factors which influenced their feeling that the time was right for parenthood. Reaching an age at which most people had children, and the expectations of family, friends, and wider society, combined with a personal feeling of being 'ready' and that it was time to embark on a new life project. Most couples did not report a conscious decision to have a baby, but instead began behaving in ways which permitted conception.

Social and cultural expectations clearly have an important impact on decision-making. Woollett, Dosanjh-Matwala, and Hadlow (1991), for example, illustrated the complex interactions between culture of origin,

extent of integration into mainstream culture, religion, and family structure in influencing preferences for family size and timing among Asian
migrants to Britain.

PERSONAL IMPACT OF TRANSITION TO MOTHERHOOD

Whatever romantic expectations may be encouraged by media images
and cultural norms, the evidence is consistent in showing that becoming
a mother is associated with decreased quality of life and general well-
being in a significant proportion of women. While expectant parents are
generally optimistic and positive, the actuality of parenthood is marked
by major unexpected upheaval and distress, especially for women (Feldman & Nash, 1984). An English study (Elliott & Huppert, 1991) concluded that the best predictor of women's well-being was the age of the
youngest child; women with children under five had lower well-being
than others, and women with several children under five had the lowest
levels of all.

Willén and Montgomery (1993) reviewed evidence which showed that
having children did not increase marital satisfaction or well-being; in
fact, at least some research shows significant negative effects. Having
a child appears to be associated with emotional separation, alienation
and disappointment, and children interfere with individual and couple
activities.

Most research focuses on the initial transition from childlessness to
parenthood, and there is little research dealing with adaptation after the
first year of motherhood. However, a four-year study by Tomlinson and
Irvin (1993) indicated that the strongest predictors of later marital
distress and family disorganization were problems with adaptation and
role reorganization in the initial few months after the baby was born.
This suggests that the birth of a baby may constitute a crisis within a
relationship, and that initial success in coping with the transition will
have a major impact on later marital quality. Belsky and Rovine (1990),
on the basis of a separate longitudinal study, though, concluded that
decreases in marital quality after the birth could be predicted from
factors which were evident during the pregnancy. It is likely that
relationships which are already under strain will degenerate more
quickly under the added pressure of parenthood (Belsky & Pensky,
1988).

HOUSEHOLD LABOUR

The mother's satisfaction with her role, and the quality of her relationship with her partner, both appear to decline with the arrival of a child,

and evidence from many countries overwhelmingly supports the view that the unexpectedly heavy and inequitably divided burden of household labour is largely responsible for these negative effects. In Australia, Terry, McHugh and Noller (1991) found that a perception that the male partner was contributing fairly to household tasks was associated with women's perceptions of increasing marital quality during the transition to parenthood, while a perception of inequity was associated with decreased marital quality. Tavecchio, van Ijzendoorn, Goossens and Vergeer (1984), in the Netherlands, found that both men and women saw an egalitarian division of labour as desirable, but in reality the women had a much greater workload. An American study (Gjerdingen & Chaloner, 1994) found that new mothers reported that the level of support, both practical and emotional, from partners, family and friends decreased steadily over the first postpartum year, and that level of satisfaction with the partner's contribution to household work was a strong predictor of psychological well-being. Similarly, Cowan and Cowan (1988), Hackel and Ruble (1992) and Ruble, Fleming, Hackel and Stangor (1988) all demonstrated that the degree of postpartum decrease in women's well-being, self-esteem and marital satisfaction could be explained by the extent to which expectations and preferences regarding the sharing of household labour were disconfirmed. In England, Nicolson (1990) found that women expected far more practical input from their partners than they actually received, and suggested that many men may allow their partners to misunderstand their intentions during the pregnancy, rather than cause conflict by openly acknowledging their actual plans to provide limited practical support. Even in lesbian families (C.J. Patterson, 1995), the biological mother has been shown to do more child caring and the non-biological mother more paid work outside the home, although lesbian couples with more equitable workloads reported greater satisfaction and more contented children.

Research evidence is consistent in showing a trend towards a more traditional sex-based division of labour following the birth of a child, and women who are unhappy with such arrangements are likely to experience the greatest decrease in satisfaction. Belsky, Lang and Huston (1986) showed that wives' marital satisfaction following the transition to motherhood was predicted by the extent to which they endorsed sex-role stereotypes, while Hock and DeMeis (1990) showed that the women who experienced most depression following childbirth were those who wanted to work outside the home but were engaged full-time in unpaid domestic labour.

Older parents seem able to resist the pressures towards sexist division of labour more effectively; Robinson, Olmsted, Garner and Gare (1988) found that older (over thirty-five) first-time mothers in Canada were more autonomous, less traditional, and more likely to return to work than younger mothers, while Coltrane (1990) found that US couples who delayed childbearing tended to be more egalitarian in the division of work; male partners were more interested and showed more commitment to the parenthood role than younger fathers. Delaying parenthood has been associated with better outcomes for parents and child, possibly because parents have had an opportunity to explore mutually satisfactory alternatives to role-based division of labour. Dion (1995) concluded that women who chose to delay motherhood were generally motivated by positive beliefs about the importance of personal maturity and the achievement of other life goals before parenthood, and Cooney, Pedersen, Indelicato and Palkovitz (1993) found that older fathers were more involved with their children and enjoyed fatherhood more. However, decisions about the timing of parenthood are clearly confounded with educational level and social class (Coltrane, 1990), and the relationship between age at first childbirth, social status and educational level is a reciprocal one.

Barkley (1993), in a series of interviews, concluded that men tended to view childbirth in romantic terms while women were horrified by the experience. In general, men maintained or increased their paid work following the birth of a baby while women stopped or cut down their work or study commitments; Barkley argued that the birth of a child was a point at which men's and women's career paths began to diverge, and that inequitable division of labour and responsibility at this time was one of the factors contributing to women's economic and career inequality.

THE TRANSITION TO MOTHERHOOD IN CONTEXT

In considering the overwhelmingly negative conclusions of research on the transition to parenthood, it is important to look at the need for adequate controls. While the transition to parenthood is associated with an increasingly traditional division of labour, less couple leisure activity, fewer positive interchanges, more arguments, and a perception of reduced love, Belsky and Pensky (1988) have argued that the same decline in relationship tends to occur in childless couples, though more gradually and without an obvious event to mark its onset. This analysis is supported by the findings of a four-year study (Kurdek, 1993) comparing couples who became parents and those who did not. Marital satisfaction, consensus and emotional expression declined equally across the four years for parents and non-parents, with the only difference being a steeper decline in joint activities for parents than for non-parents.

Tucker and Aron (1993) have compared the impact of having a first child with other marital transitions – the transition from engagement to marriage, and the transition associated with children leaving home – and found similar reductions in passionate love and marital quality at each transition. It is reasonable to assume that any change in the family structure is likely to be associated with distress and upheaval.

It has been suggested that the transition to parenthood should be studied in a broader context, for example by taking into account the role of the extended family (Fischer, 1988; Grossman, 1988) and of character-istics of the baby (Grossman, 1988). However, the majority of work continues to focus on married couples, and to study them in isolation from their social context. While some researchers (e.g. Davies & Rains, 1995) have examined women's decisions to have babies without a partner, or within a homosexual relationship (e.g. Alldred, 1996), most research still seems founded firmly on the assumption that babies are, and should be, born to married couples. Despite that fact that an increasing proportion of women are having children outside a traditional marriage, research which examines lesbian, single-parent and extended-kin families as potentially successful alternative arrangements rather than assuming such arrangements to be pathological (e.g. Benkov, 1995; Dickerson, 1995) is still unusual.

It should be emphasized that the transition to parenthood is not always associated with negative effects. Moss, Bolland, Foxman and Owen (1986), for example, found that only 10 per cent of their sample of British couples showed significantly weakened marriages, and some showed improvements in marital quality. Being older and having been married longer appeared to be protective of the relationship, but the transition to parenthood was identified as potentially a turning point in marital decline, especially when fathers lacked understanding of the difficulties faced by the mother. Palkovitz and Copes (1988) found positive effects, at least in the first month, with increases in self-esteem and nurturance for both mothers and fathers. While research discussed earlier has indicated that older parents will cope better with the transi-tion, there is a need for a more fine-grained analysis of the characteristics of individuals, couples and social contexts which are associated with a more successful transition to parenthood. One factor which seems crucial in such an analysis is the role of the male partner.

FATHERS AND THE TRANSITION TO MOTHERHOOD

What drives this seemingly consistent move towards sex-based division of labour? Moss, Bolland, Foxman and Owen (1987) found that the trend was consistent across social classes and educational levels, and that both women and men were generally dissatisfied with the arrangement. Although parents, particularly married parents, do tend to have more traditional attitudes than non-parents, this difference is only partly explained by pre-existing attitudinal differences, and seems to arise as a consequence of parenthood (Morgan & Waite, 1987).

Hawkins, Christiansen, Sargent and Hill (1993) have argued that a closer involvement by fathers in the parenting process would lead to more positive personal development among men, and a closer match between men's and women's adult development, which might serve to maintain the quality of their marital relationship. An Israeli study (Levy-Skiff, 1994) has shown that the extent of the father's involvement in both play and caregiving with his child is a good predictor of marital satisfaction for both parents, suggesting that there are measurable benefits if fathers do involve themselves with their offspring. An important predictor of fathers' involvement in childcare and family work is the type of relationship they had with their own fathers (Barnett & Baruch, 1987), suggesting that men's perceptions of the fathering role may be well established before they reach adulthood.

Western societies tend to value men for their capacity to support a family financially and their success in the public sphere, rather than in terms of their emotional and practical inputs to family life; Jordan (1990) found that new fathers had difficulty in identifying their role, perceiving that society at large saw them more as financial providers and helpers than as equal partners in the project of parenting. Social discourses for fathers are as conflictual as they are for mothers; while there is an assumption that men should be involved with their children, there continues to be a deeply ingrained cultural perception that men are, and should be, valued as providers rather than as nurturing parents (Perry-Jenkins, 1993). It has been argued that men's commitment to an anti-sexist approach to relationships is essential before women will be able to renegotiate their relationships and roles within marriage and motherhood (van Every, 1995), although the relationship between male and female partners' abilities to reconstruct their lives in more positive ways is clearly reciprocal.

Although a few writers (e.g. Ainslie & Feltey, 1991; Goldiger, 1987) have described radically different social arrangements for parenthood, such as parenting collectives, the majority of research into motherhood is based on the assumption that the nuclear family will continue to be the dominant and preferred family structure in which to raise children. This perspective needs to be challenged for two reasons. Firstly, it is clear that such a system works to the disadvantage of both parents and of the quality of their relationship, and further that the woman experiences more distress than the man in such a system; thus, there is a need to explore strategies for changing the system. Secondly, it is clear that increasing proportions of children are being raised in families which deviate from this traditional expectation, and there is a need for social research which reflects this reality without assuming that any variation on the nuclear family must be pathological. Strategies for supporting women in the difficult and socially valuable task of rearing children, and for encouraging fathers to share this responsibility, may require changes in social policy – for example, greater flexibility in patterns of employment and the development of family-friendly workplaces.

Part III

WOMEN AND WORK: A WOMAN'S WORK IS NEVER DONE

INTRODUCTION

The two chapters in this part examine the myth that certain types of work, particularly the unpaid work of running a household and caring for family members, are naturally the domain of women and are qualitatively different from paid work in the public sphere. The Victorian doctrine of separate spheres, which holds that men are naturally suited to public activities while women are, equally naturally, designed to restrict their activities to the private sphere of home and family, serves to limit women's economic power, their opportunities for personal development, and their physical and emotional health.

Chapter 8 examines the impact on women's health and well-being of the wholesale movement by women into the paid workforce which has occurred in Western countries over the past several decades. This move is best understood as prompted not by any feminist change in society, but by changing economic pressures. Changes in the relationship between hours of work and disposable income, and changes in the number of families which are supported by adult men, mean that large numbers of women need to work out of financial necessity.

Women continue to be concentrated in a small number of low-paying occupations which position them as carers, assistants, and in other extensions of their 'natural' caring role. And, no matter what formal work arrangements are involved, women continue to bear the greatest burden of unpaid domestic labour. Many women gain both personally and economically from increased opportunities to participate in the public sphere of work, but there is little evidence of a concomitant shift of responsibilities within the home. Combining paid work with domestic labour and the care of dependent children may enhance women's well-being by providing variety and a range of personal satisfactions, especially if male partners contribute to the necessary unpaid domestic labour. There is no evidence that maternal employment has any negative effects on children, nor that mothers are uniquely capable of caring for small children. Provided all family members are satisfied with the arrangements, formal childcare or non-traditional family arrangements have been shown to have no deleterious effects on children and adolescents. But if workloads exceed a reasonable threshold, overload and exhaustion will result. The literature suggests that multiple roles do indeed enhance women's health, but only up to a point.

Chapter 9 extends the examination of women's work to include the care of frail or disabled relatives, a task which is also regarded as 'naturally' that of women. In the context of social and political policies which favour deinstitutionalization and reduced welfare spending, the resource-intensive and difficult burden of caring falls inequitably on women who are often experiencing increased pressure from other roles. The concept that caregiving is naturally women's work, something that women can do effortlessly, without any training, tends to render women's caregiving invisible, neither costed nor appreciated at a political or policy level. The costs of family caregiving for women themselves, in terms of their career development, economic status, and access to leisure time, are also rendered invisible by the assumption that the role of caring for relatives is one which is freely chosen by individuals, independent of cultural context.

The predominance of women in unpaid domestic labour and in the care of children and frail relatives is usually explained in terms of gender-linked differences in ability to care, in emotional closeness to others, and in the satisfactions derived from caring. The 'separate spheres' concept, that women and men lead separate lives, continues to influence both men's and women's expectations of their family responsibilities, to limit women's personal, employment and economic opportunities, and therefore to affect women's health and well-being.

8

PAID WORK AND DOMESTIC LABOUR: THE DOUBLE SHIFT

Research on paid employment and health reflects underlying social assumptions about gender and work; research with women tends to examine hypotheses which link paid employment with stress and poor health (Baruch & Barnett, 1986; Repetti, Matthews & Waldron, 1989), while research with men is more likely to focus on the stresses associated with unemployment (e.g. Lahelma, 1992). Thus, paid work is positioned as normal for men but abnormal and potentially pathological for women. This bias is worthy of some analysis, considering the well-publicized results of a WHO survey which demonstrated that women do two-thirds of the world's work, receive 10 per cent of the world's income, and own less than 1 per cent of all property (Oakley, 1993).

The bias appears to be based on a widespread assumption, both in Western society at large and within the research community, that women who take on paid work will do this in addition to taking full responsibility for the care of children and the management of a home, while men who take on paid work will have their other responsibilities met for them.

The research does indeed indicate that women in paid employment generally continue to take a higher level of responsibility for unpaid domestic labour. However, research into paid and unpaid labour is frequently predicated on the assumptions that it is somehow natural that women should have a higher workload than men, that it is natural that childcare and most unpaid domestic labour should primarily be undertaken by women, and that it is inevitable that housework and caring for children must interfere with women's personal and career development. These assumptions serve to endanger women's physical and emotional health and to maintain inequalities between women and men. Perhaps more importantly, they undermine both the possibility of a renegotiation of social roles at a personal level, and the possibility of radical reorganization of social structures which might facilitate such renegotiation.

Further, the research literature tends to neglect those individuals and families which deviate from a rigidly sex-based allocation of paid and unpaid labour. Alternative personal and social arrangements are frequently ignored or treated as anomalous exceptions, and this again strengthens the assumption that there is something natural and inevitable in inequitable, gender-based workloads. Psychological research in particular serves to maintain this status quo by treating patterns of work and remuneration as individual choices, when it may be more useful to consider evidence that they are grounded in cultural, social and economic constraints.

CHANGING PATTERNS OF PAID EMPLOYMENT

There has been a radical change in the participation of women in the paid workforce over the last few decades. In the USA, the 'traditional' nuclear family, with a husband in formal, paid employment, a wife in unpaid domestic employment, and one or more dependent children, accounts for 28 per cent of all family households (Dalley, 1988).

Australian census data, which are typical of information on employment patterns in developed countries, indicate that 64 per cent of all women aged fifteen to sixty-four participate in the paid workforce (Australian Bureau of Statistics, 1995), while the figure for married women with children under fifteen is 40 per cent. This participation rate compares with 90 per cent of married men with children, and 80 per cent of women without children. Similarly, in Britain in 1995, 53 per cent of women and 70 per cent of men aged sixteen to sixty-four were in the paid workforce; of women with children under five, 52 per cent were in paid work (Social Trends, 1995). In the USA, 57 per cent of married and 68 per cent of unmarried women work in paid employment, while the figure for women with children under six is 29 per cent (US Bureau of the Census, 1992a). These figures suggest that a significant number of women with families are in paid employment, while at the same time the unpaid roles of wife and, particularly, mother interfere with opportunities for paid work to a much greater extent than do the roles of husband and father.

It is frequently assumed that the increased entry of women into the workforce has arisen out of the feminist movement, and has been prompted by a wider acceptance of the concept that individuals' life choices and opportunities should not be constrained by irrelevant factors such as their gender. It might be reasonable to assume, on this basis, that the large-scale move by women into paid work would be accompanied by an acceptance that unpaid work need not be allocated on the basis of gender either.

However, Hollinger (1991) has argued, on the basis of an international comparison of attitudes and work practices, that the primary motivating force behind women's entry into the paid labour market is not an ideology of egalitarianism, but changing economic pressures. Changes in the relationship between hours of work and disposable income, changes in financial and material expectations, and changes in the availability of traditional 'men's jobs' have pushed larger numbers of married women with children into paid work. While many women may appreciate their increasing freedom to choose paid employment, and many gain both financially and personally as a result, the social pressures behind this trend are not feminist attitudes but economic forces.

The maintenance of traditional gender-based divisions of labour may be demonstrated in part by the fact that the proportion of households in which traditional roles are reversed, with a woman in paid employment and a man who carries out unpaid domestic labour, continues to be very small; the US Bureau of the Census (1993) has estimated that approximately 2 per cent of US couples have such an arrangement. Increasing numbers of single-parent families have also meant an increase in the number of women who work out of necessity, to support their families; the Australian Bureau of Statistics (1995) indicated that 5.6 per cent of Australian women head single-parent households, and sole mothers, although still a minority, are a significant aspect of contemporary social reality.

That women's increased participation in the labour market is not driven by an ideology of egalitarianism is further demonstrated by evidence that women continue to be concentrated in poorly paid occupations which extend the traditionally 'feminine' roles of childcare, health care and emotional support, and are over-represented in part-time positions with few opportunities for career advancement. In the UK, one-third of all female workers are employed on a part-time basis and 75 per cent of working women are concentrated in clerical, cleaning, catering, sales, and junior or ancillary professions (Social Trends, 1995), occupations which reflect and extend women's domestic roles as carers for men. The US Bureau of Labor Statistics (1991) indicated that 45 per cent of employed women worked in clerical and service occupations and a further 22 per cent in sales.

Australian figures indicate that 39 per cent of employed women work in part-time jobs, compared to 7 per cent of men, while 31 per cent of women and 16 per cent of men are in casual employment (Australian Bureau of Statistics, 1994). Further, over 50 per cent of employed women are concentrated in the low-paid occupations of clerical, sales and personal services (Australian Bureau of Statistics, 1995). Very similar figures are found in Sweden, despite that country's reputation for gender equity; gender segregation in the workforce is as high as in any other country, and 43 per cent of employed women work part-time, in comparison with 6 per cent of male workers (Rosenthal, 1994).

Nursing and teaching, extensions of the traditional female role, are still regarded as the most appropriate professional occupations for women

(Grbich, 1995). Even in these professions, however, women are concentrated at the lower levels; in Australia in 1994, women made up 75 per cent of primary school teachers, 51 per cent of secondary school teachers, and 33 per cent of tertiary educators. At the university level, 18 per cent of senior academics were women, compared to 44 per cent of tutors, assistants and base-grade lecturers (Australian Bureau of Statistics, 1995).

In general, even highly educated women are less likely than men to attain senior positions in careers, including medicine (Cameron, Redman, Burrow & Young, 1995) and law (Kay & Hagan, 1995). The subcultures of many professions continue to be based on the assumption that the professional worker will have a full-time unpaid assistant at home, providing practical support and freeing him or her from all other responsibilities (Apter, 1993). Hooyman and Gonyea (1995) have argued that women's inferior positions in the workforce and in the home support each other: women are paid less and given fewer opportunities for career advancement because they are assumed to have duties at home which will interfere with their full involvement in the workforce, and they put in more hours of unpaid labour at home because they are assumed to be contributing less in the workforce.

Despite equal-pay legislation in most developed countries, data (e.g. Australian Bureau of Statistics, 1994) also indicate that women continue to be paid considerably less than men, even when occupational category and actual hours of employment are accounted for. US figures indicate that full-time employed women earn an average of 72 per cent of the earnings of full-time employed men (US Bureau of Labor Statistics, 1991), while in the UK the figure is around 70 per cent (Social Trends, 1995). Further, women's over-representation in part-time and casual positions means that they are more likely to be excluded from benefits such as superannuation, holiday and sick leave, training and career development programmes, and opportunities to apply for promotions (Liff, 1991). Thus, while women have entered the labour market in unprecedented numbers, they are concentrated at the bottom end of the occupational ladder and are clearly not equal partners in the employment situation.

Despite the contemporary rhetoric of egalitarianism, there has not been any major reallocation of duties within the domestic sphere. Women continue to take more responsibility than men for family maintenance, childcare and other unpaid domestic labour (e.g. Greenglass, 1991; Perry-Jenkins, 1993), and this tendency, as suggested above, interferes with women's career advancement and their economic and social power (Leonard, 1996).

Women are far more likely than men to give up paid work in order to work full-time in unpaid domestic labour. The Australian Bureau of Statistics (1995) showed that women were twice as likely as men to leave the workforce during the survey year; 61 per cent of women who had left the workforce indicated that this was because of a need to work full-time in childcare or other unpaid domestic work, compared with 7 per cent of men. Of those adults not employed or actively seeking paid employment, 33 per cent of women specified the demands of childcare and a further 13 per cent other family care for not seeking work, while only 6 per cent of men cited child and family responsibilities. A Canadian survey (Li & Currie, 1992) showed that women were less likely than men to return to paid work after an interruption to employment, and if they did return, were likely to return to part-time, casual, or less remunerative positions. This, they argued, was entirely explicable by women's inequitable level of responsibility for childcare. Broken employment histories appear to be the norm for women, and to result in reduced economic independence, as well as lowered self-esteem (Keddy, Cable, Quinn & Melanson, 1993).

The literature on family caregiving other than childcare and that on women's roles and workloads have developed largely independently of each other (Doress-Worters, 1994), and family caregiving is explored in greater detail in Chapter 9, but both literatures make it clear that a significant number of women do have to cope with high and sometimes competing demands from several different sources. A US study (Cantor, 1991) indicated that 7 per cent of women belong to the so-called 'sandwich generation', caring for children and chronically ill or otherwise dependent parents at the same time.

WORKING MOTHERS, BAD MOTHERS? EFFECTS OF MOTHERS' EMPLOYMENT ON CHILDREN

Research which problematizes women's paid labour is based on the assumption that women are, and should be, primarily responsible for unpaid work at home and particularly for the care of children. It is clear that for many women, the role of paid worker has been added to their lives without any reduction in the expectation that they will take full responsibility for unpaid domestic labour (Crosby & Jaskar, 1993; Lundberg, 1996).

The assumption that there is something inevitable about women's higher workloads is widespread in Western societies. The psychological literature overwhelmingly places the responsibility for child psychopathology and behaviour problems on the shoulders of their mothers, excusing or completely ignoring fathers (see Caplan & Hall-McCorquodale, 1985; Phares, 1992). Research with American college students indicates that respondents tend to see mothers, particularly divorced, employed mothers, as more to blame for their children's problems than fathers (Jackson & Sullivan, 1993). College students have also been shown to have markedly negative attitudes towards mothers in paid employment, especially if they were described as doing so for personal fulfilment rather than financial necessity, and expected more negative outcomes for their babies than for those of women who worked full-time at home (Bridges & Orza, 1992, 1993).

The assumption that children need the full-time attention of their biological mothers in order to develop properly, and that alternatives such as father care and paid childcare are inappropriate and unsuitable (e.g. Hojat, 1990), may be traced to the work of Bowlby (1951). His views on the sex-based allocation of childcare were embedded in the social and political context of a time in which governments were strongly motivated to move women out of the workforce to provide jobs for demobilized servicemen, but they have continued to be enormously influential. Bowlby (1951) claimed that only the mother could provide for the child's needs, marginalizing the father to the role of a largely absent breadwinner and arguing that any other form of child rearing than full-time care by the biological mother would inevitably result in terrible problems, ranging somewhat ludicrously from bedwetting to violent crime and suicide.

While it is obvious that small children need care, there is no evidence to support the notion that only full-time care by the biological mother is adequate. Bowlby's conclusions were generalized from evidence with abandoned, institutionalized and physically abused children, not with those whose mothers made responsible arrangements to leave them from time to time in the care of other competent adults. Feminist writers (e.g. Badinter, 1981; Rich, 1982; Wearing, 1984) have pointed out that the myth of the mothering instinct, and the socially constructed assumption that women are naturally more appropriate caregivers than men, serve to restrict women's choices and their economic and social power. Simultaneously, this myth also has the effect of denying the validity of men's interest in, and concern for, their children and serves to exclude men from emotional closeness and caring activities within their families (Carrigan, Connell & Lee, 1985). Further, the internalization of this myth by women themselves is one factor in the high levels of guilt and exhaustion many women experience as they strive to meet social expectations in both paid employment and the domestic sphere (Phoenix, Woollett & Lloyd, 1991).

The majority of research on this issue reaches the conclusion that, provided childcare is of good quality and mothers are satisfied with that care, employment provides clear benefits to mothers and has no negative effects on infants, children or adolescents (Lerner & Galambos, 1986; Maume & Mullin, 1993; Mischel & Fuhr, 1988; Tizard, 1991). Even with high-risk samples such as pre-term infants, and even with the infant at the relatively early age of three months, maternal employment appears to benefit both mother and child (Youngblut, Loveland-Cherry & Horan,

1991, 1994), especially if the mother feels she has had a degree of choice over her decision to return to work.

An American study with employed mothers of infants (Stifter, Coulehan & Fish, 1993) found that the level of infants' problems was explicable by their mothers' anxiety and insecurity about childcare arrangements, rather than by the amount of separation, suggesting again that it is the mother's satisfaction with the quality of the arrangements, not the mother's presence or absence, that matters.

Older children have also been shown to respond well to maternal employment; for example, a study of Australian eight- to ten-year-olds (Howie, 1996) showed that children who attended after-school care did not differ from those who went home to mothers or to other family members, in self-esteem, academic achievement, anxiety, social status and life skills. Adolescents, too, appear to suffer no ill effects from maternal employment. Armistead, Wierson and Forehand (1990) found no effect of maternal employment on adolescent cognitive or social competence, behaviour problems, or on the amount of communication between mother and child or the degree of conflict experienced. Similarly, Galambos and Maggs (1990) found no evidence that employed mothers had more conflicts with their adolescent offspring than did non-employed mothers. Employed mothers did report moderate to high levels of work-related stress, but these stresses appeared to be balanced by an increase in well-being associated with employment, so that, overall, the women generally coped well with the combination of employment and parenthood.

There is also some evidence to suggest positive psychological benefits of having a mother who is employed outside the home. For example, children of employed single mothers had higher self-esteem and positive perceptions of their families by comparison with children of unemployed single mothers (Alessandri, 1992); and college students whose mothers had been in paid employment during their childhoods showed positive androgynous characteristics (Ellis, 1994), suggesting that their families of origin had provided a basis for healthy adult development.

Maternal employment also has an effect on the extent to which fathers are involved in caring for their children (e.g. Bailey, 1994), suggesting that fathers, too, may benefit from a richer involvement in family life when mothers are in paid employment. This in turn may have positive effects on the parents' relationship (Hawkins et al., 1993).

EFFECTS OF PAID EMPLOYMENT ON WOMEN'S HEALTH

Paid employment has definite financial and personal advantages, and the majority of women who work in paid employment would not wish to change to full-time unpaid domestic labour. Scarr, Phillips and

McCartney (1989), for example, found that 21 per cent of employed mothers would prefer to be full-time housewives, while 56 per cent of housewives would prefer to work outside the home. Grbich (1995), in a survey of role-reversed couples, found that none of the women wished to exchange roles with their husbands and take on the unpaid domestic work.

The majority of research examining the relationships between women's paid work and their physical and mental health is cross-sectional in nature, making it difficult to draw causal inferences (Hibbard & Pope, 1993). It is important to note that poor physical or mental health is likely to reduce a woman's chances of obtaining paid employment (Repetti et al., 1989). The relationship between work and health is a reciprocal one (Adelmann, Antonucci, Crohan & Coleman, 1990); a longitudinal survey in New Zealand (Romans, Walton, McNoe, Herbison & Mullen, 1993) found that women without meaningful work or social roles were most likely to develop psychiatric disorders, but also that those who were experiencing psychological distress and poor health at baseline were most likely to remain without work or family. Thus, work provides psychological benefits, but women with low levels of physical or emotional well-being may be unable to find suitable work.

Despite this important caveat, longitudinal research does indicate that, in general, paid employment has a beneficial effect on women's physical and mental health. Reviere and Eberstein (1992), for example, used longitudinal data from the US National Health and Nutrition Examination Survey (NHANES) to demonstrate that formal education and paid employment were associated with significantly decreased risk of heart disease among women; unpaid domestic workers and those who left the paid workforce during the survey period had the highest level of cardiovascular disease. A longitudinal study of the relationship between employment and depression among American women (Bromberger & Matthews, 1994) also demonstrated that paid employment had a protective effect; employed women were less depressed than non-employed women, and women who became employed during the three-year study showed significant decreases in depressive symptoms. The group with the highest level of depression were unemployed women with poor education, little family support, and low marital satisfaction – those with few positive and meaningful life roles.

Despite the demonstration of clear positive effects in large-scale epidemiological surveys such as these, there is still a considerable body of research which focuses on the potential for women's paid and unpaid work to have a deleterious effect on their physical and mental health. This research generally concentrates on aspects of the roles of parent, spouse and paid worker, although recently it has been argued that the role of caregiver to elderly relatives needs more explicit attention in such an analysis (Doress-Worters, 1994). Again, this literature is frequently based on a sexist assumption that women will need to combine these roles in a way which men will be able to avoid.

A considerable body of research has examined the impact both of the number of roles occupied and of the quality of the roles occupied, and findings in this area have been somewhat conflictual. Some research (e.g. Lundberg, 1996) supports the general proposition which underlies the group of hypotheses referred to variously as the 'role conflict', 'role overload' and 'role strain' hypotheses. While the details vary, these generally argue that holding multiple roles will lead to negative outcomes to the extent that the demands of those roles are conflicting or excessive (Repetti et al., 1989). It is generally assumed that this will occur only among women, for whom the role of paid worker will simply be added to their existing 'natural' duties as wife, mother, housekeeper, cook, cleaner and so forth. Although there is evidence (e.g. Duxbury & Higgins, 1994; Shaw & Burns, 1993) that fathers also experience some degree of role conflict, sexist expectations about women and men mean that the majority of the research has focused on women. These hypotheses are supported by at least some evidence that combinations of roles can have a negative effect on women's physical health (e.g. Lundberg, 1996), and can result in high levels of guilt and anxiety (e.g. Baruch & Barnett, 1986).

Some research on conflicting roles suggests that paid work impacts differently on women and on men, and specifically that women have more difficulty in combining their work and home lives without interference. For example, Greenglass and Burke (1988), studying burnout in male and female teachers, found that burnout in men was associated mainly with direct work-related stress, while in women it was also related to perceived role strain, to marital quality, and to level of social support. Women teachers in general reported more role conflict than men teachers, and a greater degree of interdependence of work and family (Greenglass, Pantony & Burke, 1988).

Wiley (1991) has argued that findings of this nature can be explained by the different socialization experiences of women and of men, and thus the differing extents to which the role of worker or family member are important to men and to women. Employed women, mothers in particular, tend to adapt their lifestyles in order to take the primary responsibility for unpaid household work as well as meeting the demands of paid employment (Hessing, 1993); while they make use of a range of creative strategies in balancing these different roles, they still take on a greater level of responsibility for a greater amount of time each week than do men, so it is unsurprising if they experience more stress. Differences between men's and women's capacity to combine work and family lives may also be explained in terms of differing levels of autonomy and control in the work situation between men and women; even in a female-dominated profession such as teaching, women tend to be concentrated in the junior ranks, and thus may have less discretion and less flexibility in their work situations.

On the other hand, other researchers (e.g. Fallon, 1996; Frone, Russell & Cooper, 1992) have found that, although work and home duties did interfere with each other, there were no gender differences in this effect. This research has used the concept of asymmetry of the permeability of boundaries between roles (Pleck, 1977), arguing, for example, that the boundaries of the work role, with its formally defined hours and duties, are less permeable than those of the more loosely organized family roles, and thus that work has the capacity to interfere with family life to a greater extent than family life will interfere with work.

The research on role conflict can be contrasted with an equally large and diverse body of work which provides support for the 'role enhancement' hypothesis. This view holds that multiple roles will lead to positive outcomes to the extent that the different roles provide different and complementary sources of personal rewards and satisfactions. It is certainly not the case that more roles automatically means more stress, and some research (e.g. Forgays & Forgays, 1993) has found that mothers who do not have the opportunity to work outside the home are more stressed than those who balance paid work and domestic tasks, perhaps because of the limited opportunities which full-time housewives have for socializing, and for activities which society regards as productive and valuable and which develop self-esteem and coping strategies. In the USA, a fifteen-year longitudinal survey (Hibbard & Pope, 1991) indicated that, for women, paid employment was associated with longevity; there was no evidence that multiple roles had any deleterious effects on health, and some suggestion that they conferred a positive health benefit for women, although role occupancy was not a predictor of health or longevity in men.

A number of research projects from several countries support an integration of the role-overload and role-enhancement hypotheses. This research indicates that multiple roles will have a positive effect on health and well-being up to a certain total level of work, beyond which individuals will begin to suffer from tiredness, stress and overload, with resulting negative effects on their health. Given that most employed women take a higher burden of unpaid domestic labour than do men (e.g. Bittman, 1992), it is reasonable to hypothesize that these women may reach a threshold of overload at a lower level of involvement in paid labour than do men and those women whose domestic loads are more equitable.

Arber, Gilbert and Dale (1985), for example, used English data from the 1970s to indicate that paid employment seemed to benefit the health of women without children and those aged over forty, but that married women under forty with children at home (who presumably were undertaking a heavy share of unpaid domestic labour) showed health deficits if they were also in paid work. More recently, Glass and Fujimoto (1994) used national US data to show that paid work was associated with decreased symptoms of depression, but only until a threshold of total workload was reached, beyond which levels of depression increased once more.

A problem with the interpretation of much of the research on multiple roles has been that it tends to deal only with whether or not women are in paid employment of any kind, and ignores salient features of that employment such as rates of pay, length and flexibility of work hours, career development prospects, personal commitment, and job satisfaction. Similarly, it may not examine the quality of women's relationships with their children, spouse or other household members. The 'role quality' hypothesis (e.g. Facione, 1994; Muller, 1986) argues that it is not the number of roles occupied or the extent of the demands of any one of them that determines an individual's health and well-being, but the perceived quality of those roles and the degree to which the individual feels a commitment to them. Reitzes and Mutran (1994), for example, found that level of commitment to roles, rather than the number or type of roles occupied, predicted level of self-esteem in both men and women.

Waldron and Jacobs (1989) concluded that there was no evidence that the number of roles contributed to role overload or had harmful effects on women's health. They argued that the effects of each role varied, depending on the woman's social circumstances and the way in which various roles conflicted or contributed to each other; some demographic groups appeared to benefit from multiple roles to a greater extent than others, possibly because of the nature or quality of the roles available to them. As Menaghan and Parcel (1991) have pointed out, the quality of the domestic environment and of children's experiences will be influenced by the quality of the mother's job, and the mother's well-being will in turn be influenced by these factors. Since broader social forces serve to push many women, particularly mothers, into low-paying, unstable, low-status jobs which provide little intrinsic satisfaction, mothers may be more likely than others to have unsatisfactory work situations, and these may impact negatively on the quality of the home life and the children's environment. But when women are satisfied with their employment situation, both they and their families benefit.

Several authors (e.g. Piechowski, 1992; Rosenfield, 1989) have argued that jobs with a high degree of control and decision latitude are less likely to result in overload, and more likely to enhance health and well-being, than less flexible and accommodating occupations. Duxbury and Higgins (1994), for example, in a study of dual-earner couples with children, found that most parents reported some role conflicts, although these tended to be higher for mothers than for fathers. Those respondents who felt they had control over aspects of their jobs, through flexible working hours or task discretion, reported fewer role problems than those in more inflexible jobs, again suggesting that the quality of the work role affected the degree to which conflict was experienced. Naturally, employment quality is affected by variables such as education and capacity to commit oneself to a career, areas in which mothers are often forced to compromise.

Reifman, Biernat and Lang (1991) found that married professional women with pre-school children, a group of women who all occupied the same combination of roles, showed considerable variability in depression and physical symptoms. Level of symptoms, both cross-sectionally and in a twelve-month follow-up, was predictable from several measures of negative experiences in the work role, including a perceived lack of authority or influence at work, perceptions of gender discrimination, heavy workload, and work activities which interfered with leisure time. Perceived role conflict and the extent to which family responsibilities interfered with leisure, indications of the poor quality of other roles, also predicted depression and physical symptoms.

Poole and Langan-Fox (1992) have also argued that the number of roles taken on is not the crucial issue in determining women's well-being, but that it is the extent of co-operation from the family, and particularly the partner, that will determine the success with which a woman is able to combine paid and unpaid occupations. While there has been a relative neglect of the quality of non-employment roles in the research literature, it would appear that high satisfaction with family and childcare roles may help women to deal with problems in the paid work role. For example, Barnett, Marshall and Singer (1992) found that reductions in job quality led to increasing distress in single women, but that women with husbands and children did not suffer so much from negative job changes; these effects seemed to be buffered by sources of satisfaction in the women's other roles. Similar conclusions can be drawn from a Canadian study of new mothers returning to the paid workforce (Hemmelgarn & Laing, 1991); ability to cope with this transition was greatest for those with high levels of satisfaction and confidence in their performance of the motherhood role.

All this research on the effects of multiple roles on women's health is based on an apparently uncontested assumption that women who work in paid employment will still take on the majority of housework and childcare. A detailed small-scale study which examined the life histories of eighty well-educated middle-aged women (Leonard, 1996) showed that even highly privileged women are limited by these social expectations. These women generally chose careers which would enable them to cope with the double demands of work and family, 65 per cent becoming teachers because of convenient hours and the congruence of the demands of the job with the demands of caring for a family. Women's careers were still severely affected by husbands' careers and by unplanned pregnancy or children with health problems. Even these relatively privileged women's lives were overwhelmingly controlled by family care and unpaid domestic work; respondents reported a continually increasing load of paid and unpaid work over the years, and at the time of the study were working an average of eighty hours per week in paid and unpaid labour.

UNPAID DOMESTIC LABOUR

Despite egalitarian attitudes to domestic labour among most working couples (Bittman & Lovejoy, 1993), both the magnitude and the specifics of actual workload are still strongly affected by social expectations about gender-appropriate responsibilities (Greenglass, 1991; Perry-Jenkins, 1993). Surveys from a number of different countries, using a range of different methodologies (e.g. Bittman, 1992; Blair & Lichter, 1991; Social Trends, 1995; South & Spitze, 1994), are consistent in showing that women carry out more unpaid domestic labour than men, and that the division of that labour tends to be on sex-based lines, with women taking responsibility for cooking, cleaning and childcare while men predominate in home and car maintenance, gardening, and outside chores. Further, both Bittman (1992) in Australia and South and Spitze (1994) in the USA showed that married women do more unpaid domestic work than any other demographic category, while married men contribute no more than do single men. While employed wives may spend slightly less time in housework than non-employed wives, wives' paid employment has no effect on the time spent by men in household tasks; the household work is either carried out by the employed women in their 'leisure' time, or it is simply not done (Bittman, 1992; Shelton, 1990).

Blair and Lichter (1991) indicated that, among US couples, men contributed an average of fourteen hours per week, and women thirty-three hours per week, to household labour. Among working parents in the USA, Rodgers (1992) reported that employed mothers worked forty-four hours per week in their paid jobs and thirty-one hours per week in domestic labour, while the figures for fathers were forty-seven hours in the paid job and fifteen hours of unpaid work.

Trends over time can be detected in the nature of housework, but there is no evidence to suggest that the increased automation of some domestic tasks has decreased the total amount of household work. Zick and McCullough (1991), comparing diary studies undertaken with married couples in 1977 and 1987, showed that women's total work time (both paid and unpaid) had increased an average of seven hours per week while men's had increased around three and a half hours. Sanik (1990), examining time allocation among parents of infants in 1967 and in 1986, found that both fathers and mothers in the more recent survey were working longer hours.

There is evidence for cross-cultural differences in the allocation of housework, although workloads are higher for women than for men in all countries. Kamo (1994) found greater disparity of workloads, and more rigid division of labour along gender lines, among Japanese than American couples. Workloads appear to affected more by cultural and ideological assumptions than by personal factors, or by structural factors such as employment, educational levels, presence of children, or the extent of industrialization of the broader society (Sanchez, 1994). Even surveys of children and teenagers (e.g. Mauldin & Meeks, 1990) indicate that girls spend more time in household chores, and boys more time in leisure, suggesting that gender-based inequity in household duties is an aspect of gender-role socialization which is evident from a relatively early age.

Some researchers separate childcare from other unpaid domestic labour in analysing the relative contributions of men and women. There is a widespread preference for childcare over cleaning and housework, and fathers who contribute to household labour are more likely to involve themselves with childcare than with other duties (e.g. Deutsch, Lussier & Servis, 1993). Two Australian studies (Baxter & Bittman, 1995; Baxter, Gibson & Lynch-Blosse, 1991) have showed that, despite this preference, men still spent significantly less time than women in child-care, with average weekly involvement being between thirteen and eighteen hours for women and between three and eight hours for men. By contrast, a Canadian study (Hannah & Quarter, 1992) showed a reasonably equitable division of childcare labour, but mothers still taking a far greater responsibility for housework. Interestingly, although a national US survey showed that involvement in paid work was associated with decreases in depressive symptomatology, it also demonstrated that time spent in housework was positively associated with depression, especially if this was combined with a perception that household workloads were inequitably divided (Glass & Fujimoto, 1994).

While research has tended to neglect households which deviate from stereotypical expectations, there is some evidence on non-traditional households. Grbich (1995) studied twenty-five Australian families in which the mother was in paid employment and the father was responsible for housework and childcare. The men carried out most of the traditionally 'feminine' household tasks and provided emotional and practical care for their children during the day; their wives participated in childcare tasks in the evenings, but none of the women wanted to reverse their roles, and the women generally felt that they had the best of the deal. Interestingly, these men reported that they enjoyed childcare but disliked housework, seeing it as boring, repetitive and unfulfilling. The task which these men were least likely to take on, and that the women were most likely to do, was that of cleaning floors, bathrooms and toilets. It might appear that role reversal can work within certain limits, but that cleaning the toilet remains intrinsically feminine.

Gender-based inequities in workloads are often explained by individual attitudes, and research such as that of Grbich (1995) indicates that it is possible for individual couples to come to their own idiosyncratic arrangements for the allocation of household labour. However, broader structural aspects of society and of paid work put constraints on the organization of most individuals' times; in Britain, 62 per cent of couples reported that they thought housework should be divided equally, but only 27 per cent actually achieved this equity (Social Trends, 1995). Thus, it can be argued that efforts to deal with the problem of women's workloads will be unsuccessful if they focus only on individual men and women, and assume that choices about time use and the division of labour are always made freely and on an individual basis. Perhaps some women do prefer domestic employment to the stresses of a career, or of a dead-end factory job, and explanations of the continuing inequities in domestic work and the impact these have on women's career paths do need to consider women's preferences and characteristics. However, these can only be usefully considered in the context of the social forces which contribute to male power and female powerlessness (Apter, 1993).

Men and women seem to be socialized to view paid and unpaid work from different perspectives. Most men internalize the view that they have a responsibility to provide financially for their families, and that other forms of provision or support are not part of their role as husband and father (Perry-Jenkins & Crouter, 1990). Women, by contrast, are socialized to view caring for others and maintaining a household as at least as valuable a contribution to their family and to society as is providing financially (Perry-Jenkins, 1993). Women tend to see domestic labour as their responsibility, while men are more likely to see their contributions to domestic labour as 'helping out' (Gunter & Gunter, 1990).

Most social research into work and the balancing of roles accepts these socialization processes as normal and natural, and is based on the assumption that women will inevitably have to deal with household labour as well as paid employment, while men will have a choice over the extent of their unpaid contributions to the household (Hoffman, 1990). For example, Ngo (1992) explained Hong Kong women's concentration in part-time jobs, low-paid outwork, and unpaid labour in family businesses in terms of their family obligations and their need to take primary responsibility for household work and childcare; there was no consideration of the possibility that women's higher level of responsibility is a social construction, not an unavoidable and eternal truth, or that women's concentration in undesirable employment roles may be better explained by the limitations on women's educational and social opportunities than by any masochistic preference for lowly paid and unpleasant occupations.

Similar biases are not hard to find in other research. For example, Olds, Schwartz, Eisen and Betcher (1993), in a paper which purported to examine the effects of part-time employment and shared childcare on parents' well-being, in fact studied couples in which the woman worked part-time and the man full-time; the effects of part-time work among fathers was not investigated, presumably because the researchers assumed that part-time work was only appropriate for women. Again, Koch, Boose, Cohn, Mansfield, Vicary and Young (1991) examined the coping strategies that US women used to juggle the stress of work and home commitments, and suggested the need for stress management for those women, but failed to mention the possibility that men might also encounter role conflicts or stresses, or that a change in the division of labour might be more effective in reducing women's stress. These examples are typical of a large body of literature which fails to examine the assumptions we make, both about the work involvement of men and women, and about the structure of work environments.

Many researchers (e.g. Crouter & Manke, 1994; Ironson, 1992; Kahne, 1991; Lundberg, 1996) have argued for structural changes to employment practices, such as flexible working hours, options for shorter or variable working weeks without loss of the benefits associated with full-time employment, provision of family leave, and provision of childcare facilities, which would allow both women and men to combine work and family responsibilities. However, as Fallon (1997) has pointed out, contemporary changes in work practices are having the effect of reducing flexibility, increasing hours and cutting benefits; as industrial practices change and permanent unemployment becomes a fact of life, employees find themselves being required to adapt to the needs of an increasingly competitive employment market, rather than workplaces adapting to the realities of home and family lives. Full-time jobs are becoming more, not less, demanding, with the Australian Bureau of Statistics (1994) showing an increase of 5 per cent in actual hours worked by full-time employees in 1993 compared with 1983. Trends such as downsizing and forced relocations are increasing, rather than decreasing, workloads and role strain for both men and women (Fallon, 1997).

Thus, it seems unlikely that there are short-term or easy solutions to the problems of workloads, particularly those problems which women face when they are expected to combine paid employment with the majority of responsibility for unpaid domestic labour. It also seems likely that research which focuses on the individual, and ignores the effect of socially constructed gender roles in limiting employment choices and in maintaining inequities in household labour, will fail to provide a useful model of the problems of multiple workloads for women.

9

FAMILY CAREGIVING:
ANGEL IN THE HOUSE

Family caregiving includes all unpaid care provided by one family member for another, but in the research discussed in this chapter it is usually restricted to the care of adult relatives who need assistance with daily living or health care. This need may result from developmental disability, psychiatric illness, or chronic physical illness or disablement, but the majority of adults who are cared for in a family situation are the frail, physically disabled, or demented elderly. This chapter examines the gendered nature of family care, its effects on the people (mostly women) who care, and the need for changes at the level of public policy and social structure to deal more appropriately with this issue.

The literature on family caregiving, in common with much of the work reviewed in this volume, has generally focused on the individual rather than on broader social and structural variables which underlie the phenomenon. This means that the fact that the majority of family carers are women has tended to be obscured (Abel, 1991), and the extent to which women absorb the cost of caring, through unpaid caring in the home or underpaid employment in caring roles (Hooyman & Gonyea, 1995), is disguised. Social inequities, by which women's choices and opportunities are restricted by the tacit assumption that women are always available to care whenever needed and without remuneration, are positioned as normal, natural and unalterable, and this makes critical analysis of the situation difficult within the dominant discourse of contemporary society.

Hooyman and Gonyea (1995), in one of the few feminist analyses of the subject of caregiving in families, have pointed out that most research is couched in gender-neutral terms, failing to mention that the majority of carers are women, or else simply defines family caregiving as a 'women's issue'. Thus, it fails to consider why or how the preponderance of women in family caregiving has come about, or how this preponderance impacts on the lives of women.

FAMILY CAREGIVING: RHETORIC AND REALITY

The extent of family caregiving appears to have increased, at least in Western countries, as a result of a number of factors, including increased lifespans and advances in medical procedures which mean that many elderly or disabled people live longer and with a greater level of independence and dignity than was previously the case. In the current economic and political climate, formal support for the disabled and frail is inadequate, which means that the responsibility for an increasingly arduous burden falls on the family (Hollingsworth, 1994). This arrangement appears to be less costly in economic terms than the provision of adequate social services only because the costs to the caregivers, including income forgone, direct expenditure, and emotional and physical costs, are not considered (Finch & Groves, 1983; Osterbusch, Keigher, Miller & Linsk, 1987). Further, the emphasis on economic costs to the exclusion of all other factors, such as the appropriateness of the care service to the individual, suggests a deeply uncaring approach to social policy (Sommers & Shields, 1987).

An increase in the numbers of women who have entered the paid workforce might have been expected to produce a reconsideration of family caregiving at the policy level (Clulow, 1995). Instead, however, social policy in many countries promotes the ideology of family care, favours deinstutionalization of the frail and dependent, and reduces welfare spending. Policy-makers appear to ignore the reality that caring is a resource-intensive and difficult burden, which falls inequitably on women at a time when they are experiencing increased pressure from other roles (Sommers & Shields, 1987). The ideologically based concept that caregiving is 'naturally' women's work, something that women enjoy and can do effortlessly, without any training, tends to render women's caregiving invisible, neither costed nor appreciated at a political or policy level (Schiller, 1993).

The aged are a rapidly growing sector of the population, with over-sixty-fives increasing from 4 per cent of the US population in 1900 to around 13 per cent in 1990, while the over-eighty-five group is both the frailest and the fastest growing demographic group in the USA (US Bureau of the Census, 1991). Although the majority of people are in good physical, mental and emotional health for most of their old age (Seeman, 1994), many do need care, especially the very old, and formal care services are inadequate.

Hooyman and Gonyea (1995) estimated that 11.3 million Americans, about half of whom were over sixty-five, depended on others because of chronic disability, and that for every one person in formal care in the USA, there were two more in informal care who were just as severely in need. Leutz, Capitman, MacAdam and Abrahams (1992) reported that only 5 per cent of the community-living frail elderly relied completely on formal paid care; about 20 per cent had some formal support, such as meal services or day care, while 75 per cent had no formal help at all and had to rely largely on family members. Formal services for the frail elderly in the USA, as in other countries, tend to be patchy and poorly co-ordinated, so that many people fall through the gaps between different service providers and catchment areas.

Leutz et al. (1992) have estimated that families provide approximately 80 per cent of all in-home care in the USA, and the situation appears to be similar in other countries. For example, the Canadian Study of Health and Aging (1994) found that about half of all Canadians with dementia are living in the community, and of these 94 per cent are cared for by unpaid family members. Workloads associated with family caregiving are not inconsiderable. A study of care for the demented in the USA (Collins & Ogle, 1994) showed that family members cared for demented relatives at home for a mean of six years, while another study (England, 1995) showed that caregivers spent an average of four hours per day in direct caregiving activities for demented relatives.

Although there has been a decrease in the USA in the number of multi-generational households, in which elderly parents live with adult children and their families and are cared for at home if they need care (Crimmins & Ingegneri, 1990), the proportion of such families is significantly higher among Black and Latino Americans (Angel, Angel & Himes, 1992), and among those with Southern, Central, and Eastern European ancestries (Clarke & Neidert, 1992), compared to families of northwestern European extraction. In other countries, including India, Singapore, Thailand and South Korea, the multi-generation household is still common, despite increasing Westernization and other changed socioeconomic conditions (Hashimoto, 1991).

Among the ethnically and religiously diverse population of Singapore, 88 per cent of the elderly live with their children, but tradition and ethnicity are just some of the complex factors which determined household composition (Mehta, Osman & Lee, 1995). In the Philippines, elderly people generally prefer living with adult children to independent living, despite rapid socioeconomic changes (Domingo & Asis, 1995), while in Thailand there is a strong cultural expectation that elderly parents will live with and be cared for by their children (Knodel, Saengtienchai & Sittitrai, 1995). In Taiwan, the traditional arrangement is that elderly parents live with a married son and are cared for by their daughter-in-law, but a recent survey (Lee, Lin & Chang, 1995) concluded that many elderly people would like to continue living independently, provided they were well enough, mainly because of a concern of becoming a burden to the son and his younger family. Similarly in China, the expectation is that elderly parents live with a son and are cared for by a daughter-in-law, but the Chinese one-child policy has had an obvious impact on this as on many aspects of traditional Chinese life (Yu, Yu & Mansfield, 1990).

The provision of family care, thus, is a significant aspect of everyday life in many societies, although the psychological literature has been surprisingly slow to integrate family caregiving into perspectives on multiple roles and stress among women (Doress-Worters, 1994). Stone and Kemper (1989) estimated that 7.9 per cent of adult Americans had parents or spouses with disabilities, in need of care at some level from occasional assistance through to full-time personal care.

GENDER AND FAMILY CAREGIVING

The burden of family care falls most heavily on women, and particularly those of the middle generation (Gonyea, 1995). A survey of Australian women aged forty-five to fifty (Research Institute for Gender and Health, 1996) found that 19.5 per cent reported that they regularly provided care for a dependent person, while Cantor (1991) estimated that 7 per cent of US women cared for both children and parents. This situation, caring for older and younger generations of dependants in the same household, is associated with the highest levels of emotional stress for caregivers (Brody, Kleban, Hoffman & Schoonover, 1988).

Of family caregivers to the elderly in the USA, 23 per cent are wives, 29 per cent daughters or daughters-in-law, and 20 per cent are other female relatives. Of adults who care for their parents, 79 per cent are women, while of adults who care for their spouses, 68 per cent are women (Miller, McFall & Montgomery, 1991). Even after factors such as employment status are controlled for, daughters are three times as likely as sons to provide care (Dwyer & Coward, 1991). The preponderance of women in family care is also demonstrated by the finding that daughters-in-law are more likely to provide care than are sons (Stone, Cafferata & Sangl, 1987).

The situation is much the same in other countries. A Welsh survey (Wenger, 1994) found that 70 per cent of family caregivers for the demented were female, many themselves elderly and in poor health. A survey of older people in Tokyo (Tokyo Metropolitan Government, 1995) indicated that, of elderly men in need of care, 73 per cent were cared for by wives, 11 per cent by daughters and 10 per cent by daughters-in-law; of elderly women in need of care, 34 per cent were taken care of by daughters, 28 per cent by daughters-in-law and 19 per cent by husbands.

Married women in need of care are more likely than married men to be admitted to formal care (Mutchler & Bullers, 1994), in line with the social expectation that wives will naturally care for sick husbands at home while husbands will, equally naturally, make appropriate arrangements for their wives to be cared for, professionally, by other women.

Hooyman and Gonyea (1995) have argued that much of the literature on family caregiving disguises the gendered nature of care by treating it as a gender-neutral issue or by couching it as a 'women's issue'. The research literature overwhelmingly uses gender-neutral terms such as 'spouse' and 'caregiver' which, intentionally or not, disguise the fact that three-quarters of caregivers are women. For example, two recent studies of the effect of caregiving on health (Cattanach & Tebes, 1991; Pohl, Given, Collins & Given, 1994) used the term 'family caregiver' to refer exclusively to the daughters and daughters-in-law of the elderly people being cared for; sons and sons-in-law, presumably present in approximately equal numbers in the households under study, were not mentioned.

Literature which does emphasize the preponderance of women in family caregiving, according to Hooyman and Gonyea (1995), frequently constructs the problem as a women's issue, focusing on the individual needs and problems of women who care, rather than questioning the basis of this inequitable load. For example, Dippel (1991), in a chapter for medical practitioners, pointed out that, in the absence of a spouse, family care was normally provided by daughters, whose personal circumstances should be considered in making care decisions. While this seems sensible at the individual level, it of course makes a tacit assumption that daughters, rather than sons, care for the elderly. Hooyman and Gonyea (1995) argued that such an assumption 'reflects the societal expectation and ideology that the home is women's domain and caring a natural female characteristic' (p. 3), and stressed that the internalization of this ideology has major effects in restricting women's choices and their economic and social power.

IMPACT OF CARE: CAREGIVER BURDEN

Much of the research on the impact of caregiving focuses on 'caregiver burden', a multidimensional construct which includes the physical, emotional, social and financial costs to the caregiver, and most research concludes that caregiving is associated with significant subjective burden and with poor health (George & Gwyther, 1986; Snyder & Keefe, 1985). Both objective and subjective burden are higher for female than for male caregivers (Chang & White-Means, 1991; Miller & Montgomery, 1990; Morris, Woods, Davies & Morris, 1991; Mui, 1995a). Although research in both the UK (Taylor, Ford & Dunbar, 1995) and New Zealand (Falloon, Graham-Hole & Woodroffe, 1993) has found no evidence for deleterious effects of caregiving on the health of the caregivers, the majority of research does find evidence for both physical and emotional strain. As one might expect, degree of burden experienced can be predicted by the level of assistance required, the amount of dependency, the extent to which the person needs care with activities of daily living, the extent of individual responsibility for the dependant, and the availability of help from others (Jutras & Veilleux, 1991). McKinlay, Crawford and Tennstedt (1995), using data from the seven-year longitudinal Massachusetts Elder Health Program, showed that 61 per cent of carers rated their caregiving responsibilities as the most disruptive aspect of their lives, and this was particularly likely if they lived with the person cared for.

Research in the area of caregiver burden has demonstrated a range of negative effects of caregiving, including physical and emotional strain (White-Means, 1993), increased psychiatric symptoms, psychiatric illness, physical symptoms, and health care usage (Schulz, Visintainer & Williamson, 1990); depression (McNaughton, Patterson, Smith & Grant, 1995); use of psychotropic drugs (e.g. Pruchno & Potashnik, 1989); back pain, headaches, and emotional exhaustion (Snyder & Keefe, 1985); adverse effects on the immune system and resulting increases in viral illnesses (Kiecolt-Glaser & Glaser, 1994); and reduced leisure time (Miller & Montgomery, 1990; White-Means, 1993). The decision to end family caregiving by institutionalizing the frail person is also a difficult one, associated with considerable emotional stress (Gold, Reis, Markiewicz & Andres, 1995). Caregiver exhaustion appears to be as important a factor as patient deterioration in the decision to institutionalize, so this decision may frequently be accompanied by an attribution of personal failure and guilt; however, cessation of caregiving, while emotionally taxing in the short term, is associated with better physical and psychological health than is continuing to care (Gold et al., 1995).

The emotional burden seems particularly problematic. For example, Jutras and Lavoie (1995), in an analysis of the Quebec Health Survey, found that caregivers had similar physical health to other people, matched for age and socioeconomic factors, but significantly poorer psychological health. Draper, Poulos, Cole, Poulos and Ehrlich (1992) found that 46 per cent of their sample of caregivers scored at clinical levels on the General Health Questionnaire, indicating high levels of psychological distress, while Mui (1995b) concluded that level of emotional strain, rather than physical symptomatology or financial burden, was the best predictor of low levels of perceived health and well-being. Micro-social variables such as the existence of social support networks and the occupancy of other satisfying roles (e.g. Moen, Robison & Dempster-McClain, 1995; Monahan & Hooker, 1995) also affect the well-being of caregivers.

The impact of social support and of other roles is not always positive. Married women cope better with caring for elderly relatives than do single women, presumably because of the additional support provided by a spouse (Brody, Litvin, Hoffman & Kleban, 1992), but a high proportion of family caregivers are simultaneously dealing with major conflicts with at least one other member of their family, frequently over issues related to caregiving and the provision of support (Strawbridge & Wallhagen, 1991). Family conflict appears to be particularly a problem for immigrant women, who not only provide care for parents but may need to mediate between the different cultural expectations of their parents, husbands and children, and who frequently receive little help from other members of their families (Gelfand & McCallum, 1994). And although many primary caregivers do have some assistance from a family member or friend (e.g. Penrod, Kane, Kane & Finch, 1995), or make use of professional support services (Snyder & Keefe, 1985), the size of the support network does not seem to affect the amount of care which the primary caregiver provides (Penrod et al., 1995).

Research into caregiver burden has been criticized (e.g. Hooyman & Gonyea, 1995) for its focus on the individual and its neglect of the social structure and ideological expectations which have created a situation in which individual women carry an enormous and largely unacknowledged burden of caring. The problem of long-term care, Hooyman and Gonyea argue, is one of public policy and other structural conditions, not of women's coping inadequacy, need for training, or preference for the martyr role.

The focus on the individual which is apparent in research on caregiver burden is also apparent in interventions which aim to relieve this stress. The focus of this work is on individual interventions such as psychotherapy (e.g. Gallagher-Thompson & Steffen, 1994), support groups (e.g. Peak, Toseland & Banks, 1995; Toseland, Labrecque, Goebel & Whitney, 1992), and educational programmes (Magni, Zanetti, Bianchetti, Binetti & Trabucchi, 1995) to improve the performance and coping skills of caregivers, together with regular day care (e.g. Feinberg & Kelly, 1995) and occasional respite care (e.g. Bader, 1985; Caradoc-Davies & Harvey, 1995) to prevent them from collapsing under the strain. Interventions do not generally attempt to challenge the broader social structure which places intolerable demands on a powerless, frequently elderly, and overwhelmingly female section of the community. It has been argued (e.g. Abel, 1987; Brackley, 1994) that such programmes, which aim to help unpaid family carers to accept and adjust to a role in which they have no personal freedom and no opportunity for change, are in fact teaching them to connive in their own exploitation.

An example of such a programme is the anger management programme developed by Gallagher-Thompson and DeVries (1994), which trained an exclusively female group of caregivers to cope with the anger and frustration they experienced in attempting to deal with the impossible demands of caregiving and other responsibilities. In a classic example of blaming the victims of an inequitable and untenable socially constructed situation, these women were taught to use relaxation and cognitive restructuring as a solution to the lack of practical and financial support. The message here is clearly that the problem lies in a deficiency of the women themselves, rather than in the situation, and that it is their anger and frustration, not the situation, which is the real problem. Such approaches 'serve to deflect attention from broader structural problems and from social, economic and political inequities by race, gender, age or class' (Hooyman & Gonyea, 1995, p. 111).

It may be assumed that caregiving is a burden to Western women because of the individual-oriented nature of Western societies and the so-called breakdown of the mythical 'nuclear family': proponents of this view assume that contemporary society has strayed from its 'natural' structure in which men work to support a family financially while women have all their time available to attend to the needs of others. As well as blaming the victims of inequitable social systems and invoking a 'traditional' family structure which has in fact never existed, this view is challenged by findings from other cultures. In Japan, for example, the burden of caring falls excessively on daughters and daughters-in-law, who report levels of caregiver burden as high as those experienced in the USA (Harris & Long, 1993). And in the USA, a survey of caregiving among Pueblo Indians (Hennessy & John, 1995) found that the level of burden experienced was fairly similar to that of non-indigenous care-givers.

It should be acknowledged that there is a positive side to caregiving. Allen and Walker (1992), for example, have challenged the unremittingly negative view of caregiving presented in the research literature, as well as the assumption that care recipients are entirely passive and can offer nothing in return. Several surveys (e.g. Cohen, Gold, Shulman & Zucchero, 1994; Motenko, 1989; O'Connor, Pollitt, Roth, Brook & Reiss, 1990), while acknowledging the high level of burden experienced by caregivers, have noted the high degree of satisfaction which carers can experience. Hooyman and Gonyea (1995) have argued that a feminist approach to family caregiving would offer genuine choices to family members, both male and female, by providing financial and practical support to those people who were willing to care for their frail relatives. Such a social policy might see a change in the perceived balance between burdens and satisfactions.

IMPACT OF CARE: RESTRICTION OF CHOICES

Caregiving covers a huge range of responsibilities and commitments, from occasional assistance with transport or shopping through to twenty-four-hour-a-day invalid care, and thus average levels of care hide a huge degree of variability in commitment and responsibility. However, a US survey (Hu, Huang & Cartwright, 1986) concluded that the typical family caregiver was a woman who spent six and a half hours per day in direct caregiving work. A separate survey of the community-living elderly with Alzheimer's disease (Max, Webber & Fox, 1995) found that they received an average of 286 hours per month (approximately nine and a half hours per day) of informal, unpaid care, usually from a single family member.

Time spent in family caregiving is obviously time which cannot be devoted to other pursuits. Caregivers not only have reduced access to leisure time, but many find that caring interferes with employment (Abel, 1991; Wagner & Neal, 1994). Stone et al. (1987), in a large-scale US survey, found that 10 per cent of caregivers had left a paid job specifically to care for a family member, while 20 per cent of employed caregivers had reduced their working hours and 29 per cent had re-arranged their working schedules in other ways to meet the demands of their caring role. A smaller, more detailed survey by Monahan (1993) found that 14 per cent of family caregivers had left paid employment in order to care; 57 per cent of caregivers were still employed, but almost half felt their job performance and prospects were adversely affected by caregiving, 9.5 per cent had reduced their working hours, and 38 per cent had rearranged their working schedules. Those caregivers who manage to combine caregiving with full-time employment generally believe that their caregiving interferes with productivity and leads to reduced career opportunities, stress, loss of income, and negative effects on their family and social lives (Wagner & Neal, 1994).

Restriction on employment has obvious economic disadvantages, but it also involves a reduction in opportunities for personal development, social interaction, and all the other intangible benefits of successful employment (Abel, 1991; Hooyman & Gonyea, 1995). An analysis of caregiver burden by Pohl et al. (1994) concluded that giving up work in order to care tended to lead to social isolation and thus to a range of other negative consequences for caregivers.

Conversely, combining family caregiving with paid employment seems to increase the burden of caregiving, with King, Oka and Young (1994) showing that middle-aged women who combined the roles of family caregiver and paid worker tended to feel most negatively about their caregiving, and to demonstrate excess cardiovascular reactivity, an indication of chronic stress.

However, and although there have been numerous calls for employers to deal with the realities of family caregiving through the provision of family leave, work flexibility, or work-based day care for elderly relatives (e.g. Scharlach, 1995), high unemployment and other changes in the employment sector mean that employers have few incentives to consider the social and family context of their employees (Hooyman & Gonyea, 1995). Employers continue to see work–family conflicts of any kind as primarily a private issue and a 'women's problem' which is not relevant to employment conditions (Gonyea & Googins, 1992).

The ideology that women 'naturally' want to care leads not only to a preponderance of women in unpaid caring roles, but also to a preponderance of women in underpaid caring occupations such as nursing (Abel, 1991; Hooyman & Gonyea, 1995). The social construction of women as people who find emotional fulfilment in caring, and the woolly notion that people do not deserve to be paid for work (however socially useful) that they enjoy, is used to justify low wages for caring occupations. Then, the facts that women tend to have lower wages than men, and that they are more likely to be in work roles which are allied to family caring, are used as a justification for pushing women out of the paid workforce and into unpaid caring roles when the family need arises. Further, the disrupted work histories which are more characteristic of women than of men (Keddy et al., 1993) mean a reduced probability that superannuation or other retirement benefits will be adequate, forcing women into poverty and maintaining the cycle of family dependence (Hooyman & Gonyea, 1995).

Clearly family caregiving has economic benefits to the wider community. When older people live with their adult children, their use of formal services is reduced (Choi, 1994) and thus the informal family supports are saving money at a public level. The fact that this is at the expense of those families, and particularly of the women in those families, is often ignored. An examination of Hispanic families, in which usage of institutions and other formal care for the elderly tends to be low (Purdy & Arguello, 1992), concluded that reliance on informal family care for frail elders was dysfunctional, leading to a high level of dependency and, by restricting the life choices and opportunities for education and employment of the adult children, maintaining a cycle of poverty in subsequent generations.

The notion that family care is necessarily good for older people has been challenged by writers such as Strawbridge and Wallhagen (1992), who have argued that the assumptions that families are the appropriate people to provide emotional and social support for their elderly relatives, and that families want to care for their relatives, are not supported by any evidence. The assumption that all older people want to live with their children is also challenged by evidence, both from Canada (Wister, 1985) and from Taiwan (Lee et al., 1995), that older people generally prefer to live independently. When parents move in with their adult children, the primary motivation is usually ill-health, need for care, and lack of alternatives, rather than a positive desire to live in a multi-generational family (Brody, Litvin, Hoffman & Kleban, 1995; Daiewicz, 1995; Magaziner, Cadigan, Hebel & Parry, 1988; Speare & Avery, 1993).

Strawbridge and Wallhagen (1992) have stressed that a lack of alternatives to family care has particularly negative effects on the women who carry the majority of the burden of care, decreasing their economic and career opportunities and causing high levels of guilt. Further, they argued that the assumption that family care is cheaper than formal care can only be sustained if women's labour and missed opportunities for other activities are not costed. With Stommel, Collins and Given (1994) estimating that unpaid labour accounts for 71 per cent of the total costs of caregiving for dementia, even the direct costs are significant, and the cost in lost opportunities, although intangible, may be much greater.

WHY WOMEN?

Walker (1992) has argued that the predominance of women in caring roles has traditionally been explained at an individual level, and issues of gender inequity ignored; the naturalness of the arrangement has been defended by the invocation of women's presumed stronger emotional ties to family members, the assumption that caring is central to women's perceptions of themselves as 'good women', and the assumption that women are somehow 'naturally' better at caregiving than are men and more capable of altruistic self-sacrifice.

The concept of 'separate spheres', that women and men lead separate lives, with men in the public sphere, earning money to support their families and dealing with the world outside the immediate household, and women wholly responsible for the maintenance of home and family (Cott, 1977), although apparently widely rejected in contemporary society, continues to influence both men's and women's expectations of what their family responsibilities are. Our society constructs filial responsibilities differently for women and for men: the 'good son' is someone who provides financially and practically, while the 'good daughter' sacrifices her time and her self (Dalley, 1988). Thus, arranging appropriate professional care for a frail parent or spouse is seen as responsible behaviour in a man, but as uncaring in a woman. Female family members are expected to provide free of charge the type of professional care that otherwise would constitute paid employment (Abel, 1987).

Finley (1989) has described four explanatory models of why it is women who do the caring, and shown that only the gender-role social-ization view is adequately supported by the evidence. The view that women care more than men because they have more time available and fewer competing demands, Finley argues, is undermined by the fact that women who work in paid employment and care for children are as likely as other women, and more likely than men with similar levels of responsibility, to provide care. The task-specialization view, that men and women both care, but that they perform different tasks which are demarcated along gender lines, is also challenged by evidence that women are more likely than men to provide all forms of caregiving, from dealing with the frail person's financial and legal affairs to bathing and other intimate tasks. The argument that it has to do with external resources or power structures in families is also not supported, and Finley concludes that gender-role socialization, the ideology of women as natural carers, is the best explanation.

Guberman, Maheu and Maille (1992) have made the interesting point that there is a semantic confusion between the concepts of *caring about* and *caring for*: since women are believed to care more strongly *about* family members than men, they should therefore be more prepared to care *for* them.

Surveys of carers themselves support the view that women who care have internalized an ideology that women are natural caregivers, accepting that it is the place of women, rather than men, to care (Aronson, 1992). Guberman et al. (1992) identified six major themes in the explanations of women for why they provided family care: inadequacy of existing formal resources, imposition by the dependent person, and economic dependence were categorized as external or structural factors influencing caregiving, while internal reasons included feelings of family ties or affection, a personal need or desire to help others, and a sense of duty; these women, too, seemed to have internalized the dominant ideology which sees women as inevitably the ones who do the work of caring.

Over 90 per cent of paid carers, whether in community or institutional settings, are women (Leutz et al., 1992), and Hooyman and Gonyea (1995) have argued that this preponderance of women in caring roles serves to perpetuate the view that women are naturally better at caring, while that view, with its implication that caring is not really work because women do it naturally, is used to justify low rates of pay and poor conditions for paid carers. The carers themselves come to internalize the view that what they do is of little importance and thus to accept limited opportunities.

By contrast, men who perform caregiving roles do not seem to see it as naturally or inevitably their role in life. Hooyman and Gonyea (1995) have argued that 'men tend to assume primary responsibility of relatives with disabilities . . . only when a female family member is unavailable' (p. 3). While it is of course true that there are men who take on the burden of caring (Chang & White-Means, 1991), and there is evidence (e.g. Fisher, 1994; Fuller-Jonap & Haley, 1995) that these men experience the burdens and satisfactions of caring in a similar way to female caregivers, the assumption that women are natural caregivers continues to shape social and economic policy (Hooyman & Gonyea, 1995). In recent years, with a growing number of men in same-sex relationships developing AIDS and related diseases, it has been argued that the extent to which men involve themselves in caregiving may increase (e.g.

LeBlanc, Aneshensel & Wight, 1995), but it is also arguable that men who care for their male partners in homosexual relationships are not perceived as part of the social mainstream, not as men whose experiences should be seen as 'typical' or 'appropriate', and thus that this caregiving will continue to be seen as an anomaly.

In a large-scale survey of men who cared for disabled wives, Kaye and Applegate (1990) found that even these men, who averaged sixty hours per week in caregiving, felt that women were naturally better caregivers than men, and that they had been forced by circumstance into an inappropriate and arduous role. Traustadottir (1991), in a long-term and detailed study of the families of disabled children, found that the general view among these families was that fathers should contribute to caregiving by providing financial support, by recognizing and appreciating the work that the mothers carried out, and by being available to discuss options and alternatives in the child's care or treatment. If fathers involved themselves in this peripheral way, leaving mothers to do all the actual work, the mothers perceived them as deeply involved and caring, as doing as much as could possibly be expected.

It is counterproductive, however, to shift the focus of a discussion of family caregiving from individual women to individual men. The behaviours and choices of both men and women are constrained by sexist ideologies concerning appropriate behaviour. It is necessary to recognize and challenge these ideologies, and particularly to challenge the perception that women's family caregiving and other unpaid domestic labour is not real work, in order to begin to challenge social, economic and political arrangements which perpetuate inequality.

Part IV

PRETTY MAIDS ALL IN A ROW: WOMEN AS OBJECTS IN A MALE LANDSCAPE

INTRODUCTION

Gender inequity is a fundamental aspect of most human societies. Changes to the lives of at least some women, through changes in educational and employment opportunities and the removal of formal restrictions on women's participation in public life, have not changed the basically patriarchal structure of society. Society is primarily male, in the sense that men are regarded as the norm, as the standard adult. When we generalize about adults, the assumption is that we are primarily talking about men, with women as a 'special case'.

The asymmetry between the genders, whereby activities involving men are implictly regarded as more central and more important than those involving women, and the male perspective is implicitly seen as more central, more true and more universal than the female perspective, is nowhere as obvious as in the way in which women are regarded primarily as objects for the male gaze. Women are positioned as objects to be looked at, as valuable in terms of their attractiveness or usefulness to men, rather than as equal members of society whose subjectivity is as legitimate and important as that of men.

The three chapters in this part explore aspects of the woman-as-object perspective and its effects on women's health. Chapter 10 explores the issue of weight and beauty, examining both the clinical work on eating disorders and the broader issue of those social factors which lead to women's appearance being central to their social value, and to extreme thinness being viewed as desirable for women. Discontent with one's body is regarded as normal and natural for women in modern society, and disordered eating may be viewed as an extension of this discontent. Explanations for women's socially sanctioned obsession with thinness vary greatly, but tend to centre on social restrictions on women's lives and on power relations between men and women, suggesting that wholesale changes in the position of women in society may be required in order to bring about any major change in women's relationships with their bodies.

Chapter 11 deals with the issue of ageing, exploring negative stereotypes of ageing and the particularly strong stigmatization of ageing for women. Again, this can be explained by a cultural perspective which regards women as valuable only to the extent that they fulfil limited socially constrained roles, revolving around being attractive or useful to men or fulfilling domestic obligations. Older women, who may fit none of these limited roles, are assumed to have outlived their usefulness and thus to be depressed, inferior and without any meaningful social role. However, research evidence suggests that older women are in fact characterized by positive well-being, and that negative stereotypes of ageing are generally unfounded.

Chapter 12 deals with lesbians, a group of women who refuse to inhabit another aspect of women's restricted role within a patriarchal system, that of potential sexual availability to men. The prejudice faced by these women and the problems they experience in finding a way of living which is not based on a patriarchal system demonstrate both their own difficulties and those which are faced by all women who have to deal with the ingrained power asymmetries of human society.

10

UNSIGHTLY FAT:
EATING, WEIGHT AND BEAUTY

The patriarchal basis of our society, in which men are seen as valuable in and of themselves, but in which women are valuable only to the extent to which they are useful or attractive to men, is demonstrated clearly in our gendered approach to physical beauty. Socialization leads to very different attitudes towards the body in boys and in girls. From an early age, media, cultural and personal influences convey the message that boys should develop and strengthen their bodies, making them more functional and more competent. Girls, by contrast, are told that they should preserve their bodies, protect them from the rigours of normal life, and make them more attractive to look at, rather than stronger, healthier and more useful (e.g. Freedman, 1984). Being female means that how one looks is more important than what one does; men's role in society is to be active and independent, women's is primarily to be attractive and sexually available to men. Women's social position as more peripheral than men is expressed in the emphasis on their outward appearance rather than their subjective experience, and the restrictions which limit that appearance have a central impact on women's lives (Rothblum, 1994a).

As Striegel-Moore, Silberstein and Rodin (1986) pointed out in an analysis of the social importance of women's appearance, physical attractiveness has much greater benefit for women than for men. Cultural restrictions on appropriate or desirable physical appearance are much stronger for women than for men, and tolerance of diversity much weaker: 'prejudice or discrimination based on appearance has an adverse effect on all women who are not white, middle-class, heterosexual, young, thin, and able-bodied, as well as on many who are' (Rothblum, 1994a, p. 54). Thus, being overweight or physically unattractive has more negative consequences for women than for men, affecting self-esteem, confidence, and success in forming heterosexual relationships (Freeman, 1987; Harris, Walters & Waschull, 1991; Stake & Lauer, 1987). Women, from an early age, learn to make social comparisons on the basis of physical appearance more often, and with more personal investment, than do men (Martin & Kennedy, 1994). This pervasive difference in attitude has been argued to provide an explanation of girls' lower self-esteem, negative body image, and their experience of psychological conflict over success and achievement (e.g. Freedman, 1984).

A general explanation as to why appearance is more salient for women than for men can be found in patriarchal notions of women as possessions and objects rather than individual and agentic members of society (e.g. Wooley, 1994). Women are both consumers and objects of consumption in capitalist society, leading to a complex and problematic relationship between women's emotional well-being and their physical appearance which has existed for centuries (Heenan, 1996).

While some research deals with physical attractiveness more generally, most psychological and sociological analyses of the impact of appearance on women's lives focus on the central issue of body weight and shape. In recent years the pressures on women to conform to a socially approved body shape have increasingly become a concern, not only for women's autonomy and rights as full members of society, but also for women's health and their physical survival, because the body shape which is now considered desirable for women is an unhealthily and unsustainably thin one. The ideal weight for women in developed countries, as indicated by successful models and actresses, by pin-up girls and beauty queens, lies somewhere around the fifth to the tenth percentile of the normal weight range, some two standard deviations below the actual mean for normal women (Seid, 1994). Thus, not only is conformity to a physical ideal seen as essential to a woman's value as a person, but simultaneously over 90 per cent of all women are told that they are unattractively overweight.

Anti-fat prejudice affects women far more strongly than men. Fat women are unequally discriminated against in employment and other opportunities, fat women are more likely to remain single, and contemporary society views fatness, not as a physiological state, but as a moral failing (Rothblum, 1994a). This chapter explores the issue of weight and eating, with a focus on the structural factors which mean that women are the vast majority of those people whose well-being is affected by this issue.

Psychological research has tended to focus on serious, potentially life-threatening eating disorders, but there is overwhelming evidence that women with diagnosed eating disorders are not qualitatively different from other women. Rodin, Silberstein, and Striegel-Moore (1984) described a 'normative discontent' among women about their bodies; in Western countries, it is considered normal and natural for women, whatever their state of health, appearance, or success in personal and vocational domains, to be discontented or unhappy, and to attribute this to their physical appearance and particularly to their body shape (Cash & Henry, 1995; Steiner-Adair, 1994).

Psychological analyses certainly acknowledge the vast gender imbalance in disordered eating, and discussions of the role of social pressures for thinness and of the impact of gender roles and cultural experience are widespread in the psychological literature (e.g. Brownell & Fairburn, 1995; Hsu, 1990; Wilson, 1996). However, the tendency to dichotomize women into the normal and the eating-disordered, as well as psychology's traditional focus on the individual rather than the social context (Sarason, 1981), serves to maintain a discourse which contrasts a small number of disturbed, inadequate individuals with a 'normal' majority. Thus, psychological analyses have largely focused on eating-disordered women and on women exhibiting predispositions to disordered eating, on the personal characteristics which make individual women more or less able to resist social and cultural pressures, and on the strategies which will or will not help them to cope, rather than on the nature of the society which produces these maladaptive attitudes and behaviours. Although psychologists acknowledge that gender, class and race must be considered in any analysis of disordered eating and associated psychological distress (Bendfeldt-Zachrisson, 1992; Bowen, Tomoyasu & Cauce, 1991), the focus is still on the individual and her personal circumstances. This has been criticized by sociologists, who have argued that it leads to the unconsidered acceptance of cultural factors, such as the current preference for extreme thinness in women, and the centrality of physical appearance to women's personal worth, as somehow natural and universal, factors which need to be acknowledged but not challenged (e.g. Hepworth & Griffin, 1995; MacSween, 1993).

From a sociological perspective, on the other hand, the medical and psychological aspects of full-blown eating disorders often receive far less attention than the factors underlying women's 'normative discontent' with their bodies. Sociologists have tended to emphasize the role of a strongly gendered society in which political, social and economic power is vested in men to a much greater extent than in women. Perhaps the majority view among sociological analysts is that eating disorders arise from the centrality of appearance for success in the female gender role, combined with the contemporary thin ideal. These cultural imperatives are promulgated through many channels, including the media, peers and family, and are moderated at an individual level by a woman's ability to resist cultural pressures to internalize these ideals (e.g. Stice, 1994).

Attempts to integrate the sociological and psychological literatures are hampered by their almost complete incommensurability. Some sociologists (e.g. MacSween, 1993) describe individual therapy for eating disorders as a strategy which teaches the victims of culturally sanctioned restrictions to connive at their own oppression, while some psychologists (e.g. Wilson, 1996) argue that expectations of any change in broader social attitudes to eating, weight and women's bodies are unrealistic, so the only sensible strategy is to deal with these issues at the individual level. These contradictions need to be reconciled in an approach which acknowledges both the personal and the cultural influences on women's relationships with food and with their bodies.

This chapter begins with a necessarily brief description of the major clinical eating disorders, anorexia nervosa and bulimia nervosa, before moving on to a consideration of social factors which may go some way to explaining why these conditions occur overwhelmingly among women rather than among men.

ANOREXIA AND BULIMIA: DEFINITIONS, PREVALENCE AND PROGNOSIS

Eating disorders were first described in the medical literature in the 1870s by Gull in the UK and Laseque in France (Hsu, 1990). Until relatively recently, research was characterized by confusion and disagreement about the definitions of these disorders, with terms such as 'bulimarexia' and the 'dietary chaos syndrome' used to convey the overlapping nature of the conditions (Levey, McDermott & Lee, 1989), but the DSM–IV criteria (American Psychiatric Association, 1994) are now widely accepted as standard. DSM–IV defines anorexia nervosa as involving a refusal to maintain a normal body weight, leading to a weight at least 15 per cent below a minimum normal body weight (although many women reach weights significantly lower than that); an intense fear of gaining weight; a disturbed perception of the body, such as a denial of the seriousness of the problem or an insistence that one is fat; and the absence of menstruation where it would normally be expected.

Bulimia nervosa is defined primarily by two linked habitual activities: recurrent episodes of binge eating, characterized by eating a very large amount of easily digested food in a discrete period of time, while experiencing a sense of lack of control over that behaviour; and purging, involving any or all of self-induced vomiting, inappropriate use of laxatives or diuretics, prolonged fasts, or excessive exercise, in order to counteract the effects of the bingeing.

Anorexia nervosa has its onset typically in the late teens (Hsu, 1990). However, occurrence of anorexia nervosa and related eating disorders in younger age groups appears to be increasing, and research with girls as young as eight indicates a growing level of concern with body shape and a rise in the incidence of full-scale anorexia nervosa (Lask & Bryant-Waugh, 1992). Clinical eating disorders also occur among the middle-aged and elderly, showing a similar pattern of onset, and frequently associated with severe depression or obsessive-compulsive disorders (Cosford & Arnold, 1992).

The most obvious characteristic of eating disorders is that they are ten times as common among females as among males (e.g. Hsu, 1990). Both anorexia nervosa and bulimia nervosa do occur in males, although rarely, and the presentation is reasonably similar to that shown by females (Buckley, Freyne & Walsh, 1991; Carlat & Camargo, 1991). Those males who develop eating disorders tend to be involved in occupations such as modelling or dancing, or sporting activities such as diving or horse racing, which demand low body fat, and bulimia in particular seems more common in homosexual men (Carlat & Camargo, 1991). These characteristics provide support for a link between eating disorders and socialization. The gendered nature of the development of the conditions may be confused, however, by biases in diagnosis. Hepworth and Griffin (1995) have argued that contemporary medical discourses concerning anorexia nervosa and other eating disorders are so strongly gendered that men are much less likely than women to receive a diagnosis of anorexia or bulimia, and are more likely to be labelled as depressives with associated changes in appetite than to receive a primary diagnosis of eating disorder.

Anorexia nervosa usually seems to begin with dieting and to develop into a fear of fatness and preoccupation with food (Hsu, 1990). It appears to be commonest in young Caucasian females, although it is by no means unknown among Black Americans and other minority groups in developed nations (Striegel-Moore & Smolak, 1996). It does occur in developing countries (Davis & Yager, 1992), but it seems to be rare and its rate appears to be linked in some way with economic development (Hsu, 1990). A recent review (Hoek, 1993) estimated the incidence of new cases of anorexia nervosa in Western societies to be 8.1 per 100,000 population per year, with the comparable figure for bulimia nervosa at 11.4 per 100,000 per year. However, these figures are somewhat misleading, as the conditions are overwhelmingly likely to occur in young females. Hsu (1990) estimated a lifetime incidence of anorexia nervosa at around 0.1 to 0.3 per cent (100–300 per 100,000) of Western women, while Hoek (1993) put the point prevalence rate among young women at 0.28 per cent (280 per 100,000) for anorexia and 1 per cent (1,000 per 100,000) for bulimia. While reporting has increased markedly in the past decades, with increased attention in both the professional and the lay press, Fombonne (1995) has argued that there is no firm evidence for any recent increase in the actual rate of anorexia nervosa, and concluded that the point prevalence rate has been around 0.13 per cent of all women (130 per 100,000 women) for the past twenty-five years.

Anorexia nervosa has a death rate of around 5 per cent (Hsu, 1990). Undernutrition damages the cardiovascular and renal systems, while bingeing and purging cause electrolyte imbalances, and the most common cause of death, other than suicide, is heart failure (Sharp & Freeman, 1993). Although death rates have dropped since the 1950s and 1960s (Steinhausen, Rauss-Mason & Seidel, 1991), rates of recovery have not improved and there is a high level of continuing psychological and eating-related problems among former anorexics. Only about 50 per cent of individuals diagnosed with anorexia nervosa ever attain normal body weight, normal menstrual function and good psychological health (Hsu, 1990). The prognosis for bulimia nervosa is rather better, and Hsu (1990) estimated that 70 per cent would make a full recovery within one year of initial diagnosis. Contemporary treatments for disordered eating (e.g. Brownell & Fairburn, 1995; Szmukler, Dare & Treasure, 1995) tend to be behavioural and cognitive-behavioural, focusing on changing the patient's eating behaviour and her distorted view of her body and her self, in contrast to earlier psychoanalytic approaches. Increasingly, attention is also paid to family and social context.

The categories of disordered eating are by no means as separate from each other or from normal behaviour as they may appear. Firstly, many individuals who maintain a weight in the anorexic range regularly binge and purge; DSM–IV arbitrarily defines these individuals as anorexic rather than bulimic, but this appears to be because of the dangers of undernutrition, not for any reason connected with aetiology. Secondly, anorexia nervosa and bulimia nervosa frequently occur sequentially in the one person (Hsu, 1990). Further, disordered eating behaviours are not qualitatively different from normal patterns of behaviour. The obsession with food and weight which is commonly encountered among anorexic and bulimic patients is found in a majority of Western women (Rodin et al., 1984), and an overriding concern with weight and shape is widely regarded as normal and appropriate for young women (Steiner-Adair, 1994). A recent Australian survey of women aged eighteen to twenty-three (Research Institute for Gender and Health, 1996) found that over 50 per cent restricted their eating, while over 20 per cent reported bingeing and 13 per cent purging.

The psychological states associated with severely disordered eating have overlaps with other psychiatric diagnoses, particularly depression, anxiety, borderline personality disorder, and obsessive-compulsive disorder. Women with eating disorders have a high frequency of secondary diagnoses, particularly depression and borderline personality (Zerbe, Marsh & Coyne, 1993), while patients with a primary diagnosis of personality disorder frequently have disordered attitudes to eating (Dolan, Evans & Norton, 1994). Bulimia often co-occurs with alcohol abuse (Goldbloom, 1993) or substance abuse (Holderness, Brooks-Gunn & Warren, 1994), while anorexia seems to be associated with self-mutilation (Favazza, DeRosear & Conterio, 1989). Although it is frequently assumed that sexual abuse may precipitate eating disorders, the rate of sexual abuse is actually no higher among eating-disordered patients than among groups with other psychiatric diagnoses (Connors & Morse, 1993; Pope & Hudson, 1992).

One continuing problem which has been identified with explanations of anorexia and bulimia (e.g. Fairburn, 1991; Hsu, 1990) is that they are described both as a set of behaviours (fasting, bingeing, etc.) and as a set of (presumably) causal psychological states. It is not clear that the behaviours are always caused by the same set of psychological states, and it is evident that the psychological states are not always associated with abnormal eating. Thus, eating disorders seem highly heterogeneous in their causes and manifestations at the individual level, making it difficult to develop a coherent clinical understanding or to produce definitive therapeutic interventions (Fairburn, 1991). Increasingly, psychologists and sociologists alike are arguing that eating disorders must be seen less as medical or psychological diseases, and more as an extreme variation of women's normal reactions to social and cultural forces (Hepworth & Griffin, 1995).

SOCIAL AND CULTURAL ANALYSES OF DISORDERED EATING

Once one moves beyond the individual with an eating disorder, it becomes necessary to consider the nature of the social forces which are responsible for the overwhelming importance of appearance in women's lives, and for the acceptance of such a thin body shape as ideal. Such forces are assumed to interact with women's social position more generally to produce maladaptive attitudes and self-destructive behaviour. This section reviews evidence from social psychological, sociological and anthropological perspectives. While some writers (e.g. MacSween, 1993) argue that these different perspectives cannot be reconciled, because they are based on fundamentally incompatible views about the nature of the self and society, none is in itself sufficient to provide an adequate explanation of disordered eating. By juxtaposing and comparing alternative views, a more comprehensive, even if not entirely internally consistent, description of these issues may emerge. It would appear that Western women's obsession with weight and body shape is strongly over-determined; several apparently unconnected aspects of contemporary society have been advanced as partial explanations of this phenomenon, and a number of different social and cultural forces may work in combination to make it extremely difficult for women to avoid a motivation to achieve the 'thin ideal'.

Cross-cultural evidence on body shape preferences

The perception that an extremely thin body shape is attractive is somewhat singular, both historically and cross-culturally, but the pervasiveness of Western culture through economic and political forces, as well as through increasing globalization of media, mean that this local aberration has a widespread effect. Most non-Western cultures have traditionally favoured a large body size for women, associating body fat with desirable factors such as health and survival, as well as fertility, success, wealth and prestige (Cassidy, 1991). Cogan, Bhalla, Sefa-Dedeh and Rothblum (1996), for example, found that Ghanaian university students identified larger body sizes as ideal than did American students, and also reported lower levels of shape concern, dieting and restrained eating.

While non-Western societies do not appear to endorse the thin ideal to the same extent as mainstream Western societies, both anorexia nervosa and bulimia nervosa do occur in those societies (Davis & Yager, 1992; Dolan, 1991). The rates appear to be much lower than in Western societies, but Dolan (1991) has argued that biases in diagnosis and referral may contribute to at least part of the apparent difference in incidence, and it is important to remember that Western attitudes and preferences impinge on almost every culture, no matter how remote.

The process of Westernization appears to affect women's body images in unhealthy ways. Research in the South Pacific Cook Islands (Craig, Swinburn, Matenga-Smith, Matangi & Vaughan, 1996), for example, has demonstrated a shift away from a traditional preference for a large build, which seems to be associated with increasing exposure to Western media and cultural influences. This is a particular concern in countries such as the Cook Islands, where people are generally genetically predisposed to a solid, muscular body type. They are unlikely to be able to attain a thin body shape and, if they do, are more likely to be undernourished than a person with a naturally lighter build. Craig et al. (1996) have pointed out that Western weight norms are physically inappropriate for Cook Islanders, who have been shown to have a greater percentage of lean body mass, and less fat, than the average Caucasian of the same weight and height, and thus to have a somewhat higher healthy weight range.

In Hong Kong, a traditionally Chinese culture with extensive Malaysian and Indian influences, which has also been exposed to strong Western influences over several centuries, S. Lee (1993) and Lee, Leung, Lee, Yu and Leung (1996) have found high levels of unhealthy eating attitudes among students of Chinese ethnicity. They argued that Western media and attitudes were leading to a change in concepts of beauty; traditional Asian ideas of beauty which focus on facial features and on bodily grace were being replaced by the shape-oriented concepts of Western society.

Visibly different minorities in Western societies may experience particular pressures; their minority status does not make them immune to mainstream cultural forces, and finding a satisfactory self-image may be difficult if the mainstream culture presents negative views of their culture of origin or if mainstream ideals and media images of attractiveness are inappropriate because of skin colour, body shape, or cultural expectations regarding clothing and activities (Root, 1990). For example, a survey of school girls in Bradford, in the UK, found that girls from Asian families had higher rates of disordered eating than those of

Caucasian descent, and the highest levels of disorder were found among those girls who maintained a strong orientation to their family's culture of origin (Mumford, Whitehouse & Platts, 1991). Eating disorders, argued Mumford et al., may be exacerbated in those who experience conflict between personal and family values and the values of the wider society within which they live. Presented with one set of prescriptions for behaviour and appearance by their families, and a conflicting set by peers, school and media, these girls may face particular difficulties in identifying an appropriate self-image.

In the USA, by contrast, the majority of research indicates that eating disorders are less prevalent among Black, Hispanic and other minority women than they are among the cultural majority (Striegel-Moore & Smolak, 1996), and Black women have more positive body images than do women from other ethnic groups (Cash & Henry, 1995). Black men appear less negative about overweight women than are White American men (Harris et al., 1991). However, eating disorders certainly occur among American minority women, and the cultural circumstances of minority women need to be better understood in order to explore the interactions of majority and minority cultures and the effects these interactions have on individual women (Striegel-Moore & Smolak, 1996).

B.W. Thompson (1992, 1994), in a series of interviews with Black, Latina and lesbian women with eating disorders, has pointed to conflicts between minority cultural beliefs, that women are valuable for what they do rather than for how they look, and mainstream attitudes that fat is bad, ugly and a sign of failure. Thus, minority women may receive confusing and contradictory messages about desirable appearance and behaviour. Issues for lesbian women may be particularly problematic. While these women may not be personally interested in being attractive to men, they still live and work in an essentially heterosexual society and are inevitably influenced by these social forces (Rothblum, 1994b).

Media influences on the thin ideal

The media are frequently blamed for conveying and reinforcing the thin ideal, and research has demonstrated a direct relationship between women's amount of exposure to commercial media and their level of symptoms of eating disorders, extent of endorsement of traditional gender role, and body dissatisfaction (Stice, Schupak-Neuberg, Shaw & Stein, 1994). There is far less variation in the appearances of women who work in the media than is the case for men. Female actors, advertisers, models and news presenters alike are overwhelmingly young, attractive and above all thin (Kilbourne, 1994). As Rothblum (1994a) remarked, 'the occasional middle-aged or elderly woman is shown as clumsy, plump, and comical, and nearly always engaged in domestic activity' (p. 64). The message is clear: women who are not young and slim are figures of fun. To compound this problem, women have been shown to be more likely than men to compare themselves with models in advertisements, as well as to engage in social comparisons more generally on the basis of appearance (Martin & Kennedy, 1994).

Magazines which target young women present powerful messages about what should concern their readers, and content analyses show that these magazines deal overwhelmingly with physical appearance, cooking, household crafts, and heterosexual relationships (Peirce, 1990). Thus, women's value is embodied in their ability to attract a man and to be of service to him. An analysis of the content of popular magazines (Andersen & DiDomenico, 1992) found that magazines for young women had 10.5 times as many articles and advertisements promoting weight loss as did magazines for young men. In general, advertisements which target women use excessively thin models with slogans which promote a fear of fat and present body dissatisfaction as normal (Kilbourne, 1994).

Thus, contemporary culture is flooded with images of extremely thin women, conveying the message that real women's bodies are inadequate and in need of work (Wooley, 1994). These promote anxiety among women (Kilbourne, 1994) and produce widespread misapprehensions about the body shape which other people actually find attractive (Cohn & Adler, 1992). The effect of this is to distract women from other pursuits and to encourage them to concentrate on their own bodies, in a hopeless quest to meet an unhealthy and physiologically unlikely standard (Kilbourne, 1994).

Why eating and body weight?

Eating disorders are often described as attempts to gain control over a life which appears to be out of control (e.g. Lawrence, 1984). The question that this raises is why people, and women in particular, seek to control eating and body shape rather than other aspects of their lives. At one level, the explanation for this is found in society's emphasis on physical appearance, particularly for women. But there are other issues as well. Wilson (1996), writing from a psychological perspective, has argued that people may develop concerns about eating and body weight, rather than other aspects of their lives, because appearance and weight seem more controllable. The popular media, especially magazines for women, convey the message that dieting and exercise will allow any person to achieve any physical shape she desires, and that reshaping the body is simply a matter of willpower (Brownell, 1991). In fact, the extent to which body shape can be modified is to a large extent restricted by the individual's genetic make-up and weight history (Bouchard, 1995), which together affect the 'natural weight' or 'set point' (Keesey, 1995), which the body will defend through physiological control mechanisms such as small variations in basal metabolic rate (Leibel, Rosenbaum & Hirsch, 1995).

According to Wilson (1996), distressed women compound their problems by embarking on a certainly unsuccessful battle with their normal body shape, while ignoring other aspects of their lives which might be more amenable to positive change strategies. Particularly for women who are struggling with society's notions of appropriate female roles, the fact that food and food preparation is viewed as a legitimate interest of women compounds this problem (MacSween, 1993).

A factor which increases confusion for young women is widespread social and medical concern about overweight. High calorific intake, especially of saturated fats, leads to increased serum cholesterol, raised blood pressure and risk of heart disease and diabetes as well as to obesity (Epstein, 1989). Economic factors mean that high-fat, high-sugar foods are widely advertised, and often cheaper and more readily available than more healthy foods (Brownell & Wadden, 1992). Public health messages encouraging individuals to eat less fat therefore are a feature of modern Western societies. Thus, choosing to diet can be legitimized as a healthy and appropriate choice.

However, even moderate dieting may cause health problems. Insufficient iron intake, common in girls and women who avoid animal products, can result in anaemia (English & Bennett, 1990). Low calcium intake, from restriction of dairy products, also puts adolescent girls and young women at risk of failing to develop adequate bone mass, and thus at risk of later osteoporosis (Nordin, 1986).

A concern for health is certainly not solely responsible for disordered eating and concern about body shape in young women. There is ample evidence from other behaviours that health concerns are less salient than those connected with appearance, particularly for young people. Women's decisions to begin and to continue smoking, for example, are associated with the motivation to lose weight (French & Jeffrey, 1995). However, contemporary society regards health and the care of the body as a positive virtue, so health-related and appearance-related concerns overlap in the case of food and weight.

PSYCHOLOGICAL ANALYSES OF GENDER ROLE AND BODY SHAPE

Women's concern about body weight and shape cannot be understood without reference to socially constructed gender roles (e.g. Jackson, Sullivan & Rostker, 1988). Women, regardless of their actual body size or shape, are more likely to be dissatisfied with their shape, to want to lose weight, and to report dieting and other restrictive eating patterns than

men (e.g. Tiggemann & Rothblum, 1988; Tiggemann, Winefield, Winefield & Goldney, 1994; Zellner, Harner & Adler, 1989). The concept of
'normative discontent' described by Rodin et al. (1984), the notion that it
is normal for Western women to be unhappy with their bodies, has been
accepted as a natural facet of femaleness; in fact, not being concerned
about one's body shape is seen as unfeminine and somewhat odd
(Steiner-Adair, 1994).

This discontent appears to arise very early in the socialization process;
surveys with US primary school children aged as young as eight have
shown that girls have significantly more eating-related concerns, higher
body dissatisfaction, larger discrepancy between ideal and current body
shape, and lower self-esteem than boys (e.g. Oliver & Thelen, 1996;
Thelen, Powell, Lawrence & Kuhnert, 1992; Wood, Becker & Thompson,
1996). Thelen et al. (1992) did find few weight concerns and no gender
differences among second-graders, but by the fourth grade, aged around
ten, girls were already showing greater concern about their shape than
boys, whose attitudes to eating and their bodies did not seem any
different from those of younger children.

Psychological analyses of the impact of gender roles on women's
internalization of the cultural norm of thinness have tended to focus on
the gender-role perceptions of individual women. While these have
largely ignored the structural reasons why the gendered nature of society
may lead women to an obsession with their physical appearance, they do
provide evidence that gender roles are closely associated with the
problem.

Research examining the relationship between gender-role orientation
and disordered eating has been informed by two main hypotheses: one
that strong endorsement of the feminine gender role will be associated
with disordered eating, and the other that a high level of discrepancy
between perceived and ideal gender role, regardless of what that ideal is,
is associated with disordered eating (Lancelot & Kaslow, 1994). The
evidence on these two hypotheses is mixed, partly because of variations
in methodologies, definitions and populations. Some research has supported the 'femininity' hypothesis, suggesting that an androgynous or
masculine self-image appears to protect girls from the development of
eating disorders, while the adoption of a traditionally feminine sex role is
associated with increased risk. Klingenspor (1994), for example, found an
association between bulimic behaviours and low scores for psychological
masculinity among three samples of female adolescents in Germany
and the USA, while Brown, Cross and Nelson (1990) found that US
college students who engaged in bulimic behaviours tended to be more
traditionally feminine and less feminist than other students.

On the other hand, some researchers have suggested that dissatisfaction with a traditional feminine gender role, and aspirations towards
non-traditional careers and life choices, may lead to psychological stress

and increase the likelihood of disordered eating. Silverstein, Carpman, Perlick and Perdue (1990) showed that college women with non-traditional sex-role aspirations were twice as likely as others to binge and purge, and implicated gender identity conflict as a possible precursor. Perception of social pressures to conform to the demands of several stereotypes, as demonstrated in the 'superwoman' syndrome, was associated with risk of disordered eating in a separate study of US under-graduate women (Thornton, Leo & Alberg, 1991). Supporting the argument that it is a discrepancy between actual and ideal gender role, rather than a high level of psychological femininity, that is associated with eating disorders are the findings of Johnson and Petrie (1995): that gender discrepancy predicted disordered eating and weight concerns, and that the group with the highest level of symptoms were those who desired to be more masculine. A comparison of patients with eating disorders and those with other psychiatric diagnoses (Martz, Handley & Eisler, 1995) found that the eating-disordered tended to feel committed to a feminine gender role but at the same time were not meeting their own expectations in this regard.

It has been argued that, if eating disorders arise from ambiguities and tensions inherent in the traditional female gender role and in mainstream expectations of women, lesbians may be at lower risk than heterosexual women, while homosexual men, susceptible to pressures to conform to a stereotype of attractiveness which is pleasing to other men, may be more at risk than heterosexual men (Schneider, O'Leary & Jenkins, 1995). Some research does support this analysis; studies of US college students (Siever, 1994) and of San Francisco adults (Schneider et al., 1995) have found that heterosexual women and homosexual men were most vulnerable to eating disorders and dissatisfied with their bodies. However, a comprehensive review (Heffernan, 1994) concluded that results in this area are mixed and that definite conclusions regarding the role of sexual orientation in eating-related concerns cannot be reached. Homosexual people, after all, still live in a largely heterosexual society and are exposed to the same socialization processes, the same media images, and the same gendered expectations as are heterosexual people. Thus, it is perhaps unrealistic to assume that all lesbians, or even the majority of lesbians, will be unaffected by social norms of physical beauty or by other aspects of traditional female socialization.

SOCIOLOGICAL ANALYSES OF GENDER ROLE AND BODY SHAPE

Individual analyses such as those described above are widely regarded as insufficient to explain why eating disorders arise primarily in women. MacSween (1993) has argued that psychological analyses of gender roles tend to ignore the fact that such roles are artificial constructions, and to treat particular social norms as if they were natural and immutable. It is not sufficient, she argued, simply to add concepts of socialization and acculturation to an individualistic explanation of eating disorders. This leads to the implication that those women who succumb to social forces are in some way deficient, and therefore to blame for their condition. Rather than such an analysis, disordered eating needs to be understood by critically examining the social forces which underlie individual discontent, and by setting individuals within the context of a society which simultaneously promotes and resists feminism (Hepworth & Griffin, 1995; MacSween, 1993).

Avoidance of adult womanhood

Contemporary culture has been argued to place opposing and incompat-ible demands on women, expecting them to meet the expectations of their traditional gender role, to be attractive, dependent, affectionate and family-oriented, while simultaneously expecting them to meet expecta-tions of independence and success in the public sphere of education and employment (Hepworth & Griffin, 1995; MacSween, 1993). Anorexia nervosa is argued to be the response of an individual who can see no way of reconciling these conflicting demands.

Fear, reluctance or ambivalence about becoming an adult woman is a recurrent theme in sociological and psychological analyses of the aetiol-ogy of eating disorders (e.g. Crisp, 1980). Perlick and Silverstein (1994) have traced medical accounts of passivity and invalidism among female adolescents and young women over several centuries, arguing that a syndrome of depression, anxiety, headaches, and disturbances of appet-ite, sleep, menstrual function and sexual interest, can be identified as a recurring theme. They, and others, have argued that the obsolete diag-noses of chlorosis, greensickness, neurasthenia and hysteria form a continuum with eating disorders, and that all are manifestations of the same underlying distress, resulting from a reluctance to assume the social role of an adult woman.

Hepworth and Griffin (1995) and MacSween (1993) have argued that many analysts have not gone far enough, continuing to accept an individualistic and deficiency-based model, a model which assumes that adult gender roles as our culture defines them are right and good, and their adoption is the normal, healthy and desirable outcome of adoles-cent development. This acceptance of culturally defined gender roles as natural leads to the acceptance of adolescent girls' anxieties as normal and natural. Thus, it is seen as both natural and inevitable that adoles-cent girls should be more frightened of adulthood than adolescent boys, and that adult sexuality in particular is naturally more anxiety-provoking for women than for men.

Feminist writers have argued that the forces of social conservatism are served by cultural factors which make it difficult for women to take full advantage of apparently gender-neutral opportunities for educational development and the attainment of social power. Wolf (1994), for example, has argued that anorexia nervosa is more about the gendered characteristics of obedience, self-discipline and restraint than it is about physical beauty. An obsession with thinness, she argues, keeps women tired, depressed and distracted, and thus reduces their ability to achieve in traditionally masculine areas. Social forces which promote this obsession, such as the media, reinforce the notion that women are less able than men and tend to be reproduced in a society which has a considerable amount to gain by keeping women's aspirations personal and emotional, keeping their self-esteem low, and keeping women too tired and sick to demand an equal share of economic, social and political power.

Shisslak and Crago (1994) have also argued that contemporary society has a vested interest in eating disorders, because they serve to maintain power imbalances by making women distressed and anxious. Their view is that radical social change would be needed to prevent eating disorders, including a greater acceptance of diversity in physical appearance, and a weakening of the gendered nature of society that sees women primarily as objects in a male landscape, rather than as individuals who are entitled to a sense of personal authenticity and individual freedom of choice. Such changes, they argue, would also have a radical impact on equal pay, childcare, and other major issues for women by acknowledging that women's concerns are of equal importance to men's. As long as women are paid less than men, concentrated in occupations with lower power and prestige, and expected to provide the majority of unpaid domestic labour, young women will grow up with a feeling of ambivalence about adulthood. These radically feminist perspectives may seem alien from a psychological, individual-focused perspective which regards the social context either as benign or as irrelevant, but they do provide some explanation for the overwhelming femaleness of the condition, an explanation which is lacking from individual-oriented analyses.

Mother-blaming

A popular strand in both psychological and cultural analyses of disordered eating has been the mother–daughter relationship. Chernin (1986) has been a major proponent of this view, arguing that young women, growing up in a society in which their choices and opportunities are vastly greater than those available to their mothers, tend to develop feelings of guilt over the perception that, by simply being born, they had restricted their mothers' lives and opportunities and were now able to extend their own. Those young women who are unable to resolve this guilt, she argued, may develop a reluctance to eat, and therefore to grow, in an effort to compensate for their mothers' loss.

MacSween (1993), on the other hand, has argued that such an analysis only makes sense if one assumes that there are massive differences between generations in women's opportunities, and that it is only between such generations that this tension develops. These assumptions are not supported by evidence, which suggests that eating disorders have occurred over a number of generations, and that changes in women's opportunities have been quite gradual and by no means straightforward and unproblematic for individual women of any generation.

Further, a focus on the mother and her assumed inadequacies is in the tradition of mother-blaming (Caplan & Hall-McCorquodale, 1985), the perspective that any deficiency or unhappiness in an individual can be directly traced to some deficiency of that person's mother, some failure on her part to prepare her child for all the exigencies of growing up. This perspective serves to blame individual women for the difficult-ies faced by mothers in an inequitable social system which sees the care of children as women's work, simultaneously downgrading its import-ance and exonerating men from responsibility for their offspring (Davies & Welch, 1986; Hooyman & Gonyea, 1995; Perry-Jenkins, 1993). This view puts the blame on women and their relationships, citing discon-tented mothers and guilty daughters, and ignores continuing patriarchal inequities in society (MacSween, 1993).

The virtue of self-control

A third strand in sociological analyses of disordered eating has been the equation of thinness with virtue and self-control. Brownell (1991), dis-cussing our cultural obsession with appearance, points to the equation of bodily perfection with moral perfection, the assumption that physical beauty must be the result of hard work, ambition, self-control and purity, and that the overweight or unattractive are the way they are because they are lazy, self-indulgent and stupid.

While Brownell's analysis, in common with much of mainstream psychological literature in this area, is not explicitly gendered, it is clear that this myth will impinge differentially on women and on men. Seid (1994) has explored the historical context which has led to our obsession with slimness. She demonstrated that, historically, ideal body shapes for women have been considerably chubbier, and that even when a slim figure was positively regarded in earlier historical periods, factors such as soft skin, rounded arms and shoulders, and well-defined breasts were favoured. The contemporary ideal is a more masculine, firmly muscled shape with small breasts and narrow hips, a clearly unnatural attempt to suppress normal secondary sexual characteristics.

In recent years, Seid (1994) argued, physical softness has come to be equated with moral softness, and since women are seen as the guardians of moral virtue, this equation has affected women more strongly than men. The widespread social assumption that the body is infinitely perfectible (Brownell, 1991), and that dieting alone will produce a perfect body (Wilson, 1996) leads to the view that willpower is all that is needed to achieve the finely toned, hard shape of moral virtue.

Wooley (1994) argues that our society sees self-denial as good, particularly for women. Further, the idea that denial of the body serves to strengthen the spirit has a long history in Christianity and other major religions, as does the idea that women are more animal-like than men, less spiritual, and thus more in need of physical denial. In the Christian tradition, femaleness is associated with weakness and with sin, and thus looking less female, especially if it is achieved through physical self-denial, makes a woman less sinful.

Lawrence (1984) has described anorexia nervosa as being concerned with control of the self and of one's needs through self-denial. Young women in the process of developing adult sexuality must deal with the inconsistencies of desire and attractiveness on the one hand, and the role of women as gatekeepers and controllers in sexual relationships on the other. They respond to this by setting boundaries on their behaviour, which provide an illusion of safety and control. Since contemporary society sees self-denial as a virtue, and food as something women should be interested in, control of food and food intake is a logical and readily available avenue.

DIRECTIONS FOR CHANGE

While these strands are difficult to reconcile into a single coherent account of the social factors which underlie disordered eating, such factors, and particularly the patriarchal and strongly gendered nature of society, play a vital role in the development of disordered eating. The assumption that there is a specific personal deficiency in those women who develop eating disorders, and that women who make the transition to adulthood by internalizing cultural expectations of appropriate behaviour should be regarded as 'successful', has been roundly rejected by feminist sociologists (Hepworth & Griffin, 1995; MacSween, 1993). On the other hand, as Wilson (1996) has argued, radical social change is a slow and uncertain solution to the distress and suffering of individual women. Individual therapy that focuses less on conformity and more on resistance and social change may provide a compromise which satisfies at least some feminists.

Increasingly, therapeutic interventions and self-help groups for obese women (e.g. Barron & Lear, 1989; Burgard & Lyons, 1994; Srebnik & Saltzberg, 1994), as well as for those with bulimia (e.g. Katzman, Weiss & Wolchik, 1986), encourage women to accept themselves as they are and to resist the anti-fat messages of mainstream society. Some individual-focused therapists argue that body fat can, and perhaps should, be viewed as a symbol of warmth, generosity and strength (McBride, 1989), and that quality of life is more important than meeting unrealistic ideals (Burgard & Lyons, 1994).

Although the women's movement has provided girls and young women with alternative models of womanhood and of physical appearance, encouraging them to accept and appreciate diversity in appearance, there is little evidence that girls are becoming less interested in being decorative and more interested in being healthy and competent (Freedman, 1984). A solution to the problems of women's ambiguous and difficult relationships with food and with their bodies may well require a major realignment of social attitudes, a realignment which is opposed by a range of conservative forces in contemporary society. While radical feminist analyses continue to identify and to challenge these forces, there is also a continuing need for research at the individual level, to explore the processes by which some women internalize these destructive cultural messages.

11

SOMETHING TO LOOK FORWARD TO: WOMEN AND AGEING

Getting older is harder for women than for men. While older men may be perceived as wiser, more distinguished, or at least more experienced, cultural stereotypes of ageing for women focus on loss of attractiveness, loss of a valued social role, and a descent into triviality. Sexism and ageism mean that older women are generally not well represented in research or adequately served by health and welfare organizations (Belgrave, 1993; Fennell, Phillipson & Evers, 1988; Peace, 1986), even though women make up at least two-thirds of over-sixties. Negative views of ageing and old age mean that increased expectations for high standards of living and well-being have not extended to the promotion of positive and healthy lives among older people (Wells & Freer, 1988). Further, the sexist perspective which sees women as valuable only to the extent that they are attractive or useful to men, interacts with ageist assumptions about the value of older people to mean that ageing and old age are stigmatized to a greater extent among women than among men (Ford & Sinclair, 1987). A radical shift in our understanding of old age, within both professional and lay communities, may be needed in order to maximize well-being among older women.

AGEISM AND SEXISM

In Western societies, age has low status, and the entire topic of ageing is regarded as an unattractive one which is best avoided if possible. Women in particular are encouraged to disguise the visible signs of their own ageing and to lie about their age. The experience of age and ageing is shaped by sociocultural context, both formally through milestones such as ages for retirement or eligibility for pensions, and informally through family structures and assumptions about age-appropriate behaviour (Slater, 1995).

Unfounded negative assumptions about ageing lead to widespread stigmatization and avoidance of older people and of issues concerning them (Fennell et al., 1988). This means that service providers and policy-makers frequently have an inaccurate understanding of old age and are thus unable to provide the most appropriate services. Widespread but unsubstantiated assumptions about old age include the belief that most older people are sick, unhappy, cognitively impaired and isolated. Gerontological research is frequently conducted within a reductionist and biomedical model which assumes that decline is the inevitable result of individual biological ageing, and tends to ignore the social conditions which may contribute to dysfunction and distress in older people.

Such views lead to an emphasis on the negative, a confusion between normal ageing and pathology, and a lack of attention to positive aspects of ageing and to active coping strategies, which further reduces society's ability to respond to the needs of the majority of older people (Freer, 1988; Fry, 1996; Wetle, 1991). Older people are assumed to be a 'problem' group or a 'social burden', and the possibility that they may be viewed as successful survivors of life's vicissitudes, with a range of interesting experiences and potentially valuable insights and coping strategies from which others can benefit, is not generally acknowledged (Wells & Freer, 1988). Seeman (1994) and Wetle (1991) have argued that there is a need for a new research focus, on successful ageing and on the circumstances which are associated with continuing good health and social functioning, and on strategies for the empowerment of older women. Such research is more likely to lead to positive interventions which could impact on good health in old age than is present research, with its emphasis on sickness and decline.

Ageism in contemporary Western society cannot be separated from sexism; older women, to a greater extent than older men, are seen as figures of fun, as sexless, useless and stupid (Ford & Sinclair, 1987). In a sexist society in which women are defined in terms of their value to men, as sexual partners, mothers and household carers, the assumption that older women are unable to undertake any of these roles means that they are perceived to have no value. Single older women in particular are viewed with pity; widows because they have lost the main reason for their existence, their relationship with a man, and always-single women because they are assumed never to have had such a reason and to have led empty, wasted lives.

Porcino (1985) has pointed to social myths and stereotypes which characterize older women as dependent, passive, incompetent, un-attractive and sexually inactive. Women are viewed as old and un-attractive at a much earlier objective age than are men (e.g. McLellan & McKelvie, 1993), and women's self-esteem is undermined by widespread community perceptions that they are inevitably 'past it' (Fennell et al., 1988). Thus, ageing in Western society is particularly difficult for women (Fodor & Franks, 1990; Leiblum, 1990).

This interaction of ageism and sexism becomes even more a focus for concern when one considers that the majority of older people are women, and that this trend increases with increasing age. While 56 per cent of all people aged sixty-five to seventy-nine in Britain are women (Social Trends, 1995), the figure rises to 70 per cent in those aged eighty and over.

To further compound the problems of ageism and sexism, older women, despite living longer, have more health problems, both chronic and acute, make more use of health care services, and are more likely to be limited in daily functioning or to be disabled than older men (Gatz, Harris & Turk-Charles, 1995; Kutner, Schechtman, Ory & Baker, 1994). These effects are amplified for Black and minority women, whose life expectancy is shorter but who are more likely to experience negative health effects as they age (Padgett, 1988), and who start from a social position of even less power than do majority women (Ford & Sinclair, 1987).

Women are the majority of older people, they tend to be in poorer health, they are likely to have fewer economic resources than older men, and they experience greater social stigma associated with ageing. The combined impact of ageism and sexism thus has an extremely negative effect on women for a range of interconnected reasons. Research on ageing and old age, however, tends to ignore the issue of gender (Peace, 1986). The majority of the research reviewed in this chapter fails to consider the different experiences of women and men but lumps them together as 'old people', on the assumption that they are all much the same, more like each other than like younger members of their own gender. Such an assumption ignores the reality of our gendered society, and the importance of understanding ageing from a life-course perspective (Caspi & Elder, 1986; Gatz et al., 1995).

AGEING IN CONTEXT

Older people were not born old, though it seems that researchers and lay people alike are able to forget this obvious truth (Ford & Sinclair, 1987). Individuals are socialized into a gender role from the moment they are born, and it seems unlikely that the gender roles which have to a large extent determined behaviour and life course for the first sixty years of a person's life should suddenly become irrelevant. While it has been suggested that gender differences in sex-role-linked traits such as affiliation and instrumentality may decline across the lifespan (e.g. Sinnott, 1984), a large-scale cross-sectional survey of Americans found no evidence that the genders became any more similar with age (Fultz & Herzog, 1991).

The assumption that gender roles and sexual orientation become less important with age may be connected to the widespread assumption that older people are no longer sexually interested or active (Wetle, 1991), and the amused distaste with which younger people frequently regard sexuality among the elderly (Slater, 1995). However, the physiological processes of ageing seem to have little effect on sexual interest (Leiblum, 1990), and for most older people, sexual activity comes to an end only with the loss of their partner (Aiken, 1989). A national survey of married Americans (Marsiglio & Donnelly, 1991) found that 53 per cent of those over sixty, including 23 per cent of those aged over seventy-five, reported that they were currently sexually active, and it seems reasonable to assume that this figure would be considerably greater if it included those who continued to experience sexual interest but lacked appropriate opportunities for sexual expression.

Ageism and ignorance about ageing are compounded by the assumption that all old people are alike. In fact, there is a greater degree of heterogeneity among the old than among any other age group. Not only does 'old age' include a huge diversity of ethnicities and a range of sexual orientations and life histories, it also covers a huge age span. 'Old age' is usually defined as beginning at sixty (e.g. Peace, 1986) or at sixty-five (e.g. De Leon, Kasl & Jacobs, 1994). With 21 per cent of the population aged over sixty in Britain (Social Trends, 1995), average life expectancy for women now close to eighty in Western countries, and many women living well into their nineties, 'old age' is a very large category.

The young-old, up to around seventy-five, do not appear radically different from the middle aged; while the proportion in poor health or with significant disabilities may increase, the majority maintain good health and strong social networks. It is the old-old (over seventy-five) who have the highest probability of poor health and social isolation (Field & Minkler, 1993), although many maintain excellent heath and well-being into their nineties and beyond. It is worth noting that these are people who have survived longer than most of their contemporaries and that they may be a biased sample of their cohort in many important ways. Genetic and other biological characteristics may in part be responsible for their continuing good health, but the effects of individual health habits, of socioeconomic factors, education and employment, and of broader social and economic contexts over a lifetime will also be significant (e.g. Caspi & Elder, 1986).

Old age may best be understood as the culmination of a lifetime of experiences (Ford & Sinclair, 1987); life course models of ageing which emphasize the effects of childhood and earlier adult experiences are essential in understanding how people come to have different degrees of functioning in old age (Caspi & Elder, 1986; Gatz et al., 1995). Given that women's opportunities in education, careers, leisure and personal development are consistently more restricted than those of men throughout the lifespan, women will approach old age with fewer resources. At the same time, cohort effects must be considered (Gatz et al., 1995);

women who are in their eighties at the turn of the century, for example, would have been born during or shortly after World War I, have grown up during the Depression, and been active participants in World War II, circumstances which have shaped their life courses in significant ways. Those who reach their eighties in later decades will have had a quite different set of cultural and political events shaping their lives, and thus care should be taken in assuming that differences between cohorts are a result of ageing rather than sociocultural differences.

Financial context

Age is embedded in a financial as well as a social context; older people are the social group who are most likely to be poor (Wright, 1988), and women of all ages are more likely to be poor than men (Perkins, 1992). It may be, however, that older women's stronger social networks enable them to cope better with financial difficulties; De Leon, Rapp and Kasl (1994) found that financial strain was a stronger predictor of depression in older men than in older women, and that social support seemed to buffer the effect of inadequate finances, while Arber and Ginn (1994) found that older women tend to have fewer financial resources but greater social resources than older men.

Research on the impact of retirement on health and lifestyle has tended to ignore women because retirement has not traditionally been seen as an important issue for them (Ford & Sinclair, 1987). This view is based on the mistaken assumptions that most women do not work, that work is not central to women's identities, and thus that retirement is not important to women (Fennell et al., 1988). The relationship between retirement and health is a complex one which varies depending on gender, life course and career (Moen, 1996), but women are likely to have fewer financial resources than men when they retire (Perkins, 1992). One American survey showed that adjustments following retirement differed between men and women, with women increasing their social activities and showing greater life satisfaction while men showed the reverse (George, Fillenbaum & Palmore, 1984).

While a specific finding such as this may perhaps be explicable in terms of cohort effects, particularly the types of careers which were generally available to those women who were retiring in the 1980s, the more general issue of poverty in older women cannot be so easily dismissed. As Gatz et al. (1995) have pointed out, older women are the social group most likely to be below the poverty line, especially minority women and those who live alone (US Bureau of the Census, 1992b), and current social circumstances which see a high proportion of younger and middle-aged women living on pensions and benefits, heading single-parent households, and limiting their education and careers in order to care for family members, suggest that this phenomenon is likely to continue.

AGEING AND HEALTH

While health does decline in old age, the rate varies greatly between individuals (Gatz et al., 1995), and the assumption that old age is inevitably a time of infirmity and disability is not substantiated. Health, especially in the aged, may perhaps best be considered as a multi-dimensional construct encompassing all aspects of well-being. Gatz et al. (1995), writing with particular reference to older women, have described six interlinked aspects of health. These include physical health, functional health (i.e., ability to cope with the demands of everyday life), cognitive functioning, psychological health, social functioning, and economic status. Self-rated or perceived health, they argue, is based on a subjective weighting of all these 'healths', and although the majority of over-sixty-fives have at least one diagnosable medical condition, perceived health is frequently quite high. Perceived health is an excellent predictor of survival (e.g. McCallum, Shadbolt & Wang, 1994) and although it is closely related to measures of physical health (McCallum et al., 1994), it is also predicted by psychological variables such as life satisfaction and depression (Rodin & McAvay, 1992).

The Women's Health Australia project (Research Institute for Gender and Health, 1996) found that 33 per cent of older women (aged seventy to seventy-five) rated their health as very good or excellent, with 38 per cent considering it good and 24 per cent fair; only 5 per cent rated their general health as poor. Less than 50 per cent of the sample reported any limitations in climbing a flight of stairs or walking half a kilometre, and over 85 per cent reported no limitations in bathing or dressing themselves, suggesting that the majority of women in this age group were quite able to live independently without significant functional limitations.

It is notable that health problems tend to cluster together in older people to a greater extent than among younger people (Gatz et al., 1995), and that older women are more likely than older men to experience multiple medical conditions (Kutner et al., 1994). This clustering occurs not only among physical conditions but also with other aspects of health and functioning. Older people with physical health problems are also those most likely to experience cognitive impairment and psychological disorders (Lindesay, 1990). Level of depression is a good predictor of later levels of physical disability, even when sociodemographic factors, physical health and cognitive functioning are controlled for (Bruce, Seeman, Merrill & Blazer, 1994). Further, older women who show declines in cognitive functioning tend to be those with several diagnosed medical problems, and obesity, smoking, abstinence from alcohol, and sedentariness are also associated with increased risk of cognitive decline (Albert et al., 1995; Ensrud et al., 1994). Thus, a subgroup of individuals experiences a wide range of physical, cognitive, behavioural and functional declines, while the majority continue to function well across many domains.

Health habits established earlier in life will play a major role in determining functioning in old age, so at least some of the decline associated with old age may be prevented through lifestyle interventions in middle age and earlier. In studying health in older people, it is important to distinguish between normal ageing and pathological changes (Gatz et al., 1995).

For example, O'Brien and Vertinsky (1991) have estimated that regular exercise could halve the level of age-related decline in physical and psychological functioning in older women, but have simultaneously pointed to the many barriers which make exercise difficult for them. Women exercise less than men in every age group, and the rate declines with age for both sexes, suggesting that interventions which promote appropriate levels of exercise with middle-aged and older women may have great potential for the promotion of their health (Lee, 1991).

Nutrition is also often poor among older people, for reasons which include financial limitations, functional limitations in buying, preparing and serving food, poor teeth and digestion, and depression and social isolation which may reduce interest in food. Zipp and Holcomb (1992) argued that poor nutrition is a particular problem for those older people who live alone, are sedentary, and are not well educated. It is also the case that a lifetime of poor nutrition will be likely to result in diagnosable diseases, including diabetes, heart disease, osteoporosis, and some cancers, with increasing age. Again, the prevention of these diseases through the promotion of healthy diet among young and middle-aged people can contribute to better health when these people age.

COGNITIVE AND PSYCHOLOGICAL CHANGES WITH AGE

Another misconception is that cognitive decline is an inevitable and universal concomitant of normal ageing (Freer, 1988). Two European surveys of the prevalence of dementia among men and women aged over eighty-five (Fichter, Meller, Schroppel & Steinkirchner, 1995; Heeren, Lagaay, Hijmans & Rooymans, 1991) found that the great majority had normal cognitive functioning. In Munich, Fichter et al. (1995) found that only 21.1 per cent of those interviewed met clinical criteria for dementia. In the Netherlands, Heeren et al. (1991) found that 12 per cent experienced mild dementia, 7 per cent moderate, and only

4 per cent severe dementia. The prevalence did increase with age, from 19 per cent among eighty-five to eighty-nine-year-olds to 32 per cent among ninety to ninety-four and 41 per cent in the ninety-five-and-over group. But even in the oldest group, most were classified as suffering from mild dementia, characterized by slight losses in memory and concentration which do not interfere to any appreciable extent with independent living. Jorm, Korten and Henderson (1987), integrating data from a number of surveys, concluded that clinical levels of dementia occurred among 2 to 3 per cent of those aged sixty-five to seventy-four, 7 to 8 per cent of those aged seventy-five to eighty-four, and 24 per cent of those aged eighty-five and over; in other words, even in the oldest age group, most people maintain normal cognitive functioning.

The stereotypical assumption that ageing is naturally associated with increasing depression is also not substantiated by evidence (Feinson, 1991). Psychological theories of women's development tend to focus on biology and on motherhood, and to assume that women's lives are a more or less continuous decline from the age of about forty; a feminist, narrative approach, however, paints quite a different picture (Gergen, 1990), and the research on normal menopause discussed in Chapter 4 (e.g. Avis & McKinlay, 1991) shows clearly that the majority of women enter later middle age in good psychological health. If anything, the evidence suggests an improvement in psychological well-being around the age of fifty which is well maintained into old age (Fodor & Franks, 1990), and that the fifties, at least, are generally a time of good physical health and emotional stability (Mitchell & Helson, 1990).

Research on the positive and personally integrative changes associated with ageing is far less common than research on decline and depression, but evidence from several sources suggests that many people go through an active process of reorienting their values and perspectives in later middle age, and that these changes contribute to positive psychological adjustment as they grow older. For example, Niemela and Lento (1993) conducted a series of detailed interviews with Finnish women who were either just under or just over fifty, and concluded that the fiftieth birthday acts as a significant milestone in women's lives, prompting them to reflect on their personal histories and to begin planning for a positive old age. They concluded that the women who had turned fifty had gone through a largely positive reorientation to their personal lives and to their roles within their families, their careers and the broader society. As a result, they were more positive about themselves and less concerned about the possibility of illness, decline or death than were those just under fifty. Mitchell and Helson (1990), in two quantitative studies of American women, one cross-sectional and one longitudinal, also found that women in their fifties had better quality of life, better self-rated health, and higher levels of emotional security and confidence than women in their forties. A focus on personal growth and psychological well-being, rather than on the unfounded assumption that the menopause signals unhappiness and emptiness for women, might result in a more positive perception of the fifties as a time for action to prepare for a healthy old age.

An international study of human values and well-being across the lifespan (Butt & Beiser, 1987), which surveyed adults from Australia, Brazil, Canada, France, India, Italy, Japan, Korea, the Philippines, Singapore, the United Kingdom, the United States and West Germany, found that people aged over fifty had higher levels of personal contentment, life satisfaction, and stability than younger people, consistently across nations. Even in post-communist Poland, with a major economic crisis and major political uncertainty, Bien (1991) found older people to have high and increasing levels of satisfaction with their lives and their living conditions.

Surveys of age groups beyond the fifties also frequently show high levels of wellness, and positive aspects of ageing. A survey of Americans aged over sixty (Harris, Begay & Page, 1989) found that they regarded poor health as a major disadvantage of growing old, but also perceived increases in freedom of choice and in free time which they valued highly. Bearon (1989) found that life satisfaction was as high for older women as it was for middle-aged women, but that their sources of satisfaction differed, with the older women less interested in change and achievements, and more in the maintenance of their health and lifestyle. Ryff (1989) found that people in their seventies, in common with middle-aged people, considered caring, satisfactory relationships, self-acceptance, humour and a sense of enjoyment to be essential to well-being; however, older people were more likely to feel that the ability to accept change was also important. Older people appear to go through a change in value systems, re-evaluating life goals in order to deal with loss and change while maintaining a sense of personal control over their circumstances (Brandtstadter & Rothermund, 1994). Research on the experiences of older lesbians also points to the lifelong development of successful coping strategies. The concerns of older lesbians and homosexual men have many overlaps with those of other older people and include anxiety, financial difficulties, bereavement and issues surrounding intimacy, loneliness and sexuality, but they are also affected by a history of homophobia and rejection; having dealt with these issues over a lifetime and having learned to be successfully homosexual in a heterosexual culture, it is argued, gives these and other marginalized people an extra degree of flexibility and positive coping strategies which are likely to be advantageous in old age (Deevey, 1990; Kehoe, 1986; McDougall, 1993).

Life goals and aspirations change as people age. Ford and Sinclair's (1987) qualitative and descriptive research suggested that the older women they interviewed were frequently in difficult personal and financial situations but were actively striving to construct a satisfactory life for themselves. To a large extent, and despite the pressures and stereotypes of contemporary society, many older women seem to succeed in constructing such a lifestyle, rejecting the social stereotype of older women as passive and without a useful role in life, in favour of a more positive perspective of themselves.

Research which focuses on clinical levels of psychological distress among older people also fails to find the expected high levels of emotional distress. Depression and anxiety are far more common among the demented than among those who remained cognitively unimpaired (Fichter et al., 1995), again demonstrating the clustering of health problems in particular individuals. A study of Swedish people aged over ninety (Forsell, Jorm, von Strauss & Winblad, 1995) found that the prevalence of major depressive episodes was somewhere between 7.9 and 9.1 per cent, depending on the assessment method, and that disability in activities of daily living, and use of psychotropic drugs, were the best predictors of depression. A survey of Hong Kong Chinese in their seventies (Woo et al., 1994) showed that rates of depression did increase across that decade of life, but that factors associated with depression included low social class, low income, single or widowed status, poor social support, and poor health and functional ability. Similarly, Lubben (1988) found that physical health and social networks were the best predictors of psychological well-being in a sample of older Americans. These findings suggest that it is not ageing per se which leads to depression; rather, the older one is, the greater is the probability that one will have inadequate financial resources, lack social networks and support, and be in poor health. Thus, social interventions which aim to prevent poverty, isolation and illness may go a long way in the prevention of psychological distress in older people, and may be particularly important for older women, who are more likely to live alone than are older men (Social Trends, 1995).

Rodeheaver and Datan (1988) have argued that older women are at greater risk of depression than men, because the stresses of poverty, widowhood and family caregiving are more frequent among women than among men, although Feinson (1987) concluded there was no evidence for sex differences in mental health among older people. While suicide rates are high in the over-sixty-five group, the excess is almost entirely explained by suicides among White men, at least in the US (McIntosh, 1995), indicating once again the heterogeneity of ageing and the need to consider differences among individuals and groups of older people. Predictors of poor mental health in older women include low income, poor health, and few leisure activities (Riddick & Daniel, 1984), again suggesting that depression arises from a social system that neglects the aged, rather than from any factor intrinsic to ageing.

Social support

Social networks and integration appear to be an essential key to success-ful ageing (Porcino, 1985). Forster and Stoller (1992) showed that having social roles and responsibilities predicted survival, particularly for women, even when physical health status was controlled for, while Simonsick (1993) found that social support was more important to older women's well-being than was financial status.

Again, it is important to see social integration in a lifespan context; Moen, Dempster-McClain and Williams (1992) found that having held multiple roles thirty years previously was a significant predictor of good health in older women, suggesting that good social integration in the early and middle years may be an important basis for continuing well-being in old age. Older women in general have better social resources than older men and seem better able to make new friends and cope positively with changed circumstances (Arber & Ginn, 1994). Further, they have better skills in developing and maintaining intimate friend-ships (Porcino, 1985) which are increasingly valuable as social networks and opportunities for social interaction diminish with age. In Britain, 69 per cent of women aged over seventy-five live alone, compared with 35 per cent of men (Social Trends, 1995). The majority of women aged over seventy do not have a partner, and 25 per cent have no living children (Lewis, 1985), while the probability that same-age friends will die or become less able to interact socially as a result of frailness or the demands of family caregiving will increase with age (Gatz et al., 1995).

The multidimensional nature of the concept of social integration should also be considered; issues such as whether it is the number of relationships or the closeness of those relationships which is most important for well-being, the effects of practical, emotional and other types of support, and the effects of receiving or providing support have not been researched in detail but may be relevant in understanding the relationship between social integration and personal well-being (Depner & Ingersoll-Dayton, 1988). Many of these variables differ along gender lines. For example, older women are less dependent on their spouses for social support than are older men (Arber & Ginn, 1994) and in general wives provide more social support to their husbands than they receive in return (Depner & Ingersoll-Dayton, 1985). However, women's well-being seems more affected by the well-being of their spouse than is men's (Quirouette & Gold, 1992), perhaps because women are more likely to provide care to a frail or demented spouse than are men.

WIDOWHOOD

The most important social relationship in most people's lives is their marital partnership, and widowhood constitutes a major life change.

Because women live longer than men and are likely to marry men who are slightly older than they are, the great majority of widowed people are female, with the Australian Bureau of Statistics estimating that 80 per cent of all widowed Australians are women. Of women aged sixty to sixty-four, 17 per cent are widows, and this figure climbs to 72 per cent for women aged eighty-five or more (Australian Bureau of Statistics, 1995).

Loss of a spouse is almost always regarded as devastating, although reactions to that loss are highly variable (Zisook & Shuchter, 1991). Certainly bereavement, whether of a spouse or another close family member, has consistent adverse effects on the well-being of older adults (e.g. Arbuckle & de Vries, 1995), and high levels of depression and dysphoria are a normal reaction (e.g. Bruce, Kim, Leaf & Jacobs, 1990). However, it is interesting to note that the actual experiences of bereaved spouses are somewhat less negative than those expected by non-bereaved controls (Caserta & Lund, 1992) and by mental health professionals (Conway, Hayslip & Tandy, 1991).

Bereaved spouses frequently demonstrate considerable resilience and coping ability. While grief and anxiety remain high for a considerable length of time, most bereaved people also report good health, satisfactory work and role performance, and a sense that they are adjusting as well as could be expected (Zisook & Shuchter, 1991).

In general, older widows experience less extreme distress over a shorter time period than do younger widows (e.g. Zisook, Shuchter, Sledge & Mulvihill, 1993), perhaps because loss of a spouse seems more appropriate at a greater age. Also, many older women will have seen their friends experience bereavement, members of their social network may be better able to support them through the experience, and they may be more likely to have considered the possibility in advance. A minority of older bereaved people do experience severe grief-related problems; because of their smaller social networks, older people are at greater risk of becoming socially disengaged and some will become disoriented or confused following the death of their spouse (Parkes, 1992).

Adlersberg and Thorne (1990) pointed out that widowhood is not always unanticipated or unwanted, but could in some instances be a release from arduous caregiving and extreme emotional distress. They argued that those women who experience widowhood as a release need to be able to acknowledge those feelings. For women who have been in an intensive caregiving role, widowhood can mean an increase in time and opportunity. And when a spouse has been demented or in severe distress, that person's death might be seen as having some positive aspects.

Research which examines the subjective experience of the transition from caregiver to widowed person (e.g. Bass & Bowman, 1990; Bodnar &

Kiecolt-Glaser, 1994), however, has found no evidence for such a sense of relief. A comparison of the social networks of women who were caring for husbands with Alzheimer's disease, and widows who had formerly cared for such husbands, showed that widows had more free time and more social relationships (Morgan & March, 1992). But Bass and Bowman (1990) actually found that those who had experienced the most stress and difficulty in the caregiving role were also those who found bereavement most difficult.

While grief and depression are not the same phenomenon (Prigerson et al., 1995), depression is perhaps the most common emotional reaction to bereavement and research consistently finds elevated levels of depression among the recently widowed. A US study (Jacobs, Hansen, Berkman, Kasl & Ostfeld, 1989), found that 32 per cent of bereaved spouses were clinically depressed six months after bereavement, and 27 per cent were still depressed at one year. Another US study (Zisook & Shuchter, 1993) found major depression in 24 per cent of widowed men and women at two months, and 14 per cent at twenty-five months after bereavement. In Mexico, Harlow, Goldberg and Comstock (1991) found that 58 per cent of widows were clinically depressed one month after bereavement, compared with 10 per cent of non-bereaved women, but that depression scores generally returned to normal within one year. Levels of depression are high in all these samples, but it is notable that a significant proportion of widows in each study did not meet clinical criteria for depression. Stroebe, van den Bout and Schut (1994) identified a number of unsubstantiated myths about bereavement, including the inevitability of major distress and depression, and argued for a greater research emphasis on the heterogeneity of reactions to bereavement and exploration of factors associated with successful adjustment.

As one might expect, predictors of severe depression following bereavement are those which also predict depression in other circumstances. These include a history of depression (Bartrop, Hancock, Craig & Porritt, 1992) or of other psychiatric disorder (Nuss & Zubenko, 1992), poor physical health and high levels of health care usage (Zisook & Shuchter, 1993), low levels of social support (Nuss & Zubenko, 1992), poor role functioning (Zisook & Shuchter, 1993), and unemployment (Jacobs et al., 1989).

While it is sometimes argued that single status is itself a risk factor for depression (e.g. Bennett & Morgan, 1992), a survey of never-married women in their eighties found that most had satisfying lives, good social networks, and positive coping strategies (O'Brien, 1991), again illustrating the point that the well-being of older people must be understood in the context of their life history; women who have always lived independently will have different coping strategies and social networks from those who become single later in life.

Although most research does not consider the role of gender in bereavement, loss of a spouse does seem to impact differently on women and on men. Umberson, Wortman and Kessler (1992) found that level of financial strain predicted depression following bereavement in women, but problems in coping with household management were a stronger predictor of depression among men, suggesting that having to deal with other-gender-typed activities may be a source of difficulty for people who suddenly find themselves without a spouse. Several researchers (e.g. De Leon, Kasl & Jacobs, 1994; Gilbar & Dagan, 1995; Jacobs et al., 1989; Thompson, Gallagher-Thompson, Futterman, Gilewski & Peterson, 1991) have found that women experience more bereavement-related distress than men and have more difficulty adjusting to widowed life. On the other hand, widows have consistently been shown to be at considerably less risk of suicide than widowers (e.g. Li, 1995).

Coping with bereavement may be complicated by changes to financial status, and this may explain Bartrop et al.'s (1992) finding that low socioeconomic status predicts post-bereavement depression. Most women are less well off financially as a result of bereavement (Avis, Brambilla, Vass & McKinlay, 1991). Bound, Duncan, Laren and Oleinick (1991) found that women's available income fell by an average of 18 per cent following bereavement, and that 10 per cent of those whose incomes had been adequate were pushed below the poverty line. However, the financial impact of widowhood is also highly variable, and at least some widows are better off financially because they no longer have to meet the significant costs of their spouses' health care (Bound et al., 1991).

Some writers (e.g. Clayton, 1990) consider that the 'normal' grieving process should be resolved in about a year and that grief or major depression extending beyond that time can be considered pathological. This is supported by both Norwegian (Lindstrom, 1995) and American (De Leon, Kasl & Jacobs, 1994) evidence that mean levels of depression have returned to normal and the majority of widows feel they have, to a large extent, dealt with their grief by the end of one year. On the other hand, other Western research (e.g. Thompson et al., 1991) has shown that widows' grief and depression frequently continues for at least thirty months. In India, Gill and Singh (1991) found that widows reported needing at least three years to adjust to their changed life circumstances, with over 40 per cent reporting continuing adjustment problems more than ten years after the death of their husbands. Clearly adjustment to bereavement must be understood in a social and family context. Widows need both to deal with their loss and to take active steps to cope with their changed circumstances. Many widows have a large proportion of their lives ahead of them, and a society which enables widows to see the process as one which can be coped with, rather than as a devastating tragedy, may enable older women to adjust in more positive ways (Hansson & Remondet, 1988).

Widowhood and physical health

It is popularly assumed that bereavement leads to an increase in the spouse's risk of death in the short term. However, while grieving and depression do affect immune functioning (e.g, Pettingale, Hussein & Tee, 1994; Zisook, Shuchter, Irwin, Darko, Sledge & Resovsky, 1994), a longitudinal study of older widowed persons in the UK (Bowling, 1994; Bowling & Windsor, 1995) found little evidence to support the notion that bereavement poses any direct risk of death. Longitudinal surveys (e.g. Avis et al., 1991; Wolinsky & Johnson, 1992) have found no effect of widowhood on health or health care usage, although it did increase the probability that people who had been cared for by the deceased spouse would be admitted to institutional care. Stroebe (1994) concluded that social isolation was the strongest predictor of death following bereavement. However, most widows actually experience an increase in social support following bereavement (Avis et al., 1991) which may explain why they seem to be at lower risk of death than widowers (Clayton, 1990).

Widowhood involves major changes in daily routines, which may lead to changes in health habits; Rosenbloom and Whittington (1993) found that changes in the context of food preparation and eating following loss of a spouse had negative effects on calorie intake and nutrition. Such changes may interact with the loss of appetite associated with depression to mean that at least some recently widowed persons can become clinically undernourished. There is also evidence (e.g. Avis et al., 1991; Zisook, Shuchter & Mulvihill, 1990) for increases in drinking, smoking and use of psychotropic drugs following bereavement, especially among those people with poor social support.

This research suggests that widowhood, although a difficult transition associated with considerable distress, need not be devastating, and that social support in particular is useful in helping widowed people to adjust positively to their loss and to their changed life circumstances. Bereavement, like ageing, is a phenomenon which most people prefer to avoid contemplating. However, it is inevitable that a large proportion of women will become widows, and better understanding of this transition might make the experience somewhat less distressing.

POSITIVE AGEING

Ageing is a time of life during which difficult challenges, including illness, disability, bereavement and approaching death, need to be dealt with. However, unremittingly negative social and professional attitudes to ageing, especially among women, make it even more difficult for older people to cope. The re-education of health professionals, together with the empowerment of older women (Sharpe, 1995) and an increase in the focus of research on understanding positive ageing (Seeman, 1994), may be useful in the provision of appropriate services for older women and in the reduction of avoidance and rejection, so that people will prepare for old age in a more positive and optimistic way. At a broader social level, the sexist notion that older women are not valuable because they are no longer conventionally attractive, no longer fertile, and no longer caring for children serves to perpetuate negative views of older women. A broader perspective on women as people, and on older women as successful survivors, could have a major impact on women's well-being as they age.

12

LESBIAN WOMEN:
RESISTANCE AND REDEFINITION

The sexualization and objectification of women's bodies, and by extension their entire lives, results from a patriarchal social structure in which
women are valued to the extent that they are attractive or useful to men
(Millett, 1970). As the earlier chapters have shown, this means that
women who do not measure up to exacting but arbitrary standards of
physical beauty and of youth are stigmatized. Nowhere is the arbitrary
and restrictive nature of this pervasive cultural arrangement brought
into clearer focus than in the study of the lives of lesbian women.

Women who reject the basic unit of patriarchal and capitalist society,
the traditional family unit of a man and a woman whose roles and
responsibilities are divided up on gender lines and whose relative status
is defined by those roles and responsibilities, must discover new ways of
arranging their personal lives and relationships. This provides substantial challenges to those women, but also demonstrates to the rest of
society that alternatives to traditional family structures are both possible
and successful. Rejection of lesbian lifestyles by social conservatives may
be seen as resulting from a fear of those particular women's rejection of
patriarchal social structures, but also of the possibility that their example
may provide an incentive for others to explore alternative arrangements
as well.

LESBIAN AND NON-LESBIAN WOMEN: CONTINUITY OF
INTERESTS

This chapter has two aims, both to address the challenges which confront
lesbians in a heterosexist society, and to use these women's experiences
to demonstrate the viability of alternative and less restrictive life choices,
for lesbians and for non-lesbian women and their male partners. Defin-
ing oneself as lesbian means rejecting the idea that inevitable sex-based
differences in abilities and inclinations, and the resultant inescapable
gender-based division of personal and family roles, require women as a
class to operate differently in the world from men. But liberation from

this and other sexist assumptions does not require one to be a lesbian. Lesbian women are forced to discover new and non-sexist ways of constructing their personal lives (Brown, 1995); but if lesbian women can do this, so too can other people. Thus, this chapter uses an exploration of the literature on lesbians' health and health care to explore the ways in which sexist and heterosexist assumptions affect and limit all women.

The artificial creation of a dichotomous division of women into lesbians and non-lesbians, together with powerful and pervasive anti-lesbian rhetoric, is argued to restrict the behaviour of all women. Lesbian women experience social rejection, while non-lesbians are discouraged from seeking to change sexist practices by a fear of being labelled lesbians and being themselves rejected and vilified (Stevens, 1992). This serves to disguise the diversity among lesbian women, and the continuity in sexual behaviour and orientation, as well as in social and personal concerns, between lesbians and heterosexual women (Greene, 1994a). The labelling of an individual as lesbian or not on the basis of her sexual behaviour can be both irrelevant and misleading. Rothblum (1994c), for example, has argued for a need to reconsider what is meant by a lesbian relationship and what is meant, indeed, by a sexual relationship: a woman may engage in sexual activity with both men and women, or with neither, may find herself sexually attracted to women even though her sexual activity is exclusively with men, or may have a committed relationship with another woman which does not involve sexual activity as it is usually recognized. Deciding whether all or some of these women should be classified as lesbians becomes arbitrary, and unhelpful in understanding their lives.

In this chapter, I argue that it is more useful to consider all women as influenced by a culture which positions them as objects in an overwhelmingly male-dominated social structure, and thus as having central personal and political issues in common. A review by Golden (1996) suggests that sexual orientation is fluid and changeable over the life course, and reviews (Greene, 1994a; Stevens & Hall, 1991) have estimated that anywhere between 4 and 17 per cent of women may be considered to be lesbians, depending on the definition and survey method used, further emphasizing the vagueness of the boundaries between lesbian and non-lesbian.

A number of lesbian theorists have argued for a separatist approach to lesbian issues. These arguments (e.g. Burns, 1992; Kitzinger, 1993; Kitzinger & Perkins, 1993; Kitzinger & Wilkinson, 1993) are generally based on the view that an approach that minimizes or denies the hostility that lesbian women have to deal with on a daily basis, and which positions lesbians on one end of a continuum of women, does not benefit lesbian women. Seeing lesbianism as a personal matter, treating lesbianism as simply a matter of individual choice and lesbians as identical to other women in all respects except that of the gender of their sexual partner or partners, they argue, denies the social and political reality of discrimination and harassment and the fact that lesbian women's relationship with a patriarchal society must be fundamentally different from that of non-lesbian women.

The argument of this chapter, however, is that both lesbian and non-lesbian women may have more to gain from an approach which views all women as recipients of discrimination and harassment. Setting up a dichotomy divides heterosexual women from lesbians and implies that only a small proportion of women have problems with a traditional patriarchal social structure. The problems which lesbians face in dealing with sexism and oppression are definitely greater than those faced by heterosexual women, but they are not qualitatively different. If heterosexual women support lesbians' efforts to develop alternative personal, family and social lives, this may make lesbian women's lives easier and it may also provide models which heterosexual women may wish to emulate. Thus, in considering the health and well-being of all women, it is more useful to see a continuity of interests between the lesbian and the heterosexual woman and to promote an atmosphere of respect and equality between lesbian and non-lesbian women (D. Thompson, 1992).

Stevens and Hall (1991) have described how support of women's rights, and of universal suffrage in particular, was equated with lesbianism in the popular discourse of the turn of the century, when the struggle for women's legal and voting rights was at its strongest. Anyone who supported women's rights was labelled a lesbian at a time when this was regarded as evidence of inferiority, emotional instability, and a tragic lack of proper womanly fulfilment. This served to discourage women from becoming involved in the social movement or expressing emancipatory views. Thus, anti-lesbian rhetoric not only repressed lesbians, but served to repress all women, regardless of their actual sexual orientation.

Looking at society from the perspective of lesbians' lives not only enables researchers to see the ways in which lesbians have had to deal with systemic abuse, but also provides a different perspective on the lives of all women (e.g. Rothblum, 1994c). Harding (1994) has argued that a lesbian-centred perspective allows one to see that any attempt to define or describe a 'normal' woman is restrictive and artificial. More generally, she has argued that the view from the margins of any group is often better able to expose characteristics of that group which are less obvious from the mainstream. Looking at employment, or family caring, or motherhood, for example, from a lesbian perspective makes the arbitrary nature of many cultural assumptions about appropriate gender-related behaviour much clearer.

For example, contemporary society equates a woman's appearance and her sexual attractiveness to men with her value as a person, thus creating an objective and sexualized image of women which is argued to play a major role in the development of body image dissatisfaction and serious eating disorders (Rothblum, 1994a). This objectification, and the promotion of one restrictive image as an acceptable appearance for women, is largely irrelevant to women who are not interested in sexual relationships with men, although those women cannot remain unaffected by widespread norms about appearance. Lesbians' position outside heterosexual gender relationships makes it easier for them to identify the arbitrary nature of restrictions on women's appearance; their visible rejection of these standards makes it easier for non-lesbian women to see the arbitrariness of these images (Dworkin, 1988).

Thus, the experiences of lesbian women as they develop strategies to deal with a hostile society can serve as a model for all women who are seeking alternatives to traditional choices and lifestyles (Rothblum, 1988). This suggests that, far from rejecting lesbian women, non-lesbian women may have much to gain from developing solidarity with them.

It is important, however, to stress that lesbian women are not in any way in a privileged position by comparison with non-lesbian women (e.g. Burns, 1992). Nor is the study of lesbians' experiences relevant or important only insofar as it reflects or illuminates the lives of non-lesbian women. Rather, lesbians are a sizeable minority group whose interests and behaviours, both sexual and non-sexual, are of interest in themselves, and whose lives are made unnecessarily difficult by a culture which rejects them (Stevens & Hall, 1991).

Because of strong anti-lesbian forces in mainstream society, Kitzinger (1987) and Kitzinger and Perkins (1993) have argued against the apparently liberal move in psychology towards 'affirmative' research with lesbians, gay men and other traditionally rejected minorities, which is based in the liberal-humanist tradition of tolerance for diversity. Their argument is that research which focuses on the individual lesbian woman conceptualizes lesbianism as a free and neutrally valued individual choice. Such a perspective denies or minimizes the relevance of an oppressive social context which restricts the lives of all women, but is particularly hostile and repressive for lesbian women. By personalizing lesbians' experiences, individual-focused research and intervention depoliticizes those experiences and prevents researchers and therapists, and women leading lesbian lives, from recognizing the reality of structural inequity and male power, and thus from identifying the social, cultural and political roots of the oppression of lesbian women (Kitzinger, 1987; Perkins, 1991).

Despite liberal rhetoric among mainstream psychologists, however, lesbians are still widely regarded as both abnormal and inferior. Homosexual orientation and behaviour, among both men and women, was removed from the DSM classifications of mental disorders in 1973, on the grounds that there was no evidence to suggest that it was pathological. However, therapists are frequently not well informed about lesbians' lifestyles (Greene, 1994a) and many will still attempt sexual reorientation therapy (Haldeman, 1994). Lesbian lifestyles are still regarded as neces-sarily pathological (Stevens, 1992). Until relatively recently, research on lesbians' health, in common with that concerned with homosexual men, has revolved around the aetiology, prevention, diagnosis and cure of lesbianism rather than the needs of women who are lesbians. Where the pathology model of lesbianism has been rejected, Burns (1992) argues that it has not been replaced with a positive approach to the special needs and concerns of lesbians, but rather with an assumption that lesbians are basically the same as everyone else and their particular concerns can safely be ignored.

The following section reviews research on lesbians' lifestyles and health concerns, demonstrating that social hostility and heterosexist assumptions continue to be their most salient problems. The chapter then considers the implications of lesbians' lifestyles, and of the ways in which lesbians cope in a heterosexist society, for social change which can benefit all women.

DEFINING ONESELF AS LESBIAN: A DEVELOPMENTAL AND SOCIAL CHALLENGE

Coming out as lesbian in a heterosexual and frequently hostile society is a major personal challenge (Greene, 1994a), which is made particularly difficult by the fact that an awareness of one's sexual orientation nor-mally arises during early adolescence, a time at which young people are undergoing other potentially difficult developmental changes (D'Augelli & Hershberger, 1993). It is also particularly difficult for members of those minority ethnic communities which hold firmly to traditional roles and values for women and are strongly negative in their views of homo-sexuality (Greene, 1994b). The sense of loss felt by women who are excluded from traditional relationships in their families because of their sexuality is considerable, and may be greater for members of such ethnic minorities (Chan, 1987).

An issue which has yet to be addressed in the study of lesbian lives is that research on lesbian women must, by necessity, focus on women who have acknowledged their sexuality to themselves and 'come out' to others, at least to the extent of being willing to identify themselves to researchers as lesbians. Given the strongly homophobic nature of society, and the restrictions placed on all sexual expression among women and adolescent girls, many women whose sexual orientation is primarily homosexual may be unable to acknowledge these feelings to themselves, while others may be aware of their orientation but feel unable to express their sexuality openly.

It is possible that women who identify themselves as lesbians have higher than average levels of self-esteem or personal conviction, or have grown up in social milieux which are tolerant or encouraging of diversity. Thus, self-identified lesbians may be a highly selected group of women, and research with these women may not necessarily generalize to all women whose sexual orientation is homosexual. Even the most thorough and extensive of research on lesbian women's lives (e.g. Ryan & Bradford, 1993) draws its participants from social and political groups and therefore can be expected to include a high proportion of women who are publicly lesbian. Whether such women experience more or fewer problems than others with a lesbian orientation is by no means clear.

Adolescents who are beginning to identify as lesbian face difficult developmental challenges (D'Augelli, 1996). Research is generally consistent in identifying lesbian and gay adolescents as being at increased risk of severe problems, including school failure, truancy, running away from home, depression, suicide attempts, and involvement in prostitution and illegal drugs. However, these problems are not usually indicators of individual psychopathology or maladjustment, but are better seen as a reaction to a common pattern of emotional rejection and verbal and physical abuse from family and peers, and to the pressures of a cultural context which condemns homosexuality (e.g. Gonsiorek, 1988; Savin-Williams, 1994). Decisions about when, how and under what circumstances a lesbian should choose to be 'out' and when she should 'pass' as heterosexual continue throughout adult life and are the cause of considerable stress in lesbians' daily lives (Greene, 1994a).

D'Augelli and Hershberger (1993) found that the majority of the young lesbians and gay men they surveyed had become aware of their own sexual orientation at about the age of ten but had generally not disclosed this to anyone until around sixteen, which suggests that many of them will have spent most of their early adolescence feeling isolated and confused. It has been argued (e.g. Hershberger & D'Augelli, 1995; Proctor & Groze, 1994) that lesbian and gay adolescents' anxieties about their developing sexuality, and their possible exposure to victimization when they do start to express their sexual orientation, puts them at risk of suicide, especially if they lack support from family and peers or a strong sense of self-identity. However, the link between sexual orientation and suicide is by no means clear, and methodological problems preclude any definitive statement about the relationship between sexual orientation and risk of suicide (Muehrer, 1995).

A body of research has described lesbian development in adolescence, particularly the developmental tasks of self-definition, seeking support and authentication for that definition, and dealing with the hostility and ridicule of a homophobic society (e.g. Savin-Williams, 1989). What is lacking from this literature, however, is any emphasis on positive development. Research which examined the characteristics of people who make a positive and successful transition to homosexual adulthood, and identified individual strategies and social arrangements which could assist in dealing positively with this difficult developmental challenge, would be extremely valuable in providing strategies for positive development.

A lifespan perspective is also useful in understanding adult and ageing lesbians (D'Augelli & Patterson, 1995; Kertzner & Sved, 1996), as is the importance of seeing these women's lives in a sociocultural and ecological perspective. Older lesbians, for example, will have had to deal in various ways with homophobia over a lifetime, and many lesbian women have developed valuable coping skills in the process of finding a way of living in a hostile or uncaring context (Kehoe, 1986; McDougall, 1993). It is arguable that they may be better equipped than some other women for the challenges of old age, and possible that the strategies and skills they have learned may provide valuable insights into the process of successful ageing for all women.

The traditional view is that lesbianism arises from psychological disturbance (Stevens & Hall, 1991), but the evidence does not support this view. Lesbian couples, for example, are characterized by stability, affection and satisfaction equal to that observed in heterosexual couples (Kurdek, 1994). Stress and anxiety among lesbians may more reasonably be seen as arising from widespread hostility. The very existence of hate crimes against gays and lesbians has the potential for negative mental health consequences. While these are most obvious for people who have actually been targeted by such attacks, Garnets, Herek and Levy (1990) have argued that such crime also has negative effects on the partners and friends of victims of such attacks, and on the lesbian community in general, in the same way that the existence of sexual assault has negative effects on all women (Brownmiller, 1975).

In a large survey of US lesbians, Trippet and Bain (1990) found that the majority of women had 'come out' to their families and friends; families were generally described as supportive or neutral regarding the respondents' lifestyles, while friends were more likely to be supportive or very supportive. Despite this, however, respondents reported high levels of depression which they construed as resulting from the conflicts which arise from being lesbian within a predominantly heterosexual and homophobic society. Another large-scale survey of American lesbians (Bradford, Ryan & Rothblum, 1994) also found that most self-identified lesbians had supportive relationships with their family and friends, but the majority felt the need to keep their lesbian identity secret from at least some family members and work colleagues, for fear of negative reactions ranging from embarrassment and ostracism to physical violence. Secrecy and fear are commonplace for these women in a way which is not the case for non-lesbian women.

Evidence for higher rates of depression among lesbians than among other women, therefore, may be explained as a result of having to deal with homophobia, with the pressures and anxieties of coming out as lesbian, and with the problems which lesbians face on a daily basis of living in a culture in which they differ from what is assumed to be normal (Rothblum, 1990). Similarly, lesbians are higher users of alcohol and marijuana than are other women (Skinner, 1994), but this may also be explained by reference to a lifetime of experience of anti-lesbian prejudices and stereotypes. Historically, lesbianism has been seen as a sin, a moral failing or a disease, arising from an individual failure to develop appropriate womanly attitudes (Stevens & Hall, 1991). This failure is assumed to arise from a history of rape or incest or simply from a particular woman's inadequacy, and to lead inevitably to aggression, hostility and psychiatric disturbance. Despite clear evidence to the contrary, these views continue to have widespread currency among both lay and professional communities. While some would argue that this overt and institutionalized hostility means that lesbians need to maintain their separateness from other women, an alternative viewpoint is that all women need to agitate for social change, towards a society in which people are not labelled and graded according to their gender and sexual preferences, and that solidarity between lesbian and non-lesbian women is an important component of this process.

LESBIANS AND HEALTH CARE

Research has consistently shown negative stereotypes of lesbians among members of the health professions, which mirror those in society more generally. Negative attitudes among health care providers are likely to impact on lesbians' ability to access appropriate health care services (e.g. Eliason, Donelan & Randall, 1992; Smith, 1993). When lesbian women approach health care professionals with specific problems such as relationship violence (Hammond, 1988) or drug abuse (MacEwan, 1994), it is frequently assumed that it is the client's sexual orientation and not the presenting problem which is in need of intervention, and lesbians' actual wants and needs may receive secondary attention or be dismissed as 'symptoms' of their underlying 'pathology'.

Even those health care providers who are not actively hostile or pathologizing in their attitudes towards lesbians tend to assume that all clients are heterosexual and thus fail to be sensitive to lesbians' needs (Banks & Gartrell, 1996; Robertson, 1992). Many lesbians prefer not to reveal their sexual orientation unless they can be sure of a non-hostile response (Stevens & Hall, 1990), and because of the power differentials inherent in the health care provider–client relationship, it is necessary for health care professionals to convey a positive attitude of respect.

However, evidence since the 1970s has shown consistently negative views of lesbians and lesbian lifestyles among health care students and professionals (Stevens, 1992). This research indicates that lesbianism continues to be viewed as pathological and lesbians as emotionally disturbed; a significant minority of health care providers also state that they would refuse to provide health care to lesbians and believe that it is not appropriate for lesbians to work as health care professionals. Widespread attitudes such as these clearly make it difficult for those lesbians who do work in health care to 'come out' publicly about their own sexuality, making those women's professional lives difficult and further reducing the probability that lesbian clients will be greeted with warmth and acceptance.

Despite some attempts to educate health care providers, however, Stevens' (1992) review showed that lesbians generally perceived interactions with health care providers to be hostile, intimidating and humiliating. In a qualitative study of the health care experiences of lesbians, Stevens (1994) found that the vast majority of recalled instances were negative; respondents reported a lack of genuine caring and openness and felt that health professionals had been either intrusive or dismissive.

Stereotypes and prejudices on the part of health care providers, and negative expectations on the part of lesbians themselves, mean that lesbians may conceal their sexual orientation from health care providers (e.g. MacEwan, 1994), or avoid seeking health care (Robertson, 1992; Stevens & Hall, 1990, 1991). When lesbians do seek health care, ignorance on the part of providers may mean that their needs are not addressed. For example, many health care providers believe that lesbians do not ever have sex with men, and thus assume that they are not at risk for sexually transmitted diseases and do not need Pap smears. However, the majority of lesbian women have had sexual relationships with men at some stage of their life, and a significant minority report injecting drugs or otherwise putting themselves in danger of infection with HIV or hepatitis (Einhorn & Polgar, 1994).

A particular issue identified by lesbian women is that they want health care professionals to include lesbian partners in discussion and decision-making in the same way that they would heterosexual partners (Banks & Gartrell, 1996; Rankow, 1995). The need for better education of health care providers, to help them deal with a range of lifestyles, is demonstrated by research with specific groups of women. Deevey (1990), for example, points to the needs of frail older lesbians in nursing homes. Kanuha (1990) discussed the issues that arise for lesbians of colour in violent relationships and pointed out that the assumptions of a male-dominated, white-dominated, heterosexist health care system make it almost impossible for these women to find appropriate help. In a similar vein, Orzek (1988) points to the problems in obtaining appropriate professional help for lesbians who have been raped. While rape crisis centres are normally run by women, not all women have access to these centres, and even there the staff still assume that their clients are heterosexual and may be unable to respond appropriately to lesbian clients. Taking a more general perspective, Gentry (1992) has pointed out that health care providers need to understand the existence of a long history of stigmatization of lesbianism and the reluctance that many lesbian women feel about seeking health care or identifying themselves as lesbian to health care providers, as well as becoming aware of the lifestyles and health concerns of lesbian and gay clients, which have important overlaps with, and important differences from, the concerns of non-lesbian clients.

Lesbians frequently report that heterosexist assumptions about their lifestyles lead to inappropriate advice and treatment, but fear rejection, inadequate care or even violence if they do reveal their sexual orientation to health care providers (Stevens, 1992). Surveys of lesbians' needs in general health care (Lucas, 1992; Trippet & Bain, 1992) have found that participants wanted a more holistic approach, an emphasis on pre-vention, education and health maintenance, more female health care professionals, and a more open, accepting attitude to lesbianism. Over-whelmingly, research has shown that the male domination of health care is a major factor contributing to lesbians' dissatisfaction, and that larger numbers of female counsellors and health professionals, even if they are not themselves lesbians, would make the experience of seeking health care substantially more positive for lesbians (e.g. Modrcin & Wyers, 1990; Stevens, 1992). Of course, it is not only lesbians who would benefit from a holistic, prevention-focused, less male-dominated health care service, demonstrating once more that the needs of lesbian and non-lesbian women overlap and that the creation of an artificial dichotomy between two different types of woman serves to isolate lesbians and to reduce the likelihood of changes that would benefit all users of health care services.

Heterosexist assumptions in the health care system impact negatively on lesbians at a systemic as well as an individual level (Stevens, 1995; Trippet, 1994). Structures which fail to recognize same-sex couples, for example insurance programmes which do not allow one to nominate a same-sex partner, and hospital visiting and next-of-kin arrangements which have restrictive definitions of 'family' or refuse to recognize lesbian partnerships as equivalent to marriage (Trippet, 1994), make life more difficult for lesbian couples.

LESBIAN MOTHERS

One aspect of lesbian women's health and interaction with health care services which generates heated resistance from social conservatives is motherhood. Alldred (1996) has identified strong sociocultural assumptions that a child needs a 'normal' family including a mother and a father in order to develop adequately. She argues that lesbianism is widely seen as evidence of emotional immaturity, and thus that it is assumed that lesbian women are not fit to be mothers. Interestingly, when lesbians decide to have children, this is not seen as evidence that they are normal women who are able to make reasoned decisions about their lives, but as evidence of even greater perversion.

The concept of lesbian motherhood, and of children raised by lesbian couples or in lesbian communes, is something which is frequently obstructed by legal restrictions. While feminists such as Radford (1993) have argued that lesbians need to resist pressures which restrict the rights of lesbian mothers and of their partners and to promote the legal recognition of lesbian families, others (e.g. Robson, 1994) have questioned the appropriateness of lesbian families, arguing that women who have babies in non-traditional circumstances should be agitating for the recognition of other structures such as parenthood collectives or extended community groups rather than seeking acknowledgement for their ability to emulate the sort of traditional patriarchal family which they have rejected.

While some lesbian women have children in heterosexual relationships before changing to a lesbian lifestyle, for others the lesbianism comes first and the wish for children later (Patterson, 1994). Lesbian individuals or couples planning parenthood face unique issues, including decisions on how to conceive, problems in telling their families and friends about the pregnancy, and dealing with a frequently hostile and ignorant health care system (Kenney & Tash, 1992). Most assisted reproduction clinics refuse their services to lesbians on principle, regardless of those women's personal circumstances, assuming that they cannot possibly be appropriate mothers (Campion, 1995; Oakley, 1993). This means that lesbians need to lie to people in positions of authority or use informal networks to seek information and make decisions about how best to conceive.

The literature, however, is unanimous in showing that children raised by lesbian women are psychologically healthy and socially well integrated. The assumption that lesbians are not appropriate mothers is not supported by the evidence, which throws doubt more generally on traditional assumptions about sex roles in parenthood (Benkov, 1995). The children of lesbian mothers are similar to other children in emotional health, interpersonal relationships and gender development (Patterson, 1994), while lesbian mothers have the same levels of parenting skills and psychological health as do other mothers (Victor & Fish, 1995). Adults, both men and women, who were raised by lesbian mothers have been demonstrated to have good psychological health and strong family relationships (Tasker & Golombok, 1995). Several studies (Tasker & Golombok 1995; Victor & Fish, 1995) have shown that these people are no more likely than others to become gay or lesbian themselves, although Alldred (1996) has pointed out that the presentation of this finding as evidence for positive outcomes of lesbian motherhood serves only to support the unfounded assumption that healthy people should be heterosexual, and that raising heterosexual offspring is better than raising homosexuals. Ainslie and Feltey (1991) have described lesbian mothers living in a feminist community as striving to raise children who are feminist, politically aware, open-minded and respecting diversity, values which are positively regarded by many non-lesbian parents. Once again, the concerns of lesbians have significant overlaps with those of non-lesbians.

Lesbian motherhood is just one of many difficult challenges faced by lesbians, and psychology has failed to provide support or useful strategies for change. Garnets and D'Augelli (1994) have called for community psychologists to involve themselves in the empowerment of lesbian and gay communities by dealing with structural barriers to equality, including systemic prejudice and hostility, discrimination and violence, restrictions in civil rights, and the enhancement of positive mental health and self-images. However, the individual focus and the pretence of political neutrality in much of mainstream psychology means that this continues to be a relatively isolated perspective.

The main factor which militates against the well-being of lesbian women is the heterosexist and homophobic nature of society (Burns, 1992). The socially perceived 'inferiority' and 'deviance' of the lesbian woman restricts lesbians' rights and interferes with their ability to lead their lives as they wish. But it also creates an artificial dichotomy between the 'bad' lesbian who agitates for social change because of her own inadequacies, and the 'good' heterosexual woman who, by implication, is perfectly happy with institutionalized sexism, with the sexist objectification of her body as a commodity for men's consumption, and with family and social structures which reinforce her powerlessness.

This division of women into two opposing groups serves to reduce the capacity of women in general for change (D. Thompson, 1992). An examination of the social forces which impinge on lesbians' lives illuminates the way in which social structures limit all women, both lesbian and non-lesbian. Rothblum (1988) has argued that lesbians can be seen as positive role models for all women, and while we must remember that lesbians' needs are important in and of themselves, it is also true that the view from the edge can illuminate the centre in unique ways (Harding, 1994). Solidarity among women, combined with a genuine respect for diversity, is more likely to produce social change than an acceptance of the traditional good woman/bad woman dichotomy favoured by social conservatives.

Part V

13

MAKING A DIFFERENCE: FEMINIST APPROACHES TO RESEARCH IN THE PSYCHOLOGY OF WOMEN'S HEALTH

The psychology of women's health is a rich and dynamic research area. The thoughtful combination of quantitative and qualitative research, and the use of developmental models and longitudinal designs, are serving to develop a psychology of women's health which sets women in their social context, which understands their health as a complex, inter-active and multiply determined phenomenon, and which recognizes the diversity of women's voices and experiences (Gallant, Coons & Morokoff, 1994; Striegel-Moore, 1994).

Calls for psychological research which examines diversity and sets individuals in context, however, need to be understood in relation to the strengths and weaknesses of the discipline of psychology as a whole. Psychology does not, traditionally, take a social-action perspective. Both historically and in the present day, psychology has emphasized the subjective and the individual in a way which turns its focus away from the physical world and from the social contexts in which people lead their lives (Lee, 1998).

PSYCHOLOGY AND FEMINISM

This book highlights a tension between mainstream psychology and women's health research, particularly feminist women's health research, a sense that the two start from incompatible epistemological standpoints. This results both from the individualistic focus of psychology and from its position within an empiricist, positivist and experimental tradition. Sarason (1981) has argued that 'from its inception a hundred years ago . . . psychology has been quintessentially a psychology of the individual organism, a characteristic that . . . has severely and adversely affected psychology's contribution to human welfare' (p. 827). More recently, Prilleltensky (1989) has criticized psychology's focus on the individual and on cognitive adjustment, rather than on practical change, by arguing that it promotes a world-view in which 'solutions for human predicaments are to be found within the self, leaving the social order unaffected' (p. 796). A characteristic of a feminist approach to scholarship, by contrast, is that it aims to explore, rather than eliminate, contextual and sociopolitical perspectives on its subject matter. In this way, it conflicts directly with the values of mainstream psychology (Bailey & Eastman, 1994; Howard, 1985).

An empiricist approach to science generally has led to a focus on single problems which can be isolated from their contexts, so it is not surprising that a good deal of traditional, empiricist research on women's health has focused on specific diseases, specific causes of death, and specific illness-associated behaviours such as smoking, or medical-care-related behaviours such as cancer screening. These specific behaviours or disease endpoints fit neatly with a focus on the individual and on circumscribed problems. Such problems can, apparently, be disembedded from their untidy contexts. However, such research misses the point, which is that women's health is not a series of isolated problems which can, one by one, be understood and then subtracted from women's lives, until they have no health problems left. Women's health, from a feminist and contextualist perspective, is a complex interacting pattern of positive and negative experiences which can only be understood in their social, cultural and political context.

What the individualism and subjectivism of psychology mean for the psychological study of women's health is that psychological theories, methods and assessment strategies sit uneasily with such an approach. Stanton and Gallant (1995a) have pointed out that, for psychologists, there are very sound practical reasons for focusing on our traditional research strengths. Studies of stress and heart disease among individual women, for example, are consistent with the positivist and reductionist epistemology of science which has been emphasized in psychologists' professional socialization. By contrast, non-empiricist and explicitly political work, such as exploration of cultural images of the feminine, challenges that epistemology and breaks many of the conventions of the expected and the publishable.

Research carried out on aspects of women's health within the empiricist traditions of psychological science is, of course, of great value. But, as Stanton and Gallant (1995a) pointed out, a concentration on such research makes it easy to forget that this is a partial view of women's health, a view which can readily lead to biological reductionism, to a fragmentation of research and of health care into isolated problem areas, to a focus on illness rather than on health in its broadest sense, and to research which is atheoretical and problem-focused and which fails to contribute to a coherent overall picture of women's health.

Within psychology, the structure of the discipline means that work which is qualitative, which deals primarily with sociocultural context, which is openly political, or which is expressly feminist is less likely to be regarded as worthy of publication and, when it does appear, is likely to appear in specialist feminist journals which are read largely by an already-converted minority (Striegel-Moore, 1994). This chapter examines the tensions between psychological and feminist approaches to the study of women's health, and suggests that, while different views of what constitutes legitimate research and legitimate knowledge may be essentially incommensurable, a rapport can perhaps be achieved through acceptance of diversity in research methods, in epistemological standpoints, and in conceptions of women's health.

NEGLECT OF WOMEN IN ILLNESS RESEARCH

It is frequently pointed out that research on illness and its treatment has traditionally been conducted with male subjects, and it is by no means clear which results do, and which do not, generalize to women (e.g. Rodin & Ickovics, 1990; Stanton, 1995). Further, research has often failed to consider diversity both between and within cultural, racial and ethnic groups, because a reductionist focus on physiological and intra-individual variables assumes that cultural differences will not be relevant. Thus, the particular needs and problems of the poor, minorities, the disabled and older people have often not been directly addressed in basic research on the precursors and consequences of illness (Stanton, 1995).

Explanations for the neglect of women in illness-related research seem very reasonable when viewed solely from an individualistic and biomedical perspective, being generally couched in terms of protecting women from unnecessary biological risks. Stanton (1995) has identified the most frequently specified reason as a concern for damage to women's reproductive capacity or to children conceived during or subsequent to a research project (although it is notable that men are not excluded from basic research as a general principle, for fear that their reproductive capacity might be affected). Methodological issues such as the potential for complex interactions between treatments and hormonal fluctuations are also frequently raised, as is the fact that women have a lower risk of death across any finite study period, and many important diseases and risk factors are more common in men, meaning that much larger sample sizes would be needed for research to focus on women. At a more practical level, recruitment issues such as the convenience of workplace or armed-forces samples, who are predominantly male, have been raised, and Stanton (1995) has also pointed to an unfounded assumption that women are less likely to comply with intervention regimes and to accept random assignment to research groups than are men; such a view is presumably based on the stereotype that women are less reliable and less intelligent than men.

While some of these reasons may appear justifiable, it can be observed that the results of research on men are frequently generalized to include women; in pharmacological trials in particular, the end result is that an exclusion of women from controlled research, justified in terms of avoiding possible damage to female subjects' reproductive health, means that the drugs may later be made available in uncontrolled, unevaluated clinical usage to much larger numbers of women, with unknown effects on their reproductive health (Hamilton, 1986). The male domination of research and of the health care system, the concentration of money and of power among men, and the problems women report with access and appropriateness of health care services (Rodin & Ickovics, 1990) are also worth considering in attempting to understand the reasons for the neglect of women in basic illness research.

The need for a better level of basic understanding of women's health and illness, though, derives not only from biological differences between men and women, but also from the social and cultural differences which have been the focus of this book. However, within the culture of traditional science the need to study women specifically is most readily appreciated where the differences in illnesses or in prevalence may be seen as being related to biological differences between men and women.

Research in psychopharmacology, for example, has neglected female subjects, and thus little is known about the effect of female sex-related hormones and their interactions with medication (e.g. Stanton, 1995), despite the fact that the majority of medicinal and psychoactive drugs are taken by women (Ogur, 1986). Viewing this as a problem is quite consistent with empiricism and reductionism and, perhaps because of this, it has been discussed at length in both the mainstream (e.g. Hamilton, 1986) and the feminist (e.g. Hamilton & Jensvold, 1995) literature.

Such arguments, however, are made less often with reference to the social and psychological aspects of drug use. Research on the abuse of drugs and alcohol has also concentrated on men despite major psycho-social differences between male and female drug users (Broom, 1995; Hamilton, 1986; D.G. Patterson, 1995). Female drug abusers, for example, encounter specific obstacles to accessing services, differ from men in their patterns of drug use, and report that their drug use is associated with gender-specific issues such as body image problems, domestic violence and sexual abuse (Broom, 1995). These issues are central to understanding and dealing with women's abuse of drugs, but are less likely to be perceived as legitimate topics for research than are those concerning women's physiological reactions to drugs.

Research on illness and specific risk factors, therefore, needs to be expanded in order to include women: this involves a traditionally empiricist focus on problems which are unique to women, problems which are commoner in women than in men, and problems which have special relevance to women, but it also requires a broader, contextualist approach to all these (Rodin & Ickovics, 1990). Further, it needs to adopt a range of methods and perspectives. Basic experimental research which includes women is essential, but it can only be applied effectively if the contexts and patterns of women's illnesses and illness-related behaviour are also understood.

RESEARCH METHODS AND WOMEN'S HEALTH

As discussed in Chapter 1, one approach to the topic of women's health has been the generation of lists of specific topics in which woman-oriented research would be valuable. However, such lists frequently derive from a point of view which is both reductionist and sexist, focusing exclusively on the individual rather than her social context, and emphasizing sexual and reproductive issues, and any list of disconnected items must be somewhat idiosyncratic. The psychology of women's health cannot be defined by making lists of important topics, but must be approached as an integrated perspective, one which may be applied to almost any subject area, from the traditional issues of childbirth and menopause through contemporary issues such as violence, harassment and the division of household labour, to as yet unconsidered issues which will concern the women of the future. Illnesses, illness behaviours, and lists of current 'hot topics' are of course relevant, but in order to understand them from a feminist perspective it is necessary to see these and other topics in the context of culture; a culture which limits and prescribes women's behaviour in many ways, and which perpetuates sex-based inequities in economic and political power through the promulgation of myths about women's 'natural' role as unworldly, subservient, emotion-oriented, family-bound carers.

In order to challenge these culturally based assumptions, it may be necessary to explore a broader range of research methods derived from a number of alternative approaches to scientific epistemology.

Research strategies for the psychology of women's health

Positivist, empiricist approaches are frequently rejected by feminist writers because they are based on the assumption that values play no part in research. Traditional empirical methods emphasize rigid control and isolation of a single variable, removed from its context (Stanton &

Gallant, 1995a; Striegel-Moore, 1994). Feminist approaches, by contrast, emphasize and explore bias and context, assume the existence of ambiguity, and embrace the concept that reality depends on the observer's standpoint (Striegel-Moore, 1994).

Quantitative and qualitative research strategies Qualitative research methods are a group of approaches which aim to allow the voices of research participants to be heard, rather than imposing the world view of the researcher on them. They include descriptive or interpretive content analysis of semi-structured interviews and focus groups; the use of discourse analysis or narrative analysis to explore participants' conceptual frameworks; and various types of participant observation. Psychologists frequently justify qualitative research as a useful developmental strategy which identifies possible hypotheses or models for later empirical tests (e.g. Stanton & Gallant, 1995a), and while this is a valuable use for qualitative methods it is by no means the only argument in their favour.

Researchers trained in an empiricist tradition may find it difficult to appreciate the value of qualitative methods, but the intelligent and appropriate use of alternative approaches has the potential to make psychology much more inclusive and socially relevant (Bohan, 1992), by exploring diversity and context, or by dealing with issues which have been excluded from a traditional scientific approach. Renzetti (1995), for example, has discussed the problems inherent in conducting research which aims to understand and assist lesbians who have been the victims of partner abuse. The stigmatized nature both of relationship violence and of lesbianism means that quantitative, positivist methods are very unlikely to obtain a sample of research volunteers or encourage them to describe their experiences. A feminist participatory research model, in which the participants are initially approached as equal partners in the research process, with a voice in the design of the investigation and the use to which the findings are put, may be the only way in which it is possible to establish the extent to which a phenomenon such as lesbian partner abuse is a serious problem and, if it is, to explore the contexts in which it arises and to develop potentially useful interventions (Renzetti, 1995).

Because mainstream psychology emphasizes quantitative methods and either rejects alternative approaches as non-scientific or accords them a minimal role in the informal, developmental, stages of research, there is a tendency for some feminist researchers to go to the opposite extreme and imply that only qualitative research methods are of any value. While qualitative research strategies do enable researchers to approach topics in ways that might otherwise be impossible, they do have limitations, and several writers (e.g. Chesney & Ozer, 1995; Stanton & Gallant, 1995a) have pointed to the need for a thoughtful combination of qualitative and quantitative methods, and a selection of method on the basis of what will most appropriately address the research question.

There are many questions in women's health research for which either qualitative or quantitative methods, or a combination of both, would be appropriate, and it is important to appreciate the different biases and thus the different outcomes which will arise from these different approaches. Saint-Germain, Bassford and Montano (1993), for example, conducted a direct comparison of quantitative and qualitative methods, in an investigation of barriers to health care usage in older Hispanic women in the USA. Comparing a structured, individually administered survey with a series of focus groups, they found that the two techniques produced broadly similar findings, but that focus groups were more useful in revealing group norms, community attitudes, and social reasons behind women's individual behaviour, while the survey provided more information at an individual level. Thus, the focus groups enabled the researchers to understand the context within which women were making individual choices, while the surveys provided information on how this context was interpreted by individual women.

Contextualism A contextualist approach to psychology does not require qualitative methods, although they will be appropriate in some instances. Contextualist research emphasizes the meaning of the context and its impact on individual behaviour, using methods which range from the qualitative to those derived from the behavioural tradition (Jaeger & Rosnow, 1988). Whatever the methods, though, contextualism is based on a perception that the focus of analysis should not be the individual, but the individual-in-context (Morris, 1988).

Landrine (1995) has argued that a contextualist approach is appropriate for health research, particularly in understanding the effects of culture and ethnicity on individual health-related choices. For example, adolescent girls' decisions about the use of condoms are embedded in the context of the cultural meaning of sex; among Hispanic Americans, for example, pressures on girls to be sexually active but simultaneously to remain virgins may explain a high incidence of anal sex, and a perception of condoms as being for contraception rather than disease prevention may explain their low rate of condom usage. A purely individual-focused approach to health promotion, particularly by a researcher who was unaware of these cultural constructions, could miss these factors and result in health-promotion interventions that were inappropriate and ineffective.

Cultural sensitivity An inclusive approach and the use of participants from diverse cultural, ethnic and racial backgrounds is an essential aspect of a contextualist approach to women's health research (Chesney & Ozer, 1995), but research with participants from cultures other than

one's own can be difficult, and it appears to be particularly difficult
for researchers who are themselves members of dominant cultures to
avoid the perception among potential research participants that their
approach is stereotyping, biasing or otherwise inappropriate (Henderson, Sampselle, Mayes & Oakley, 1992; Wyche, 1993).

Research which treats culture or ethnicity simply as a category
assumes that members of minorities are all the same. Ethnicity is better
understood as a multidimensional and variable concept, experienced
very differently by people in different circumstances. Landrine (1995)
and Stanton and Gallant (1995a) have criticized mainstream research
whose approach to ethnic or cultural factors has been simply to compare
responses from different ethnic groups, without any appreciation of
diversity within cultural groups, any underlying model of the role of
ethnicity in health or health behaviour, or any a priori hypotheses about
the strength or direction of differences. Explanations of cultural differences, where they are made, are frequently speculative and stereotyping.

Measurement issues One implication of the male orientation of most
mainstream research is that many standard questionnaires and assessment measures are developed for men or from a male perspective on
health, and these may not always be appropriate for women, especially
for culturally diverse groups of women. A number of health science
researchers (e.g. Chesney & Ozer, 1995; Gallant et al., 1994; Stanton &
Gallant, 1995a) have identified a need for the development and evaluation of gender-appropriate measures and variables. The assessment of
health-related physical activity, for example, is a very different issue
among women than among men. Women are more likely to engage in
incidental and moderate-intensity activity, which is notoriously difficult
to assess reliably and validly, while men are more likely to attend formal
exercise sessions or play competitive sport (C. Lee, 1993).

Further, there are some experiences which are ignored by male-
oriented research. In psychology, concepts can obtain legitimacy through
the development and use of standardized questionnaires for their assessment. For example, standardized measures of menstrual-related distress
are one way in which the supposed existence of premenstrual syndrome
is legitimized as scientific fact (Ussher, 1992a). In a similar fashion, the
existence of scales for the assessment of postpartum depression implies
that there is something specific about depression following childbirth.

It is notable, however, that questionnaires which assess socially
mediated distress among women are not accorded the same degree of
legitimacy. While scales such as the Schedule of Sexist Events (Klonoff &
Landrine, 1995) are developed and shown to have predictive validity
(Landrine, Klonoff, Gibbs, Manning & Lund, 1995), they tend to be
published in the less prestigious and more specialized women's health

journals. Questionnaires which assess minor issues in the lives of the socially privileged (e.g. the Psychology Student Stress Questionnaire; Cahir & Morris, 1991) appear in mainstream journals such as the *Journal of Clinical Psychology*. The implicit view here is that the experiences of psychology students are 'naturally' more important, more central, than those of the majority of women. A woman-centred psychology challenges this assumption.

RESEARCH IN PSYCHOLOGY AND WOMEN'S HEALTH: DEALING WITH HEALTH, WITH CONTEXT, WITH DIVERSITY, WITH POLITICS

Feminist research deals with the psychology of women's health from a perspective which differs in four main ways from traditional health psychology. Firstly, feminist women's health research focuses on health and well-being in its widest sense, rather than simply on illnesses. Secondly, it emphasizes the broader social, cultural and political context which shapes the behaviours of individuals. Thirdly, it aims to explore and understand diversity among groups and individuals, rather than taking the more traditional perspective that sociocultural differences simply interfere with well-designed research. And fourthly, it has an openly political purpose, in that its final aim is to promote social change and to work towards a more equitable society.

Focus on health

A focus on illness or on specific illness-related behaviours or attitudes is consistent with an empiricist approach but fails to consider health in its broadest biopsychosocial context. The earlier chapters of this book have illustrated that women's health is more than physiological functioning and more than the absence of illness; health encompasses an individual's physiological state, psychological well-being, and social context. From a biopsychosocial perspective, women's health encompasses normal physiological processes such as growth and ageing, childbirth and menopause; it includes the relationships between women and their families; it includes women's interactions with the wider society in which they live; it includes both positive and negative aspects of the broader culture, including discrimination, harassment, violence and homophobia on the one hand, and respect and tolerance on the other; and it includes women's economic and political power and influence.

Focus on context

Psychology's tendency to emphasize the personal and to focus on subjective intra-individual causes of distress (e.g. Prilleltensky, 1989), when applied to those whose lives are constrained by social inequities, poverty or the threat of violence, can lead to an implicit blaming of those people for their problems (Lee, 1998; Stanton & Gallant, 1995a). Women's behaviour and their health are affected in obvious ways by violence, harassment and discrimination (Rodin & Ickovics, 1990). They are also affected more subtly by a sexist and heterosexist society, and by the myths and stereotypes which this book has explored. Women's choices are constrained by a social context which values them for their appearance, for their relationships with men, for subservience and self-sacrifice. The interactions between this context and any individual woman's choices or behaviours regarding her health are complex, but must be understood if the psychology of women's health is to reflect this reality. As Striegel-Moore (1994) has argued, women's health research needs to take account of systemic imbalances in power and resources between women and men, as well as of sociocultural assumptions about appropriate or expected behaviour for women and men.

Focus on diversity

Psychology assumes that cognitive events are more important and more central to an understanding of the psychology of the individual than are social or cultural circumstances (Sampson, 1988), so cultural context, social conditions, and cultural diversity have tended to be marginalized in our explanations of behaviour (Jahoda, 1988). Psychological textbooks and journals frequently give the impression that research is carried out in a cultural vacuum; the implication of an individual-centred approach to both data and theory is the assumption that 'the particular historical period or sociocultural context in which data have been collected is . . . of little or no importance' (Spence, 1985, p. 1285), and thus that, while society and culture may affect minor details, they have no impact on the real relationships between important variables.

This lack of contextual awareness has led to a tendency to treat local and temporary cultural arrangements as natural and proper reflections of a permanent, indisputable reality (Lee, 1998). Even within cross-cultural psychology, it is often assumed that a mere shifting of surface detail will suffice for a mainstream theory to apply in a non-Western culture (Jahoda, 1988), despite analyses (e.g. Markus & Kitayama, 1991; Rogoff & Chavajay, 1995; Spence, 1985) which suggest that many of the apparent absolutes in psychological theory are in fact the result of culture-specific socialization.

Thus, it is frequently assumed that minorities, including ethnic, religious or racial minorities, lesbians, and people with disabilities or special needs, are basically the same as the White, middle-class, heterosexual men who are implicitly regarded as 'standard' human beings throughout much of the psychological literature, and that their different needs can be accommodated through minor modifications of existing theories, models and intervention strategies. Traditional science is embedded in a cultural discourse which describes some human attributes as normal and natural, and others as anomalous and in need of explanation. The 'normal human being' is implicitly assumed to be White, male, heterosexual, middle-class and able-bodied. Where others differ from the 'norm', they are positioned as inevitably problematic and in need of investigation and correction (Harding, 1986). Thus, gender differences in self-esteem are explained in terms of women's personal deficiencies, rather than in terms of men's excessive self-confidence. Homosexuality is theorized while heterosexuality is assumed to be natural and in need of no explanation (Kitzinger & Wilkinson, 1993). Feminist research challenges these assumptions.

Research as a political process

Mainstream psychological research, in which questionnaires designed to assess trivial issues among the powerful are perceived as legitimate while those which seek to quantify the experiences of powerless people are accorded only peripheral attention, serves to maintain the status quo in many ways. The assumption that politics is something which can be politely left out of psychological discourse cannot be upheld. Clearly, decisions about what to study, and in what way, are embedded in a sociopolitical context (Lee, 1998), and political perspective is something which must be addressed in considering the implications of any theoretical stance (Bohan, 1992; Prilleltensky, 1990), including that of the traditional mainstream. For example, Biglan et al. (1990) have argued that smoking cessation interventions which focus on the individual, ignoring both the economic structures which encouraged tobacco companies to promote smoking, and the social context which positions smoking as a mature and sexy choice, are as much grounded in a political perspective as are those which directly confront these social, political and economic realities.

Feminist research in the psychology of women's health examines such issues as the subordinate position of women in society, and the difficulties which face women who want to make positive health-related changes in their own and others' lives. Such research, by challenging cultural assumptions such as the naturalness of women's roles as subordinates and caregivers (Gallant et al., 1994), must challenge dominant attitudes to women and to social structure.

As Striegel-Moore (1994) has argued, it is not possible to eliminate political bias or assumptions from research. Data are always political, psychology is already a political and moral force, and the question is not whether to imbue psychology with a political perspective but which political perspective to take (Lee, 1998). Although psychological research has not traditionally embraced reflexivity, an analysis of the researcher's experience, assumptions and social perspectives can be valuable in identifying the biases inherent in research which may otherwise be construed as completely objective and unbiased.

Oakley's (1993) well-known account of her experiences when interviewing women during their pregnancies and subsequent adjustment to motherhood is an example of a researcher's reflexive analysis of the process of research. Oakley contrasted the standard assumptions of questionnaire research – that the researcher will not become involved or offer opinions, that the interviewee will not ask questions of her own, and that the relationship between researcher and interviewee will remain formal and distant – with this experience. Many interviewees asked questions about childbirth and motherhood which she could not, ethically, avoid answering. Further, she found that a series of lengthy and detailed interviews over a period of months inevitably led to personal relationships with many of the interviewees, and frequently found herself helping the interviewees with housework or childcare during the interview. Oakley (1993) argued that this sort of 'contamination' is common, indeed inevitable, in applied research and that failure to answer the women's questions or to help in other ways would have been both exploitative of the women and damaging for the research project.

Research questions do need to be framed with a consideration of the assumptions and preconceptions that the researchers bring to the work (Stanton & Gallant, 1995a). While qualitative and reflexive analyses are by no means impervious to bias, it is possible that they will have different biases and thus provide a different perspective. For a complete understanding of the psychology of women's health, a diverse range of research strategies which looks from as wide a range of perspectives as possible does not confuse the situation, but rather enables one to develop a fuller picture. Traditional science and feminism may have a somewhat uneasy relationship, but the development of an understanding of the social and psychological issues which affect women's health requires that researchers combine the two.

REFERENCES

Abbey, A., Andrews, F.M., & Halman, L.J. (1991). Gender's role in responses to infertility. *Psychology of Women Quarterly, 15*, 295–316.

Abbey, A., Andrews, F.M., & Halman, L.J. (1994). Infertility and parenthood: Does becoming a parent increase well-being? *Journal of Consulting and Clinical Psychology, 62*, 398–403

Abel, E.K. (1987). *Love is not enough: Family care for the frail elderly.* Washington, DC: American Public Health Association.

Abel, E.K. (1991). *Who cares for the elderly? Public policy and the experiences of adult daughters.* Philadelphia, PA: Temple University Press.

Abidoye, R.O., & Agbabiaka, B.A. (1994). Incidence and management of menstrual disorders and foods implicated among Nigerian adolescents. *International Journal of Adolescence and Youth, 4*, 271–283.

Adelmann, P.K., Antonucci, T.C., Crohan, S.E., & Coleman, L.M. (1990). A causal analysis of employment and health in midlife women. *Women and Health, 16*, 5–20.

Adelson, P.L., Frommer, M.S., & Weisberg, E. (1995). A survey of women seeking termination of pregnancy in New South Wales. *Medical Journal of Australia, 163*, 419–422.

Aderibigbe, Y.A., Gureje, O., & Omigbodun, O. (1993). Postnatal emotional disorders in Nigerian women: A study of antecedents and associations. *British Journal of Psychiatry, 163*, 645–650.

Adesso, V.J., Reddy, D.M., & Fleming, R. (eds). (1994). *Psychological perspectives on women's health.* Washington, DC: Taylor & Francis.

Adler, N.E. (1992). Unwanted pregnancy and abortion: Definitional and research issues. *Journal of Social Issues, 48*, 19–35.

Adler, N.E., Boyce, T., Chesney, M.A., Cohen, S., Folkman, S.M., Kahn, R.L., & Syme, S.L. (1994). Socioeconomic status and health: The challenge of the gradient. *American Psychologist, 49*, 15–24.

Adler, N.E., David, H.P., Major, B.N., Roth, S.H., Russo, N.F., & Wyatt, G.E. (1992). Psychological factors in abortion: A review. *American Psychologist, 47*, 1194–1204.

Adlersberg, M., & Thorne, S. (1990). Emerging from the chrysalis: Older widows in transition. *Journal of Gerontological Nursing, 16* (1), 4–8.

Aganoff, J.A., & Boyle, G.J. (1994). Aerobic exercise, mood states and menstrual cycle symptoms. *Journal of Psychosomatic Research, 38*, 183–192.

Aiken, L.R. (1989). *Later life.* 3rd edn. Hillsdale, NJ: Lawrence Erlbaum Associates.

Ainscough, C.E. (1990). Premenstrual emotional changes: A prospective study of symptomatology in normal women. *Journal of Psychosomatic Research, 34,* 35–45.

Ainslie, J., & Feltey, K.M. (1991). Definitions and dynamics of motherhood and family in lesbian communities. *Marriage and Family Review, 17,* 63–85.

Albert, M.S., Jones, K., Savage, C.R., Berkman, L., Seeman, T., Blazer, D., & Rowe, J.W. (1995). Predictors of cognitive change in older persons: MacArthur studies of successful aging. *Psychology and Aging, 10,* 578–589.

Albright, A. (1993). Postpartum depression: An overview. *Journal of Counseling and Development, 71,* 316–320.

Alessandri, S.M. (1992). Effects of maternal work status in single-parent families on children's perception of self and family and school achievement. *Journal of Experimental Child Psychology, 54,* 417–433.

Alldred, P. (1996). 'Fit to parent'? Developmental psychology and 'non-traditional' families. In E. Burman, C. Bewlay, B. Goldberg, C. Heenan, D. Marks, J. Marshall, K. Taylor, R. Ullah, & S. Warner (eds), *Challenging women: Psychology's exclusions, feminist possibilities* (pp. 141–159). Buckingham, UK: Open University Press.

Allen, K.R., & Walker, A.J. (1992). A feminist analysis of interviews with elderly mothers and their daughters. In J.F. Gilgun, K. Daly & G. Handel (eds), *Qualitative methods in family research* (pp. 198–214). Newbury Park, CA: Sage.

American Cancer Society (1994). *Cancer facts and figures, 1994.* Atlanta, GA: Author.

American Psychiatric Association (1994). *Diagnostic and statistical manual of mental disorders, 4th edition.* Washington, DC: Author.

Andersen, A.E., & DiDomenico, L. (1992). Diet vs. shape content of popular male and female magazines: A dose-response relationship to the incidence of eating disorders? *International Journal of Eating Disorders, 11,* 283–287.

Andrews, F.M., Abbey, A., & Halman, L.J. (1991). Stress from infertility, marriage factors, and subjective well-being of wives and husbands. *Journal of Health and Social Behavior, 32,* 238–253.

Angel, R.J., Angel, J.L., & Himes, C.L. (1992). Minority group status, health transitions, and community living arrangements among the elderly. *Research on Aging, 14,* 496–521.

Apgar, B.S., & Churgay, C.A. (1993). Spontaneous abortion. *Primary Care: Clinics in Office Practice, 20,* 621–627.

Apter, T. (1993). *Professional progress: Why women still don't have wives.* Basingstoke, UK: Macmillan.

Arber, S., Gilbert, G.N., & Dale, A. (1985). Paid employment and women's health: A benefit or a source of role strain? *Sociology of Health and Illness, 7,* 375–400.

Arber, S., & Ginn, J. (1994). Women and aging. *Reviews in Clinical Gerontology, 4,* 349–358.

Arbuckle, N.W., & de Vries, B. (1995). The long-term effects of later life spousal and parental bereavement on personal functioning. *Gerontologist, 35,* 637–647.

Armistead, L., Wierson, M., & Forehand, R. (1990). Adolescents and maternal employment: Is it harmful for a young adolescent to have an employed mother? *Journal of Early Adolescence, 10,* 260–278.

Aronson, J. (1992). Women's sense of responsibility for the care of old people: 'But who else is going to do it?' *Gender and Society, 6,* 8–29.

Asso, D. (1992). A reappraisal of the normal menstrual cycle. *Journal of Reproductive and Infant Psychology, 10,* 103–109.

August, E.R. (1985). *Men's studies: A selected and annotated interdisciplinary bibliography.* Littleton, CO: Libraries Unlimited.

Australian Bureau of Statistics (1994). *Australian women's yearbook 1994.* Canberra: Australian Government Publishing Office.

Australian Bureau of Statistics (1995). *Australian women's yearbook 1995.* Canberra: Australian Government Publishing Office.

Avis, N.E., Brambilla, D., McKinlay, S.M., & Vass, K. (1994). A longitudinal analysis of the association between menopause and depression: Results from the Massachusetts Women's Health Study. *Annals of Epidemiology, 4,* 214–220.

Avis, N.E., Brambilla, D.J., Vass, K., & McKinlay, J.B. (1991). The effect of widowhood on health: A prospective analysis from the Massachusetts Women's Health Study. *Social Science and Medicine, 33,* 1063–1070.

Avis, N.E., & McKinlay, S.M. (1991). A longitudinal analysis of women's attitudes toward the menopause: Results from the Massachusetts Women's Health Study. *Maturitas, 13,* 65–79.

Bader, J.B. (1985). Respite care: Temporary relief for caregivers. *Women and Health, 10,* 39–52.

Badinter, E. (1981). *The myth of motherhood: An historical overview of the maternal instinct.* London: Souvenir Press.

Bailey, J.R., & Eastman, W.N. (1994). Positivism and the promise of the social sciences. *Theory and Psychology, 4,* 505–524.

Bailey, W.T. (1994). A longitudinal study of fathers' involvement with young children: Infancy to age 5 years. *Journal of Genetic Psychology, 155,* 331–339.

Ballard, C.G., Davis, R., Cullen, P.C., Mohan, R.N., & Dean, C. (1994). Prevalence of postnatal psychiatric morbidity in mothers and fathers. *British Journal of Psychiatry, 164,* 782–788.

Ballinger, C.B. (1977). Psychiatric morbidity and the menopause: Survey of a gynaecological outpatient clinic. *British Journal of Psychiatry, 131,* 83–89.

Ballinger, C.B. (1990). Psychiatric aspects of the menopause. *British Journal of Psychiatry, 156,* 773–787.

Bancroft, J. (1993). The premenstrual syndrome: A reappraisal of the concept and the evidence. *Psychological Medicine, 24 (Monog. Suppl.),* 1–53.

Bancroft, J., Rennie, D., & Warner, P. (1994). Vulnerability to perimenstrual mood change: The relevance of a past history of depressive disorder. *Psychosomatic Medicine, 56,* 225–231.

Banks, A., & Gartrell, N.K. (1996). Lesbians in the medical setting. In R.P. Cabaj & T.S. Stein (eds), *Textbook of homosexuality and mental health* (pp. 659–671). Washington, DC: American Psychiatric Press.

Barkley, M.L. (1993). Balancing work and family: The experience of new parents. *Australian Journal of Marriage and the Family, 14,* 143–150.

Barnes, L. (1991). HRT suggested for all women. *New Zealand Doctor, 1,* 17–23.

Barnett, P.A., & Gotlib, I.H. (1988). Psychosocial functioning and depression: Distinguishing among antecedents, concomitants, and consequences. *Psychological Bulletin, 104,* 97–126.

Barnett, R.C., & Baruch, G.K. (1987). Determinants of fathers' participation in family work. *Journal of Marriage and the Family, 49,* 29–40.

Barnett, R.C., Marshall, N.L., & Singer, J.D. (1992). Job experiences over time, multiple roles, and women's mental health: A longitudinal study. *Journal of Personality and Social Psychology, 62*, 634–644.

Barnett, W., Freudenberg, N., & Wille, R. (1992). Partnership after induced abortion: A prospective controlled study. *Archives of Sexual Behavior, 21*, 443–455.

Barrett-Connor, E. (1992). Hormone replacement and cancer. *British Medical Bulletin, 48*, 345–355.

Barrett-Connor, E. (1994). Heart disease in women. *Fertility and Sterility, 62*, 127–132.

Barrieto, T., Campbell, O.M., Davies, J.L., Fauveau, V., Filippi, V.G., Graham, W.J., Mamdani, M., Rooney, C.I., & Toubla, N.F. (1992). Investigating induced abortion in developing countries: Methods and problems. *Studies in Family Planning, 23*, 159–170.

Barron, N., & Lear, B.H. (1989). Ample opportunity for fat women. *Women and Therapy, 8*, 79–92.

Bartrop, R.W., Hancock, K., Craig, A., & Porritt, D.W. (1992). Psychological toxicity of bereavement: Six months after the event. *Australian Psychologist, 27*, 192–196.

Baruch, G.K., & Barnett, R. (1986). Role quality, multiple role involvement, and psychological well-being in midlife women. *Journal of Personality and Social Psychology, 51*, 578–585.

Bass, D.M., & Bowman, K. (1990). The transition from caregiving to bereavement: The relationship of care-related strain and adjustment to death. *Gerontologist, 30*, 35–42.

Baumeister, L.M., Flores, E., & Marin, B.V. (1995). Sex information given to Latina adolescents by parents. *Health Education Research, 10*, 233–239.

Baxter, J., & Bittman, M. (1995). Measuring time spent on housework: A comparison of two approaches. *Australian Journal of Social Research, 1*, 21–46.

Baxter, J., Gibson, D., & Lynch-Blosse, M. (1991). *Doubletake: The links between paid and unpaid work.* Canberra: Australian Government Publishing Service.

Bearon, L.B. (1989). No great expectations: The underpinnings of life satisfaction for older women. *Gerontologist, 29*, 772–778.

Beaurepaire, J., Jones, M., Thiering, P., Saunders, D., & Tennant, C. (1994). Psychosocial adjustment to infertility and its treatment: Male and female responses at different stages of IVF/ET treatment. *Journal of Psychosomatic Research, 38*, 229–240.

Beck, C.T. (1992). The lived experience of postpartum depression: A phenomenological study. *Nursing Research, 41*, 166–170.

Becker, G., & Nachtigall, R.D. (1994). 'Born to be a mother': The cultural construction of risk in infertility treatment in the US. *Social Science and Medicine, 39*, 507–518.

Belgrave, L.L. (1993). Discrimination against older women in health care. In J.D. Garner & A.A. Young (eds), *Women and healthy aging: Living productively in spite of it all* (pp. 181–199). New York: Haworth Press.

Bell, A.J., Land, N.M., Milne, S., & Hassanyeh, F. (1994). Long-term outcome of post-partum psychiatric illness requiring admission. *Journal of Affective Disorders, 31*, 67–70.

Belsky, J., Lang, M., & Huston, T.L. (1986). Sex typing and division of labor as determinants of marital change across the transition to parenthood. *Journal of Personality and Social Psychology, 50*, 517–522.

Belsky, J., & Pensky, E. (1988). Marital change across the transition to parenthood. *Marriage and Family Review, 12*, 133–156.

Belsky, J., & Rovine, M. (1990). Patterns of marital change across the transition to parenthood: Pregnancy to three years postpartum. *Journal of Marriage and the Family, 52*, 5–19.

Benazon, N., Wright, J., & Sabourin, S. (1992). Stress, sexual satisfaction, and marital adjustment in infertile couples. *Journal of Sex and Marital Therapy, 18*, 273–284.

Bendfeldt-Zachrisson, F. (1992). The causality of bulimia nervosa: An overview and social critique. *International Journal of Mental Health, 21*, 57–82.

Benkov, L. (1995). Lesbian and gay parents: From margin to center. In K. Weingarten (ed.), *Cultural resistance: Challenging beliefs about men, women, and therapy* (pp. 49–64). New York: Harrington Park Press.

Bennett, K.M., & Morgan, K. (1992). Health, social functioning, and marital status: Stability and change among elderly recently widowed women. *International Journal of Geriatric Psychiatry, 7*, 813–817.

Berg, B.J., & Wilson, J.F. (1991). Psychological functioning across stages of treatment for infertility. *Journal of Behavioral Medicine, 14*, 11–26.

Berg, B.J., Wilson, J.F., & Weingartner, P.J. (1991). Psychological sequelae of infertility treatment: The role of gender and sex-role identification. *Social Science and Medicine, 33*, 1071–1080.

Berg, D.H., & Coutts, L.B. (1994). The extended curse: Being a woman every day. *Health Care for Women International, 15*, 11–22.

Beyene, Y. (1986). Cultural significance and physiological manifestations of menopause: A biocultural analysis. *Culture, Medicine and Psychiatry, 10*, 47–71.

Bien, B. (1991). A socio-medical survey of the old citizens of Bialystok, Poland: 5 years longitudinal observation. *Journal of Cross-Cultural Gerontology, 6*, 101–108.

Biglan, A., Glasgow, R.E., & Singer, G. (1990). The need for a science of larger social units: A contextual approach. *Behavior Therapy, 21*, 195–215.

Bittman, M. (1992). *Juggling time: How Australian families use their time.* Canberra: Australian Government Publishing Service.

Bittman, M., & Lovejoy, F. (1993). Domestic power: Negotiating an unequal division of labour within a framework of equality. *Australian and New Zealand Journal of Sociology, 29*, 302–321.

Black, A.L., & Koulis-Chitwood, A. (1990). The menstrual cycle and typing skill: An ecologically-valid test of the 'raging hormones' hypothesis. *Canadian Journal of Behavioural Science, 22*, 445–455.

Blair, S.L., & Lichter, D.T. (1991). Measuring the division of household labor: Gender segregation of housework among American couples. *Journal of Family Issues, 12*, 91–113.

Blair, S.N., Kohl, H.W., Paffenbarger, R.S., Clark, D.G., Cooper, K.H., & Gibbons, L.W. (1989). Physical fitness and all-cause mortality: A prospective study of healthy men and women. *Journal of the American Medical Association, 262*, 2395–2401.

Blumberg, L. (1994). The politics of prenatal testing and selective abortion. *Sexuality and Disability, 12,* 135–153.

Blumenthal, S.J. (1991). Psychiatric consequences of abortion: Overview. In N.L. Stotland (ed.), *Psychiatric aspects of abortion* (pp. 17–37). Washington, DC: American Psychiatric Press.

Blumenthal, J.A., Emery, C.F., Madden, D.J., George, L.K., Coleman, R.E., Riddle, M.W., McKee, D.C., Reasoner, J., & Williams, R.S. (1989). Cardiovascular and behavioral effects of aerobic exercise training in healthy older men and women. *Journal of Gerontology: Medical Sciences, 44,* 147–157.

Bodnar, J.C., & Keicolt-Glaser, J.K. (1994). Caregiver depression after bereavement: Chronic stress isn't over when it's over. *Psychology and Aging, 9,* 372–380.

Bohan, J.S. (1992). Prologue: Re-viewing psychology, re-playing women – an end searching for a means. In J.S. Bohan (ed.), *Seldom seen, rarely heard: Women's place in psychology* (pp. 9–53). Boulder, CO: Westview Press.

Bonilla-Becerra, N., Quintero-Zurek, M.C., & Vela-Ortega, C.F. (1991). Actitudes de las mujeras hacia la vivencia de su sexualidad en la menopausia. [Women's attitudes toward sexual experiences after menopause.] *Revista Latinoamericana de Sexología, 6,* 167–181.

Bouchard, C. (1995). Genetic influences on body weight and shape. In K.D. Brownell & C.G. Fairburn (eds), *Eating disorders and obesity* (pp. 21–26). New York: Guilford Press.

Boulet, M.J., Oddens, B.J., Lehert, P., Vemer, H.M., & Visser, A. (1994). Climacteric and menopause in seven south-east Asian countries. *Maturitas, 19,* 157–176.

Bound, J., Duncan, G.J., Laren, D.S., & Oleinick, L. (1991). Poverty dynamics in widowhood. *Journals of Gerontology, 46,* S115-S124.

Bowen, D.J., Tomoyasu, N., & Cauce, A.M. (1991). The triple threat: A discussion of gender, class, and race differences in weight. *Women and Health, 17,* 123–143.

Bowlby, J. (1951). *Maternal care and mental health.* Geneva: World Health Organization.

Bowling, A. (1994). Mortality after bereavement: An analysis of mortality rates and associations with mortality 13 years after bereavement. *International Journal of Geriatric Psychiatry, 9,* 445–459.

Bowling, A., & Windsor, J. (1995). Death after widow(er)hood: An analysis of mortality rates up to 13 years after bereavement. *Omega Journal of Death and Dying, 31,* 35–49.

Boyce, P., Hickie, I., & Parker, G. (1991). Parents, partners or personality? Risk factors for post-natal depression. *Journal of Affective Disorders, 21,* 245–255.

Boyle, G.J., & Grant, A.F. (1992). Prospective versus retrospective assessment of menstrual cycle symptoms and moods: Role of attitudes and beliefs. *Journal of Psychopathology and Behavioral Assessment, 14,* 307–321.

Boyle, M. (1992). The abortion debate: An analysis of psychological assumptions underlying legislation and professional decision-making. In P. Nicolson & J. Ussher (eds), *The psychology of women's health and health care* (pp.124–151). Basingstoke, UK: Macmillan.

Brackley, M.H. (1994). The plight of American family caregivers: Implications for nursing. *Perspectives in Psychiatric Care, 30* (4), 14–20.

Bradford, J., Ryan, C., & Rothblum, E.D. (1994). National lesbian health care survey: Implications for mental health care. *Journal of Consulting and Clinical Psychology, 62,* 228–242.

Brandtstadter, J., & Rothermund, K. (1994). Self-percepts of control in middle and later adulthood: Buffering losses by rescaling goals. *Psychology and Aging, 9,* 265–273.

Bridges, J.S., & Orza, A.M. (1992). The effects of employment role and motive for employment on the perceptions of mothers. *Sex Roles, 27,* 331–343.

Bridges, J.S., & Orza, A.M. (1993). Effects of maternal employment–childrearing pattern on college students' perceptions of a mother and her child. *Psychology of Women Quarterly, 17,* 103–117.

Brockington, I.F., Martin, C., Brown, G.W., Goldberg, D., & Margison, F. (1990). Stress and puerperal psychosis. *British Journal of Psychiatry, 157,* 331–334.

Brody, E.M., Kleban, M.H., Hoffman, C., & Schoonover, C.B. (1988). Adult daughters and parent care: A comparison of one-, two- and three-generation households. *Home Health Care Services Quarterly, 9,* 19–45.

Brody, E.M., Litvin, S.J., Hoffman, C., & Kleban, M.H. (1992). Differential effects of daughters' marital status on their parent care experiences. *Gerontologist, 32,* 58–67.

Brody, E.M., Litvin, S.J., Hoffman, C., & Kleban, M.H. (1995). Marital status of caregiving daughters and co-residence with dependent parents. *Gerontologist, 35,* 75–85.

Bromberger, J.T., & Matthews, K.A. (1994). Employment status and depressive symptoms in middle-aged women: A longitudinal investigation. *American Journal of Public Health, 84,* 202–206.

Brooks-Gunn, J. (1986). Differentiating premenstrual symptoms and syndromes. *Psychosomatic Medicine, 48,* 385–387.

Brooks-Gunn, J., & Ruble, D.N. (1986). Men's and women's attitudes and beliefs about the menstrual cycle. *Sex Roles, 14,* 287–299.

Broom, D.H. (1995). Rethinking gender and drugs. *Drug and Alcohol Review, 14,* 411–415.

Brown, J.A., Cross, H.J., & Nelson, J.M. (1990). Sex-role identity and sex-role ideology in college women with bulimic behavior. *International Journal of Eating Disorders, 9,* 571–575.

Brown, L.S. (1995). New voices, new visions: Toward a lesbian/gay paradigm for psychology. In N.R. Goldberger & J. B. Veroff (eds), *The culture and psychology reader* (pp. 559–574). New York: New York University Press.

Brown, S., Lumley, J., Small, R., & Astbury, J. (1994). *Missing voices. The experience of motherhood.* Melbourne: Oxford University Press.

Brown, W.A. (1993). 'Menstrually related disorders: Points of consensus, debate, and disagreement': Commentary. *Neuropsychopharmacology, 9,* 23–24.

Browne, A. (1993). Violence against women by male partners: Prevalence, outcomes, and policy implications. *American Psychologist, 48,* 1077–1087.

Brownell, K.D. (1991). Dieting and the search for the perfect body: Where physiology and culture collide. *Behavior Therapy, 22,* 1–12.

Brownell, K.D., & Fairburn, C.G. (eds). (1995). *Eating disorders and obesity: A comprehensive handbook.* New York: Guilford Press.

Brownell, K.D., & Wadden, T.A. (1992). Etiology and treatment of obesity: Understanding a serious, prevalent, and refractory disorder. *Journal of Consulting and Clinical Psychology, 60,* 505–517.

Brownmiller, S. (1975). *Against our will: Men, women and rape.* London: Secker & Warburg.

Bruce, M.L., Kim, K., Leaf, P.J., & Jacobs, S. (1990). Depressive episodes and dysphoria resulting from conjugal bereavement in a prospective community sample. *American Journal of Psychiatry, 147,* 608–611.

Bruce, M.L., Seeman, T.E., Merrill, S.S., & Blazer, D.G. (1994). The impact of depressive symptomatology on physical disability: MacArthur studies of successful aging. *American Journal of Public Health, 84,* 1796–1799.

Bryan, J.W., & Freed, F.W. (1993). Abortion research: Attitudes, sexual behavior, and problems in a community college population. *Journal of Youth and Adolescence, 22,* 1–22.

Buckley, P., Freyne, A., & Walsh, N. (1991). Anorexia nervosa in males. *Irish Journal of Psychological Medicine, 8,* 15–18.

Burgard, D., & Lyons, P. (1994). Alternatives in obesity treatment: Focusing on health for fat women. In P. Fallon, M.A. Katzman & S.C. Wooley (eds), *Feminist perspectives on eating disorders* (pp. 212–230). New York: Guilford Press.

Burns, J. (1992). The psychology of lesbian health care. In P. Nicolson & J. Ussher (eds), *The psychology of women's health and health care* (pp. 225–248). Basingstoke, UK: Macmillan.

Burns, L.H. (1995). An overview of sexual dysfunction in the infertile couple. *Journal of Family Psychotherapy, 6,* 25–46.

Burrage, J., & Schomer, H. (1993). The premenstrual syndrome: Perceived stress and coping efficacy. *South African Journal of Psychology, 23,* 111–115.

Busch, C.M., Zonderman, A.B., & Costa, P.T. (1994). Menopausal transition and psychological distress in a nationally representative sample: Is menopause associated with psychological distress? *Journal of Aging and Health, 6,* 209–228.

Butler, R.R., & Koraleski, S. (1990). Infertility: A crisis with no resolution. *Journal of Mental Health Counseling, 12,* 151–163.

Butt, D.S., & Beiser, M. (1987). Successful aging: A theme for international psychology. *Psychology and Aging, 2,* 87–94.

Cahir, N., & Morris, R.D. (1991). The psychology student stress questionnaire. *Journal of Clinical Psychology, 47,* 414–417.

Callan, V.J. (1986). The impact of the first birth: Married and single women preferring childlessness, one child, or two children. *Journal of Marriage and the Family, 48,* 261- 269.

Callan, V. J. (1987). The personal and marital adjustment of mothers and of voluntarily and involuntarily childless wives. *Journal of Marriage and the Family, 49,* 847–856.

Callan, V.J., & Hennessey, J.F. (1989). Psychological adjustment to infertility: A unique comparison of two groups of infertile women, mothers and women childless by choice. *Journal of Reproductive and Infant Psychology, 7,* 105–112.

Cameron, R., Redman, S., Burrow, S., & Young, B. (1995). Comparison of career patterns of male and female graduates of one Australian medical school. *Teaching and Learning in Medicine, 7,* 218–224.

Campbell, E. (1983). Becoming voluntarily childless: An exploratory study in a Scottish city. *Social Biology, 30,* 307–317.

Campion, M.J. (1995). *Who's fit to be a parent?* London: Routledge.

Canadian Study of Health and Aging. (1994). Patterns of caring for people with dementia in Canada. *Canadian Journal on Aging, 13*, 470–487.

Cantor, M.H. (1991). Family and community: Changing roles in an aging society. *Gerontology, 31*, 337–346.

Caplan, P.J., & Hall-McCorquodale, I. (1985). The scapegoating of mothers: A call for change. *American Journal of Orthopsychiatry, 55*, 610–613.

Caplan, P.J., McCurdy-Myers, J., & Gans, M. (1992). Should 'premenstrual syndrome' be called a psychiatric abnormality? *Feminism and Psychology, 2*, 27–44.

Caradoc-Davies, T.H., & Harvey, J.M. (1995). Do 'social relief' admissions have any effect on patients or their care-givers? *Disability and Rehabilitation, 17*, 247–251.

Carlat, D.J., & Camargo, C.A. (1991). Review of bulimia nervosa in males. *American Journal of Psychiatry, 148*, 831–843.

Carolan, M.T. (1994). Beyond deficiency: Broadening the view of menopause. *Journal of Applied Gerontology, 13*, 193–205.

Carrigan, T., Connell, R., & Lee, J. (1985). Toward a new sociology of masculinity. *Theory and Society, 14*, 551–604.

Carroll, D., Bennett, P., & Davey Smith, G. (1993). Socio-economic health inequalities: Their origins and implications. *Psychology and Health, 8*, 295–316.

Caserta, M.S., & Lund, D.A. (1992). Bereavement stress and coping among older adults: Expectations versus the actual experience. *Omega Journal of Death and Dying, 25*, 33–45.

Cash, T.F., & Henry, P.E. (1995). Women's body images: The results of a national survey in the USA. *Sex Roles, 33*, 19–28.

Caspi, A., & Elder, G.H. (1986). Life satisfaction in old age: Linking social psychology and history. *Psychology and Aging, 1*, 18–26.

Cassidy, C.M. (1991). The good body: When big is better. *Medical Anthropology, 13*, 181–213.

Cattanach, L., & Tebes, J.K. (1991). The nature of elder impairment and its impact on family caregivers' health and psychosocial functioning. *Gerontologist, 31*, 246–255.

Cauley, J.A., Seeley, D.G., Ensrud, K., Ettinger, B., Black, D., & Cummings, S.R. (1995). Estrogen replacement therapy and fractures in older women. *Annals of Internal Medicine, 122*, 9–16.

Cecil, R. (1994). 'I wouldn't have minded a wee one running about': Miscarriage and the family. *Social Science and Medicine, 38*, 1415–1422.

Centers for Disease Control and Prevention (1995a). Abortion surveillance: Preliminary data – United States, 1992. *Journal of the American Medical Association, 273*, 371.

Centers for Disease Control and Prevention (1995b). Differences in maternal mortality among black and white women – United States, 1990. *Journal of the American Medical Association, 273*, 370–371.

Chan, C.S. (1987). Asian lesbians: Psychological issues in the 'coming out' process. *Asian American Psychological Association Journal, 12*, 16–18.

Chan, Y.F., O'Hoy, K.M., Wong, A., & So, W.K. (1989). Psychosocial evaluation in an IVF IFT program in Hong Kong. *Journal of Reproductive and Infant Psychology, 7*, 67-77.

Chandra, P.S., & Chaturvedi, S.K. (1989). Cultural variations of premenstrual experience. *International Journal of Social Psychiatry, 35,* 343–349.

Chang, C.F., & White-Means, S.I. (1991). The men who care: An analysis of male primary caregivers who care for frail elderly at home. *Journal of Applied Gerontology, 10,* 343–358.

Chaturvedi, S.K., & Chandra, P.S. (1990). Stress-protective functions of positive experiences during the premenstrual period. *Stress Medicine, 6,* 53–55.

Chernin, K. (1986). *Women, eating and identity.* London: Virago.

Chesney, M.A., & Ozer, E.M. (1995). Women and health: In search of a paradigm. *Women's Health: Research on Gender, Behavior, and Policy, 1,* 3–26.

Choi, N.G. (1994). Patterns and determinants of social service utilization: Comparison of the childless elderly and elderly parents living with or apart from their children. *Gerontologist, 34,* 353–362.

Choi, P.Y.L., & Salmon, P. (1995). How do women cope with menstrual cycle changes? *British Journal of Clinical Psychology, 34,* 139–151.

Choquet, M., & Manfredi, R. (1992). Sexual intercourse, contraception, and risk-taking behavior among unselected French adolescents aged 11–20 years. *Journal of Adolescent Health, 13,* 623–630.

Chrisler, J.C., Johnston, I.K., Champagne, N.M., & Preston, K.E. (1994). Menstrual joy: The construct and its consequences. *Psychology of Women Quarterly, 18,* 375–387.

Chrisler, J.C., & Levy, K.B. (1990). The media construct a menstrual monster: A content analysis of PMS articles in the popular press. *Women and Health, 16,* 89–104.

Christensen, A.P., Board, B.J., & Oei, T.P. (1992). A psychosocial profile of women with premenstrual dysphoria. *Journal of Affective Disorders, 25,* 251–259.

Christiansen, C., & Riis, B.J. (1990). 17-Beta-estradiol and continuous norethisterone: a unique treatment for established osteoporosis in elderly women. *Journal of Clinical Endocrinology and Metabolism, 71,* 836–841.

Clare, A.W., & Tyrrell, J. (1994). Psychiatric aspects of abortion. *Irish Journal of Psychological Medicine, 11,* 92–98.

Clarke, A.E., & Ruble, D.N. (1978). Young adolescents' beliefs concerning menstruation. *Child Development, 49,* 231–234.

Clarke, C.J., & Neidert, L.J. (1992). Living arrangements of the elderly: An examination of differences according to ancestry and generation. *Gerontologist, 32,* 796–804.

Clayton, P.J. (1990). Bereavement and depression. *Journal of Clinical Psychiatry, 51,* 34–40.

Clulow, C. (1995). Who cares? Implications of caring responsibilities for couples and families. *Sexual and Marital Therapy, 10,* 63–68.

Cogan, J.C., Bhalla, S.K., Sefa-Dedeh, A., & Rothblum, E.D. (1996). A comparison study of United States and African students on perceptions of obesity and thinness. *Journal of Cross-Cultural Psychology, 27,* 98–113.

Cohan, C.L., Dunkel-Schetter, C., & Lydon, J. (1993). Pregnancy decision making: Predictors of early stress and adjustment. *Psychology of Women Quarterly, 17,* 223–239.

Cohen, C.A., Gold, D.P., Shulman, K.I., & Zucchero, C.A. (1994). Positive aspects in caregiving: An overlooked variable in research. *Canadian Journal on Aging, 11,* 378–391.

Cohn, L.D., & Adler, N.E. (1992). Female and male perceptions of ideal body shapes. *Psychology of Women Quarterly, 16,* 69–79.

Colditz, G.A., Hankinson, S.E., Hunter, D.J., Willett, W.C., Manson, J.E., Stampfer, M.J., Hennekens, C., Rosner, B., & Speizer, F.E. (1995). The use of estrogens and progestins and the risk of breast cancer in postmenopausal women. *New England Journal of Medicine, 332,* 1589–1593.

Cole, E., & Rothblum, E. (1990). Commentary on 'sexuality and the midlife woman'. *Psychology of Women Quarterly, 14,* 509–512.

Collins, C., & Ogle, K. (1994). Patterns of predeath service use by dementia patients with a family caregiver. *Journal of the American Geriatrics Society, 42,* 719–722.

Collins, N.L., Dunkel-Schetter, C., Lobel, M., & Scrimshaw, S.C. (1993). Social support in pregnancy: Psychosocial correlates of birth outcomes and post-partum depression. *Journal of Personality and Social Psychology, 65,* 1243–1258.

Coltrane, S. (1990). Birth timing and the division of labor in dual-earner families: Exploratory findings and suggestions for future research. *Journal of Family Issues, 11,* 157–181.

Coney, S. (1993). *The menopause industry.* Melbourne, Australia: Spinifex Press.

Congleton, G.K., & Calhoun, L.G. (1993). Post-abortion perceptions: A comparison of self-identified distressed and non-distressed populations. *International Journal of Social Psychiatry, 39,* 255–265.

Connidis, I.A., & McMullin, J.A. (1993). To have or have not: Parent status and the subjective well-being of older men and women. *Gerontologist, 33,* 630–636.

Connolly, K.J., Edelmann, R.J., Cooke, I.D., & Robson, J. (1992). The impact of infertility on psychological functioning. *Journal of Psychosomatic Research, 36,* 459–468.

Connors, M.E., & Morse, W. (1993). Sexual abuse and eating disorders: A review. *International Journal of Eating Disorders, 13,* 1–11.

Conway, S.W., Hayslip, B., & Tandy, R.E. (1991). Similarity of perceptions of bereavement experiences between widows and professionals. *Omega Journal of Death and Dying, 23,* 37–51.

Cook, R., Parsons, J., Mason, B., & Golombok, S. (1989). Emotional, marital and sexual functioning in patients embarking upon IVF and AID treatment for infertility. *Journal of Reproductive and Infant Psychology, 7,* 87–93.

Cooney, T.M., Pedersen, F.A., Indelicato, S., & Palkovitz, R. (1993). Timing of fatherhood: Is 'on-time' optimal? *Journal of Marriage and the Family, 55,* 205-215.

Corney, R., & Stanton, R. (1991). A survey of 658 women who report symptoms of PMS. *Journal of Psychosomatic Research, 35,* 471–482.

Cosford, P.A., & Arnold, E. (1992). Eating disorders in later life: A review. *International Journal of Geriatric Psychiatry, 7,* 491–498.

Cott, N. (1977). *The bonds of womanhood: Women's sphere in New England, 1780–1835.* New Haven, CT: Yale University Press.

Cowan, C.P., & Cowan, P.A. (1988). Who does what when partners become parents: Implications for men, women, and marriage. *Marriage and Family Review, 12,* 105–131.

Cox, J.L. (1988). Childbirth as a life event: Sociocultural aspects of postnatal depression. *Acta Psychiatrica Scandinavica, 78,* 75–83.

Cox, J.L., Holden, J.M., & Sagovsky, R. (1987). Detection of postnatal depression: Development of the 10-item Edinburgh Postnatal Depression Scale. *British Journal of Psychiatry, 150,* 782–786.

Cox, J.L., Murray, D., & Chapman, G. (1993). A controlled study of the onset, duration and prevalence of postnatal depression. *British Journal of Psychiatry, 163,* 27–31.

Cozzarelli, C. (1993). Personality and self-efficacy as predictors of coping with abortion. *Journal of Personality and Social Psychology, 65,* 1224–1236.

Craig, P.L., Swinburn, B.A., Matenga-Smith, T., Matangi, H., & Vaughan, G. (1996). Do Polynesians still believe that big is beautiful? Comparison of body size perceptions and preferences of Cook Islands Maori and Australians. *New Zealand Medical Journal, 109,* 200–203.

Creatsas, G.K. (1993). Sexuality: Sexual activity and contraception during adolescence. *Current Opinion in Obstetrics and Gynaecology, 5,* 774–783.

Crimmins, E.M., & Ingegneri, D.G. (1990). Interaction and living arrangements of older parents and their children: Past trends, present determinants, future implications. *Research on Aging, 12,* 3–35.

Crisp, A.H. (1980). *Anorexia nervosa: Let me be.* New York: Grune & Stratton.

Crosby, F.J., & Jaskar, K.L. (1993). Women and men at home and at work: Realities and illusions. In S. Oskamp & M. Costanzo (eds), *Gender issues in contemporary society. Claremont Symposium on Applied Social Psychology, Vol. 6* (pp. 143–171). Newbury Park, CA: Sage.

Crouter, A., & Manke, B. (1994). The changing American workplace: Implications for individuals and families. *Family Relations, 43,* 117–224.

Dagg, P.K. (1991). The psychological sequelae of therapeutic abortion – denied and completed. *American Journal of Psychiatry, 148,* 578–585.

Daiewicz, S.C. (1995). When parents can't live alone: Choosing multi-generational households. *Journal of Gerontological Social Work, 23(3–4),* 47–63.

Dalley, G. (1988). *Ideologies of caring: Rethinking community and collectivism.* London: Macmillan.

Dalton, K. (1969). *The menstrual cycle.* New York: Pantheon.

Dalton, K. (1984). *The premenstrual syndrome and progesterone therapy.* London: Heinemann.

Daly, E., Gray, A., Barlow, D., McPherson, K., Roche, M., & Vessey, M. (1993). Measuring the impact of menopausal symptoms on quality of life. *British Medical Journal, 307,* 836–840.

Daniluk, J.C. (1991). Strategies for counseling infertile couples. *Journal of Counseling and Development, 69,* 317–320.

D'Augelli, A.R. (1996). Lesbian, gay, and bisexual development during adolescence and young adulthood. In R.P. Cabaj & T.S. Stein (eds), *Textbook of homosexuality and mental health* (pp. 267–288). Washington, DC: American Psychiatric Press.

D'Augelli, A.R., & Hershberger, S.L. (1993). Lesbian, gay, and bisexual youth in community settings: Personal challenges and mental health problems. *American Journal of Community Psychology, 21,* 421–448.

D'Augelli, A.R., & Patterson, C.J. (eds). (1995). *Lesbian, gay, and bisexual identities over the lifespan: Psychological perspectives.* New York: Oxford University Press.

David, H.P. (1992a). Abortion in Europe, 1920–91: A public health perspective. *Studies in Family Planning, 23,* 1–22.

David, H.P. (1992b). Born unwanted: Long-term developmental effects of denied abortion. *Journal of Social Issues, 48,* 163–181.

David, H.P. (1994). Reproductive rights and reproductive behavior: Clash or convergence of private values and public policies? *American Psychologist, 49,* 343–349.

David, H.P., Dytrych, Z., Matějček, Z., & Schüller, V. (1988). *Born unwanted: Developmental effects of denied abortion.* New York: Springer.

Davies, B., & Welch, D. (1986). Motherhood and feminism: Are they compatible? The ambivalence of mothering. *Australian and New Zealand Journal of Sociology, 22,* 411–426.

Davies, L., & Rains, P. (1995). Single mothers by choice? *Families in Society, 76,* 543–550.

Davis, C., & Yager, J. (1992). Transcultural aspects of eating disorders: A critical literature review. *Culture, Medicine and Psychiatry, 16,* 377–394.

Deevey, S. (1990). Older lesbian women: An invisible minority. *Journal of Gerontological Nursing, 16,* 35–37.

Delaney, J., Lupton, M.J., & Toth, E. (1988). *The curse: A cultural history of menstruation.* Urbana, IL: University of Illinois Press.

De Leon, C.F.M., Kasl, S.V., & Jacobs, S. (1994). A prospective study of widowhood and changes in symptoms of depression in a community sample of the elderly. *Psychological Medicine, 24,* 613–624.

De Leon, C.F.M., Rapp, S.S., & Kasl, S.V. (1994). Financial strain and symptoms of depression in a community sample of elderly men and women: A longitudinal study. *Journal of Aging and Health, 6,* 448–468.

Demyttenaere, K., Lenaerts, H., Nijs, P., & Van Assche, F.A. (1995). Individual coping style and psychological attitudes during pregnancy predict depression levels during pregnancy and during postpartum. *Acta Psychiatrica Scandinavica, 91,* 95–102.

Denmark, F., Russo, N.F., Frieze, I.H., & Sechzer, J.A. (1988). Guidelines for avoiding sexism in psychological research. *American Psychologist, 43,* 582–585.

Dennerstein, L., Brown, J.B., Gotts, G., Morse, C.A., Farley, T.M.M., & Pinol, A. (1993). Menstrual cycle hormonal profiles of women with and without premenstrual syndrome. *Journal of Psychosomatic Obstetrics and Gynecology, 14,* 259–268.

Dennerstein, L., Smith, A., Morse, C., Burger, H., Green, A., Hopper, J. & Ryan, M. (1993). Menopausal symptoms in Australian women. *Medical Journal of Australia, 159,* 232–236.

Depner, C.E., & Ingersoll-Dayton, B. (1985). Conjugal social support: Patterns in later life. *Journal of Gerontology, 40,* 761–766.

Depner, C.E., & Ingersoll-Dayton, B. (1988). Supportive relationships in later life. *Psychology and Aging, 3,* 348–357.

De Souza, R.P., de Almeida, A.B., Wagner, M.B., Zimmerman, I.I., de Almeida, S.B., & Caleffi, A. (1993). A study of the sexual behavior of teenagers in South Brazil. *Journal of Adolescent Health, 14,* 336–339.

Deutsch, F.M., Lussier, J.B., & Servis, L.J. (1993). Husbands at home: Predictors of paternal participation in childcare and housework. *Journal of Personality and Social Psychology, 65,* 1154–1166.

Deutsch, H. (1947). *The psychology of women. Volume 2: Motherhood.* London: Love & Malcolmson.

Dickerson, B.J. (ed.). (1995). *African American single mothers: Understanding their lives and families*. Thousand Oaks, CA: Sage.

Dickson, G.L. (1990). A feminist poststructuralist analysis of the knowledge of menopause. *Advances in Nursing Science, 12(3)*, 15–31.

Dion, K.K. (1995). Delayed parenthood and women's expectations about the transition to parenthood. *International Journal of Behavioral Development, 18*, 315–333.

Dippel, R.L. (1991). The caregivers. In R.L. Dippel & J.T. Hutton (eds), *Caring for the Alzheimer patient: A practical guide*, 2nd edn (pp. 17–27). Buffalo, NY: Prometheus Books.

Dixon-Mueller, R. (1990). Abortion policy and women's health in developing countries. *International Journal of Health Services, 20*, 297–314.

Dolan, B. (1991). Cross-cultural aspects of anorexia nervosa and bulimia: A review. *International Journal of Eating Disorders, 10*, 67–79.

Dolan, B., Evans, C., & Norton, K. (1994). Disordered eating behavior and attitudes in female and male patients with personality disorders. *Journal of Personality Disorders, 8*, 17–27.

Domingo, L.J., & Asis, M.M.B. (1995). Living arrangements and the flow of support between generations in the Philippines. *Journal of Cross-Cultural Gerontology, 10*, 21–51.

Doress-Worters, P.B. (1994). Adding elder care to women's multiple roles: A critical review of the caregiver stress and multiple roles literatures. *Sex Roles, 31*, 597–616.

Dowlatshahi, D., & Paykel, E.S. (1990). Life events and social stress in puerperal psychoses: Absence of effect. *Psychological Medicine, 20*, 655–662.

Downey, J., & McKinney, M. (1992). The psychiatric status of women presenting for infertility evaluation. *American Journal of Orthopsychiatry, 62*, 196–205.

Doyal, L. (1995). *What makes women sick*. Basingstoke, UK: Macmillan.

Draper, B.M., Poulos, C.J., Cole, A.M., Poulos, R.G., & Ehrlich, F. (1992). A comparison of caregivers for elderly stroke and dementia victims. *Journal of the American Geriatrics Society, 40*, 896–901.

Dunnewold, A.L., & Sanford, D. (1992). Postpartum depression: A spectrum of treatment options. In L. van de Creek, S. Knapp & T.L. Jackson (eds), *Innovations in clinical practice: A sourcebook* (pp. 39–51). Sarasota, FL: Professional Resource Press.

Duxbury, L., & Higgins, C. (1994). Interference between work and family: A status report on dual-career and dual-earner mothers and fathers. *Employee Assistance Quarterly, 9*, 55–80.

Dworkin, S.H. (1988). Not in man's image: Lesbians and the cultural oppression of body image. *Women and Therapy, 8*, 27–39.

Dwyer, J.W., & Coward, R.T. (1991). A multivariate comparison of the involvement of adult sons versus daughters in the care of impaired parents. *Journals of Gerontology, 46*, S259-S269.

Eckerd, M.B., Hurt, S.W., & Severino, S.K. (1989). Late luteal phase dysphoric disorder: Relationship to personality disorders. *Journal of Personality Disorders, 3*, 338–344.

Edelmann, R.J., Connolly, K.J., & Bartlett, H. (1994). Coping strategies and psychological adjustment of couples presenting for IVF. *Journal of Psychosomatic Research, 8*, 355–364.

Edelman, R.J., & Golombok, S. (1989). Stress and reproductive failure. *Journal of Reproductive and Infant Psychology, 7,* 79–86.

Einhorn, L., & Polgar, M. (1994). HIV-risk behavior among lesbians and bisexual women. *AIDS Education and Prevention, 6,* 514–523.

Eliason, M., Donelan, C., & Randall, C. (1992). Lesbian stereotypes. *Health Care for Women International, 13,* 131–144.

Elliott, B.J., & Huppert, F.A. (1991). In sickness and in health: Associations between physical and mental well-being, employment and parental status in a British nationwide sample of married women. *Psychological Medicine, 21,* 515–524.

Ellis, J.B. (1994). Children's sex-role development: Implications for working mothers. *Social Behaviour and Personality, 22,* 131–136.

Endicott, J. (1993). The menstrual cycle and mood disorders. *Journal of Affective Disorders, 29,* 193–200.

England, M. (1995). Crisis and the filial caregiving situation of African American adult offspring. *Issues in Mental Health Nursing, 16,* 143–163.

English, R., & Bennett, S. (1990). Iron status of Australian schoolchildren. *Medical Journal of Australia, 153,* 502–503.

Ensrud, K.E., Nevitt, M.C., Yunis, C., Cauley, J.A., Seeley, D.G., Fox, K.M., & Cummings, S.R. (1994). Correlates of impaired function in older women. *Journal of the American Geriatrics Society, 42,* 481–489.

Epstein, F.H. (1989). The relationship of lifestyle to international trends in coronary heart disease. *International Journal of Epidemiology, 18,* S203–S209.

Everson, S.A., Matthews, K.A., Guzick, D.S., Wing, R.R., & Kuller, L.H. (1995). Effects of surgical menopause on psychological characteristics and lipid levels: The Healthy Women Study. *Health Psychology, 14,* 435–443.

Eyer, D.E. (1994). Mother–infant bonding: A scientific fiction. *Human Nature, 5,* 69–94.

Facione, N.C. (1994). Role overload and health: The married mother in the waged labor force. *Health Care for Women International, 15,* 157–167.

Fairburn, C.G. (1991). The heterogeneity of bulimia nervosa and its implications for treatment. *Journal of Psychosomatic Research, 35* (Suppl. 1), 3–9.

Fallon, B.J. (1996). Work-family conflict: How permeable are the boundaries for Australian workers? Paper presented at the XXVI International Congress of the International Union of Psychological Science, Montreal, August.

Fallon, B.J. (1997). The balance between paid work and home responsibilities: Personal problem or corporate concern? *Australian Psychologist, 32,* 1–9.

Falloon, I.R.H., Graham-Hole, V., & Woodroffe, R. (1993). Stress and health of informal carers of people with chronic mental disorders. *Journal of Mental Health, 2,* 165–173.

Favazza, A.R., DeRosear, L., & Conterio, K. (1989). Self-mutilation and eating disorders. *Suicide and Life Threatening Behavior, 19,* 352–361.

Feinberg, L.F., & Kelly, K.A. (1995). A well-deserved break: Respite programs offered by California's statewide system of caregiver resource centers. *Gerontologist, 35,* 701–705.

Feinson, M.C. (1987). Mental health and aging: Are there gender differences? *Gerontologist, 27,* 703–711.

Feinson, M.C. (1991). Reexamining some common beliefs about mental health and aging. In B.B. Hess & E.W. Markson (eds), *Growing old in America*, 4th edn (pp. 125–135). New Brunswick, NJ: Transaction Publishers.

Feldman, S.S., & Nash, S.C. (1984). The transition from expectancy to parenthood: Impact of the firstborn child on men and women. *Sex Roles, 11*, 61–78.

Fennell, G., Phillipson, C., & Evers, H. (1988). *The sociology of old age*. Milton Keynes, UK: Open University Press.

Ferguson, K.J., Hoegh, C., & Johnson, S. (1989). Estrogen replacement therapy: A survey of women's knowledge and attitudes. *Archives of Internal Medicine, 149*, 133–136.

Fichter, M.M., Meller, I., Schroppel, H., & Steinkirchner, R. (1995). Dementia and cognitive impairment in the oldest old in the community: Prevalence and comorbidity. *British Journal of Psychiatry, 166*, 621–629.

Field, D., & Minkler, M. (1993). The importance of family in advanced old age: The family is 'forever'. In P.A. Cowan, D.A. Hansen, A. Skolnick & G.E. Swanson (eds), *Family, self, and society: Toward a new agenda for family research* (pp. 331–351). Hillsdale, NJ: Lawrence Erlbaum Associates.

Finch, J., & Groves, D. (eds). (1983). *A labour of love: Women, work and caring*. London: Routledge & Kegan Paul.

Finley, N.J. (1989). Theories of family labor as applied to gender differences in caregiving for elderly parents. *Journal of Marriage and the Family, 51*, 79–86.

Fischer, L.R. (1988). The influence of kin on the transition to parenthood. *Marriage and Family Review, 12*, 201–219.

Fisher, M. (1994). Man-made care: Community care and older male carers. *British Journal of Social Work, 24*, 659–680.

Fitzgerald, M.H. (1990). The interplay of culture and symptoms: Menstrual symptoms among Samoans. *Medical Anthropology, 12*, 145–167.

Florack, E.I., Zielhuis, G.A., & Rolland, R. (1994). Cigarette smoking, alcohol consumption, and caffeine intake and fecundability. *Preventive Medicine, 23*, 175–180.

Fodor, I.G., & Franks, V. (1990). Women in midlife and beyond: The new prime of life? *Psychology of Women Quarterly, 14*, 445–449.

Fombonne, E. (1995). Anorexia nervosa: No evidence of an increase. *British Journal of Psychiatry, 166*, 462–471.

Fontana, A.M., & Palfai, T.G. (1994). Psychosocial factors in premenstrual dysphoria: Stressors, appraisal, and coping processes. *Journal of Psychosomatic Research, 38*, 557–567.

Ford, J., & Sinclair, R. (1987). *Sixty years on: Women talk about old age*. London: Women's Press.

Forgays, D.K., & Forgays, D.G. (1993). Personal and environmental factors contributing to parenting stress among employed and nonemployed women. *European Journal of Personality, 7*, 107–118.

Forrest, J.D. (1994). Epidemiology of unintended pregnancy and contraceptive use. *American Journal of Obstetrics and Gynecology, 170*, 1485–1489.

Forrest, L., & Gilbert, M.S. (1992). Infertility: An unanticipated and prolonged life crisis. *Journal of Mental Health Counseling, 14*, 42–58.

Forsell, Y., Jorm, A.F., von Strauss, E., & Winblad, B. (1995). Prevalence and correlates of depression in a population of nonagenarians. *British Journal of Psychiatry, 167*, 61–64.

Forster, L.E., & Stoller, E.P. (1992). The impact of social support on mortality: A seven-year follow-up of older men and women. *Journal of Applied Gerontology, 11*, 173–186.

Fradkin, B., & Firestone, P. (1986). Premenstrual tension, expectancy, and mother–child relations. *Journal of Behavioral Medicine, 9*, 245–259.

France, K., Lee, C., & Schofield, M. (1996). Hormone replacement therapy: Knowledge, attitudes and well-being among mid-aged Australian women. *International Journal of Behavioral Medicine, 3*, 202–220.

Freedman, R.J. (1984). Reflections on beauty as it relates to health in adolescent females. *Women and Health, 9* (2–3), 29–45.

Freeman, E.K., Rickels, K., Sondheimer, S., & Polansky, M. (1990). Ineffectiveness of progesterone suppository treatment for premenstrual syndrome. *Journal of the American Medical Association, 264*, 349–353.

Freeman, H.R. (1987). Structure and content of gender stereotypes: Effects of somatic appearance and trait information. *Psychology of Women Quarterly, 11*, 59–68.

Freer, C. (1988). Old myths: Frequent misconceptions about the elderly. In N. Wells & C. Freer (eds), *The ageing population: Burden or challenge?* (pp. 3–15). Basingstoke, UK: Macmillan.

French, S.A., & Jeffrey, R.W. (1995). Weight concerns and smoking: A literature review. *Annals of Behavioral Medicine, 17*, 234–244.

Frone, M.R., Russell, M., & Cooper, M.L. (1992). Prevalence of work-family conflict: Are work and family boundaries asymmetrically permeable? Journal of Organizational Behavior, *13*, 723–729.

Fry, C.L. (1996). Age, aging, and culture. In R.H. Binstock, L.K. George, V.W. Marshall, G.C. Myers, & J.H. Schulz (eds), *Handbook of aging and the social sciences*, 4th edn (pp. 117–136). San Diego, CA: Academic Press.

Fuller-Jonap, F., & Haley, W.E. (1995). Mental and physical health of male caregivers of a spouse with Alzheimer's disease. *Journal of Aging and Health, 7*, 99–118.

Fultz, N.H., & Herzog, A.R. (1991). Gender differences in affiliation and instrumentality across adulthood. *Psychology and Aging, 6*, 579–586.

Funkhouser, S.W., & Moser, D.K. (1990). Is health care racist? *Advances in Nursing Science, 12*(2), 47–55.

Gabriel, A., & McAnarney, E.R. (1983). Parenthood in two subcultures: White, middle-class couples and Black, low-income adolescents in Rochester, New York. *Adolescence, 18*, 595–608.

Galambos, N.L., & Maggs, J.L. (1990). Putting mothers' work-related stress in perspective: Mothers and adolescents in dual-earner families. *Journal of Early Adolescence, 10*, 313–328.

Gallagher-Thompson, D., & DeVries, H.M. (1994). 'Coping with frustration' classes: Development and preliminary outcomes with women who care for relatives with dementia. *Gerontologist, 34*, 548–552.

Gallagher-Thompson, D., & Steffen, A.M. (1994). Comparative effects of cognitive-behavioral and brief psychodynamic psychotherapies for depressed family caregivers. *Journal of Consulting and Clinical Psychology, 62*, 543–549.

Gallant, S.J., & Hamilton, J.A. (1992). 'Using daily ratings to confirm premenstrual syndrome/late luteal phase dysphoric disorder: I. and II.': Response. *Psychosomatic Medicine, 54*, 725–728.

Gallant, S.J., Coons, H.L., & Morokoff, P.J. (1994). Psychology and women's health: Some reflections and future directions. In V.J. Adesso, D.M. Reddy & R. Fleming (eds), *Psychological perspectives on women's health* (pp. 315–346). Washington, DC: Taylor & Francis.

Gallant, S.J., Popiel, D.A., Hoffman, D.M., Chakraborty, P.K., & Hamilton, J.A. (1992). Using daily ratings to confirm premenstrual syndrome/late luteal phase dysphoric disorder: I. Effects of demand characteristics and expectations. *Psychosomatic Medicine, 54,* 149–166.

Gannon, L. (1988). The potential role of exercise in the alleviation of menstrual disorders and menopausal symptoms: A theoretical synthesis of recent research. *Women and Health, 14,* 105–127.

Gannon, L. (1993). Menopausal symptoms as consequences of dysrhythmia. *Journal of Behavioral Medicine, 16,* 387–401.

Gannon, L., & Ekstrom, B. (1993). Attitudes toward menopause: The influence of sociocultural paradigms. *Psychology of Women Quarterly, 17,* 275–288.

Gannon, L., Luchetta, T., Pardie, L., & Rhodes, K. (1989). Perimenstrual symptoms: Relationships with chronic stress and selected lifestyle variables. *Behavioral Medicine, 15,* 149–159.

Garnets, L.D., & D'Augelli, A.R. (1994). Empowering lesbian and gay communities: A call for collaboration with community psychology. *American Journal of Community Psychology, 22,* 447–470.

Garnets, L.D., Herek, G.M., & Levy, B. (1990). Violence and victimization of lesbians and gay men: Mental health consequences. *Journal of Interpersonal Violence, 5,* 366–383.

Garton, M., Reid, D., & Rennie, E. (1995). The climacteric, osteoporosis and hormone replacement: Views of women aged 45–49. *Maturitas, 21,* 7–15.

Gath, D., Osborn, M., Bungay, G., Iles, S., Day, A., Bond, A., & Passingham, C. (1987). Psychiatric disorder and gynaecological symptoms in middle-aged women: A community survey. *British Medical Journal, 294,* 213–218.

Gatz, M., Harris, J.R., & Turk-Charles, S. (1995). The meaning of health for older women. In A.L. Stanton & S.J. Gallant (eds), *The psychology of women's health: Progress and challenges in research and application* (pp. 491–529). Washington, DC: American Psychological Association.

Gavey, N. (1989). Feminist poststructuralism and discourse analysis: Contributions to feminist psychology. *Psychology of Women Quarterly, 13,* 459–475.

Gelfand, D.E., & McCallum, J. (1994). Immigration, the family, and female caregivers in Australia. *Journal of Gerontological Social Work, 22*(3–4), 41–59.

Gentry, S.E. (1992). Caring for lesbians in a homophobic society. *Health Care for Women International, 13,* 173–180.

George, L.K., Fillenbaum, G.G., & Palmore, E.B. (1984). Sex differences in the antecedents and consequences of retirement. *Journal of Gerontology, 39,* 364–371.

George, L.K., & Gwyther, L.P. (1986). Caregiver well-being: A multidimensional examination of family caregivers of demented adults. *Gerontologist, 26,* 253–259.

Gergen, M.M. (1990). Finished at 40: Women's development within the patriarchy. *Psychology of Women Quarterly, 14,* 471–493.

Gerson, M-J., Posner, J-A., & Morris, A.M. (1991). The value of having children as an aspect of adult development. *Journal of Genetic Psychology, 152,* 327–339.

Giannini, A.J., Melemis, S.M., Martin, D.M., & Folts, D.J. (1994). Symptoms of premenstrual syndrome as a function of beta-endorphin: Two subtypes. *Progress in Neuro-Psychopharmacology and Biological Psychiatry, 18,* 321–327.

Gifford, S.M. (1994). The change of life, the sorrow of life: Menopause, bad blood and cancer among Italian-Australian working class women. *Culture, Medicine and Psychiatry, 18,* 299–319.

Gilbar, O., & Dagan, A. (1995). Coping with loss: Differences between widows and widowers of deceased cancer patients. *Omega Journal of Death and Dying, 31,* 207–220.

Gill, S., & Singh, G.M. (1991). Widowhood: Perceptions and coping strategies. *Indian Journal of Behaviour, 15,* 14–19.

Gimenez, M.E. (1989). The feminization of poverty: Myth or reality? *International Journal of Health Services, 19,* 45–61.

Gjerdingen, D.K., & Chaloner, K. (1994). Mothers' experience with household roles and social support during the first postpartum year. *Women and Health, 21,* 57–74.

Glass, J., & Fujimoto, T. (1994). Housework, paid work, and depression among husbands and wives. *Journal of Health and Social Behavior, 35,* 179–191.

Glover, V. (1992). Do biochemical factors play a part in postnatal depression? *Progress in Neuro-Psychopharmacology and Biological Psychiatry, 16,* 605–615.

Glover, V., Liddle, P., Tayler, A., Adams, D., & Sandler, M. (1994). Mild hypomania (the highs) can be a feature of the first postpartum week: Association with later depression. *British Journal of Psychiatry, 164,* 517–521.

Goddard, M.K. (1992). Hormone replacement therapy and breast cancer, endometrial cancer and cardiovascular disease: Risks and benefits. *British Journal of General Practice, 42,* 120–125.

Gold, D.P., Reis, M.F., Markiewicz, D., & Andres, D. (1995). When home caregiving ends: A longitudinal study of outcomes for caregivers of relatives with dementia. *Journal of the American Geriatrics Society, 43,* 10–16.

Goldbloom, D.S. (1993). Alcohol misuse and eating disorders: Aspects of an association. *Alcohol and Alcoholism, 28,* 375–381.

Golden, C. (1996). What's in a name? Sexual self-identification among women. In R.C. Savin-Williams & K.M. Cohen (eds), *The lives of lesbians, gays, and bisexuals: Children to adults* (pp. 229–249). Fort Worth, TX: Harcourt Brace.

Goldiger, B. (1987). Kollektivt foraldraskap [Collective parenthood]. *Psykisk Halsa, 28,* 147–153.

Gonsiorek, J.C. (1988). Mental health issues of gay and lesbian adolescents. *Journal of Adolescent Health Care, 9,* 114–122.

Gonyea, J.G. (1995). Middle age. In D. Levinson (ed.), *Encyclopedia of marriage and the family.* New York: Macmillan.

Gonyea, J.G., & Googins, B.K. (1992). Linking the worlds of work and family: Beyond the productivity trap. *Human Resource Management, 31,* 209–226.

Gordon, H.W., & Lee, P.A. (1993). No difference in cognitive performance between phases of the menstrual cycle. *Psychoneuroendocrinology, 18,* 521–531.

Gotlib, I.H., Whiffen, V.E., Mount, J.H., Milne, K., & Cordy, N.I. (1989). Prevalence rates and demographic characteristics associated with depression in pregnancy and the postpartum. *Journal of Consulting and Clinical Psychology, 57,* 269–274.

Gottlieb, L.N., & Mendelson, M.J. (1995). Mothers' moods and social support when a second child is born. *Maternal-Child Nursing Journal, 23,* 3–14.

Grbich, C.F. (1995). Male primary caregivers and domestic labour: Involvement or avoidance? *Journal of Family Studies, 1,* 114–129.

Greene, B. (1994a). Lesbian and gay sexual orientations: Implications for clinical training, practice, and research. In B. Greene & G.M. Herek (eds), *Lesbian and gay psychology: Theory, research and clinical applications, Volume 1* (pp. 1–24). Thousand Oaks, CA: Sage.

Greene, B. (1994b). Ethnic-minority lesbians and gay men: Mental health and treatment issues. *Journal of Consulting and Clinical Psychology, 62,* 243–251.

Greenglass, E.R. (1991). Burnout and gender: Theoretical and organizational implications. *Canadian Psychology, 32,* 562–574.

Greenglass, E.R., & Burke, R.J. (1988). Work and family precursors of burnout in teachers: Sex differences. *Sex Roles, 18,* 215–229.

Greenglass, E.R., Pantony, K.L., & Burke, R.J. (1988). A gender-role perspective on role conflict, work stress and social support. *Journal of Social Behavior and Personality, 3,* 317–328.

Greer, G. (1991). *The change.* London: Penguin.

Greil, A.L., Porter, K.L., & Leitko, T.A. (1989). Sex and intimacy among infertile couples. *Journal of Psychology and Human Sexuality, 2,* 117–138.

Grewal, R.P., & Urschel, J.D. (1994). Why women want children: A study during phases of parenthood. *Journal of Social Psychology, 134,* 453–455.

Grossman, F.K. (1988). Strain in the transition to parenthood. *Marriage and Family Review, 12,* 85–104.

Guberman, N., Maheu, P., & Maille, C. (1992). Women as family caregivers: Why do they care? *Gerontologist, 32,* 607–617.

Gunter, N.C., & Gunter, B.G. (1990). Domestic division of labor among working couples: Does androgyny make a difference? *Psychology of Women Quarterly, 14,* 355–370.

Guthrie, J.R., Smith, A.M.A., Dennerstein, L., & Morse, C. (1994). Physical activity and the menopause experience: A cross-sectional study. *Maturitas, 20,* 71–80.

Hackel, L.S., & Ruble, D.N. (1992). Changes in the marital relationship after the first baby is born: Predicting the impact of expectancy disconfirmation. *Journal of Personality and Social Psychology, 62,* 944–957.

Haines, C.J., Chung, T.K.H., & Leung, D.H.Y. (1994). A prospective study of the frequency of acute menopausal symptoms in Hong Kong Chinese women. *Maturitas, 18,* 175–181.

Haldeman, D.C. (1994). The practice and ethics of sexual orientation conversion therapy. *Journal of Consulting and Clinical Psychology, 62,* 221–227.

Hamilton, J.A. (1986). An overview of the clinical rationale for advancing gender-related psychopharmacology and drug abuse research. *National Institute on Drug Abuse Research Monograph Series, 65,* 14–20.

Hamilton, J.A., & Jensvold, M.F. (1995). Introduction: Feminist psychopharmacology. *Women and Therapy, 16,* 1–7.

Hammarback, S., Damber, J., & Backstrom, T. (1989). Relationship between symptom severity and hormone changes in women with premenstrual syndrome. *Journal of Clinical Endocrinology and Metabolism, 68,* 125–130.

Hammer, M., Berg, G., & Lindgren, R. (1990). Does physical exercise influence the frequency of postmenopausal hot flushes? *Acta Obstetricia et Gynaecologica Scandinavica, 69,* 407–412.

Hammond, C.B. (1989). Estrogen replacement therapy: What the future holds. *American Journal of Obstetrics and Gynecology, 161,* 1864–1868.

Hammond, N. (1988). Lesbian victims of relationship violence. *Women and Therapy, 8,* 89–105.

Hannah, J., & Quarter, J. (1992). Sharing household labour: 'Could you do the bedtime story while I do the dishes?' *Canadian Journal of Community Mental Health, 11,* 147–162.

Hansson, R.O., & Remondet, J.H. (1988). Old age and widowhood: Issues of personal control and independence. *Journal of Social Issues, 44,* 159–174.

Harding, J.J. (1989). Postpartum psychiatric disorders: A review. *Comprehensive Psychiatry, 30,* 109–112.

Harding, S. (1986). *The science question in feminism.* Milton Keynes, UK: Open University Press.

Harding, S. (1994). Thinking from the perspective of lesbian lives. In A.C. Herrmann & A.J. Stewart (eds), *Theorizing feminism: Parallel trends in the humanities and social sciences* (pp. 343–357). Boulder, CO: Westview Press.

Harlow, S.D., Goldberg, E.L., & Comstock, G.W. (1991). A longitudinal study of the prevalence of depressive symptomatology in elderly widowed and married women. *Archives of General Psychiatry, 48,* 1065–1068.

Harris, B. (1994). Biological and hormonal aspects of postpartum depressed mood: Working towards strategies for prophylaxis and treatment. *British Journal of Psychiatry, 164,* 288–292.

Harris, M.B., Begay, C., & Page, P. (1989). Activities, family relationships and feelings about aging in a multicultural elderly sample. *International Journal of Aging and Human Development, 29,* 103–117.

Harris, M.B., Walters, L.C., & Waschull, S. (1991). Gender and ethnic differences in obesity-related behaviors and attitudes in a college sample. *Journal of Applied Social Psychology, 21,* 1545–1566.

Harris, P.B., & Long, S.O. (1993). Daughter-in-law's burden: An exploratory study of caregiving in Japan. *Journal of Cross-Cultural Gerontology, 8,* 97–118.

Harris, R.B., Laws, A., Roddy, V.W., King, A., & Haskell, W.L. (1990). Are women using postmenopausal estrogens? A community survey. *American Journal of Public Health, 80,* 1266–1268.

Hashimoto, A. (1991). Living arrangements of the aged in seven developing countries: A preliminary analysis. *Journal of Cross-Cultural Gerontology, 6,* 359–381.

Hawkins, A.J., Christiansen, S.L., Sargent, K.P., & Hill, E.J. (1993). Rethinking fathers' involvement in child care: A developmental perspective. *Journal of Family Issues, 14,* 531–549.

Hawton, K., Gath, D., & Day, A. (1994). Sexual function in a community sample of middle-aged women with partners: Effects of age, marital, socioeconomic, psychiatric, gynecological, and menopausal factors. *Archives of Sexual Behavior, 23,* 375–395.

Heenan, C. (1996). Women, food and fat: Too many cooks in the kitchen? In E. Burman, C. Bewlay, B. Goldberg, C. Heenan, D. Marks, J. Marshall, K. Taylor,

R. Ullah & S. Warner (eds), *Challenging women: Psychology's exclusions, feminist possibilities* (pp. 19–35). Buckingham, UK: Open University Press.

Heeren, T.J., Lagaay, A.M., Hijmans, W., & Rooymans, H.G. (1991). Prevalence of dementia in the 'oldest old' of a Dutch community. *Journal of the American Geriatrics Society, 39,* 755–759.

Heffernan, K. (1994). Sexual orientation as a factor in risk for binge eating and bulimia nervosa: A review. *International Journal of Eating Disorders, 16,* 335–347.

Heikkinen, E., Waters, W., & Brzezinski, Z. (eds). (1993). *The elderly in eleven countries – a sociomedical survey* (Public health in Europe no. 21). Copenhagen: World Health Organization.

Heilbrun, A.B., & Frank, M.E. (1989). Self-preoccupation and general stress level as sensitizing factors in premenstrual and menstrual distress. *Journal of Psychosomatic Research, 33,* 571–577.

Hemmelgarn, B., & Laing, G. (1991). The relationship between situational factors and perceived role strain in employed mothers. *Family and Community Health, 14,* 8–15.

Hemminki, E., Malin, M., & Topo, P. (1993). Selection to postmenopausal therapy by women's characteristics. *Journal of Clinical Epidemiology, 46,* 211–219.

Henderson, D.J., Sampselle, C., Mayes, F., & Oakley, D. (1992). Toward culturally sensitive research in a multicultural society. *Health Care for Women International, 13,* 339–350.

Hennessy, C.H., & John, R. (1995). The interpretation of burden among Pueblo Indian caregivers. *Journal of Aging Studies, 9,* 215–229.

Hepworth, J., & Griffin, C. (1995). Conflicting opinions? 'Anorexia nervosa', medicine and feminism. In S. Wilkinson & C. Kitzinger (eds), *Feminism and discourse: Psychological perspectives* (pp. 68–85). London: Sage.

Herold, J.M., Thompson, N.J., Valenzuela, M.S., & Morris, L. (1994). Unintended pregnancy and sex education in Chile: A behavioural model. *Journal of Biosocial Science, 26,* 427–439.

Herrera, E., Gomez-Amor, J., Martinez-Selva, J.M., & Ato, M. (1990). Relationship between personality, psychological and somatic symptoms, and the menstrual cycle. *Personality and Individual Differences, 11,* 457–461.

Hershberger, S.L., & D'Augelli, A.R. (1995). The impact of victimization on the mental health and suicidality of lesbian, gay, and bisexual youths. *Developmental Psychology, 31,* 65–74.

Hessing, M. (1993). Mothers' management of their combined workloads: Clerical work and household needs. *Canadian Review of Sociology and Anthropology, 30,* 37–63.

Hibbard, J.H., & Pope, C.R. (1991). Effect of domestic and occupational roles on morbidity and mortality. *Social Science and Medicine, 32,* 805–811.

Hibbard, J.H., & Pope, C.R. (1993). The quality of social roles as predictors of morbidity and mortality. *Social Science and Medicine, 36,* 217–225.

Hobfoll, S.E., Ritter, C., Lavin, J., Hulsizer, M.R., & Cameron, R.P. (1995). Depression prevalence and incidence among inner-city pregnant and postpartum women. *Journal of Consulting and Clinical Psychology, 63,* 445–453.

Hock, E., & DeMeis, D.K. (1990). Depression in mothers of infants: The role of maternal employment. *Developmental Psychology, 26,* 285–291.

Hoek, H.W. (1993). Review of the epidemiological studies of eating disorders. *International Review of Psychiatry, 5*, 61–74.

Hoffman, L.W. (1990). Bias and social responsibility in the study of maternal employment. In C.B. Fisher & W.W. Tryon (eds), *Ethics in applied developmental psychology: Emerging issues in an emerging field* (pp. 253–271). Norwood, NJ: Ablex.

Hojat, M. (1990). Can affectional ties be purchased? *Journal of Social Behavior and Personality, 5*, 493–502.

Holderness, C.C., Brooks-Gunn, J., & Warren, M.P. (1994). Comorbidity of eating disorders and substance abuse: Review of the literature. *International Journal of Eating Disorders, 16*, 1–34.

Hollinger, F. (1991). Frauenerwerbstätigkeit und Wandel der Geschlechtsrollen im internationalen Vergleich. [Female employment and changing sex roles: An international comparison.] *Kölner Zeitschrift für Soziologie und Sozialpsychologie, 43*, 753–771.

Hollingsworth, E. (1994). Falling through the cracks: Care of the chronically mentally ill in the United States. In J. Hollingsworth & E. Hollingsworth (eds), *Care of the chronically and severely ill* (pp. 145–172). New York: Aldine de Gruyter.

Hooyman, N.R., & Gonyea, J. (1995). *Feminist perspectives on family care: Policies for gender justice.* Thousand Oaks, CA: Sage.

Hopkins, J., Campbell, S., & Marcus, M. (1989). Postpartum depression and postpartum adaptation: Overlapping constructs? *Journal of Affective Disorders, 17*, 251–254.

Hopkins, J., Marcus, M., & Campbell, S. (1984). Postpartum depression: A critical review. *Psychological Bulletin, 95*, 498–515.

Howard, G.S. (1985). The role of values in the science of psychology. *American Psychologist, 40*, 255–265.

Howie, P.M. (1996). After-school care arrangements and maternal employment: A study of the effects on third and fourth grade children. *Child and Youth Care Forum, 25*(1), 29–48.

Hsu, L.K.G. (1990). *Eating disorders.* New York: Guilford Press.

Hu, T., Huang, L., & Cartwright, W.W. (1986). Evaluation of the costs of caring for the senile demented elderly: A pilot study. *Gerontologist, 26*, 158–163.

Huffman, L.C., Lamour, M., Bryan, Y.E., & Pederson, F.A. (1990). Depressive symptomatology during pregnancy and the postpartum period: Is the Beck Depression Inventory applicable? *Journal of Reproductive and Infant Psychology, 8*, 87–97.

Humphrey, M., Humphrey, H., & Ainsworth-Smith, I. (1991). Screening couples for parenthood by donor insemination. *Social Science and Medicine, 32*, 273–278.

Hunt, K. (1994). A 'cure for all ills'? Construction of the menopause and the chequered fortunes of hormone replacement therapy. In S. Wilkinson & C. Kitzinger (eds), *Women and health: Feminist perspectives* (pp. 141–165). London: Taylor & Francis.

Hunter, M.S. (1990). Psychological and somatic experience of the menopause: A prospective study. *Psychosomatic Medicine, 52*, 357–367.

Hurt, S.W., Schnurr, P.P., Severino, S.K., Freeman, E.W., Gise, L.H., Rivera-Tovar, A., & Steege, J.F. (1992). Late luteal phase dysphoric disorder in 670 women evaluated for premenstrual complaints. *American Journal of Psychiatry, 149*, 525–530.

Hurwitz, N. (1989). The psychological aspects of in-vitro fertilization. *Pre- and Peri-Natal Psychology Journal, 4*, 43–50.

Hynes, G.J., Callan, V.J., Terry, D.J., & Gallois, C. (1992). The psychological well-being of infertile women after a failed IVF attempt: The effects of coping. *British Journal of Medical Psychology, 65*, 269–278.

Iles, S., & Gath, D. (1993). Psychiatric outcome of termination of pregnancy for foetal abnormality. *Psychological Medicine, 23*, 407–413.

Iles, S., Gath, D., & Kennerley, H. (1989). Maternity blues: II. A comparison between post-operative women and post-natal women. *British Journal of Psychiatry, 155*, 363–366.

Ironson, G. (1992). Work, job stress and health. In S. Zedeck (ed.), *Work, families and organisations* (pp. 33–69). San Francisco: Jossey-Bass.

Jackson, L.A., & Sullivan, L.A. (1993). Parental role participation and perceptions of responsibility for children's school adjustment. *Sex Roles, 28*, 485–491.

Jackson, L.A., Sullivan, L.A., & Rostker, R. (1988). Gender, gender role, and body image. *Sex Roles, 19*, 429–443.

Jacobs, S., Hansen, F., Berkman, L., Kasl, S., & Ostfeld, A. (1989). Depressions of bereavement. *Comprehensive Psychiatry, 30*, 218–224.

Jaeger, M.E., & Rosnow, R.L. (1988). Contextualism and its implications for psychological inquiry. *British Journal of Psychology, 79*, 63–75.

Jahoda, G. (1988). J'accuse. In M.H. Bond (ed.), *The cross-cultural challenge to social psychology* (pp. 86–95). Thousand Oaks, CA: Sage.

Jarvis, T.J., & McCabe, M.P. (1991). Women's experience of the menstrual cycle. *Journal of Psychosomatic Research, 35*, 651–660.

Johnson, C.E., & Petrie, T.A. (1995). The relationship of gender discrepancy to eating disorder attitudes and behaviors. *Sex Roles, 33*, 405–416.

Jones, J. (1994). Embodied meaning: Menopause and the change of life. *Social Work in Health Care, 19*, 43–65.

Jordan, P.L. (1989). Support behaviors identified as helpful and desired by second-time parents over the perinatal period. *Maternal-Child Nursing Journal, 18*, 133–145.

Jordan, P.L. (1990). Laboring for relevance: Expectant and new fatherhood. *Nursing Research, 39*(1), 11–16.

Jorm, A.F., Korten, A.E., & Henderson, A.S. (1987). The prevalence of dementia: A quantitative integration of the literature. *Acta Psychiatrica Scandinavica, 76*, 465–479.

Jutras, S., & Lavoie, J-P. (1995). Living with an impaired elderly person: The informal caregiver's physical and mental health. *Journal of Aging and Health, 7*, 46–73.

Jutras, S., & Veilleux, F. (1991). Informal caregiving: Correlates of perceived burden. *Canadian Journal on Aging, 10*, 40–55.

Kahne, H. (1991). Economic perspectives on work and family issues. In M.T. Notman & C.C. Nadelson (eds), *Women and men: New perspectives on gender differences* (pp. 9–22). Washington, DC: American Psychiatric Press.

Kamo, Y. (1994). Division of household work in the United States and Japan. *Journal of Family Issues, 15*, 348–378.

Kang, M.S., & Zador, D.A. (1993). Sexual behaviour and contraceptive practices of Year 10 schoolgirls in inner metropolitan Sydney. *Australian Journal of Marriage and the Family, 14*, 137–142.

Kanuha, V. (1990). Compounding the triple jeopardy: Battering in lesbian of color relationships. *Women and Therapy, 9*, 169–184.

Kaspi, S.P., Otto, M.W., Pollack, M.H., Eppinger, S., & Rosenbaum, J.F. (1994). Premenstrual exacerbation of symptoms in women with panic disorder. *Journal of Anxiety Disorders, 8*, 131–138.

Katzman, M.A., Weiss, L., & Wolchik, S.A. (1986). Speak don't eat! Teaching women to express their feelings. *Women and Therapy, 5*, 143–157.

Kaufert, P.A., Gilbert, P., & Tate, R. (1992). The Manitoba Project: A re-examination of the link between menopause and depression. *Maturitas, 14*, 143–155.

Kaur, H.P. (1991). Knowledge regarding family planning methods among rural women of Faridkot District of Punjab. *Indian Journal of Behaviour, 15*, 49–55.

Kay, F.M., & Hagan, J. (1995). The persistent glass ceiling: Gendered inequalities in the earnings of lawyers. *British Journal of Sociology, 46*, 279–310.

Kaye, L.W., & Applegate, J.S. (1990). *Men as caregivers to the elderly: Understanding and aiding unrecognised family support.* Lexington, MA: Lexington Books.

Keddy, B., Cable, B., Quinn, S., & Melanson, J. (1993). Interrupted work histories: Retired women telling their stories. *Health Care for Women International, 14*, 437–446.

Kedem, P., Bartoov, B., Mikulincer, M., & Shkolnik, T. (1992). Psychoneuro-immunology and male infertility: A possible link between stress, coping and male immunological infertility. *Psychology and Health, 6*, 159–173.

Keenan, P.A., Lindamer, L.A., & Jong, S.K. (1992). Psychological aspects of premenstrual syndrome: II. Utility of standardized measures. *Psychoneuro-endocrinology, 17*, 189–194.

Keesey, R.E. (1995). A set-point model of body weight regulation. In K.D. Brownell & C.G. Fairburn (eds), *Eating disorders and obesity* (pp. 46–50). New York: Guilford Press.

Kehoe, M. (1986). Lesbians over 65: A triply invisible minority. *Journal of Homosexuality, 12*, 139–152.

Kendell, R.E., Chalmers, J.C., & Platz, C.L. (1987). Epidemiology of puerperal psychoses. *British Journal of Psychiatry, 150*, 662–673.

Kenney, J.W., & Tash, D.T. (1992). Lesbian childbearing couples' dilemmas and decisions. *Health Care for Women International, 13*, 209–219.

Kertzner, R.M., & Sved, M. (1996). Midlife gay men and lesbians: Adult development and mental health. In R.P. Cabaj & T.S. Stein (eds), *Textbook of homosexuality and mental health* (pp. 289–303). Washington, DC: American Psychiatric Press.

Ketting, E., & Visser, A.P. (1994). Contraception in the Netherlands: The low abortion rate explained. *Patient Education and Counseling, 23*, 161–171.

Kiecolt-Glaser, J.K., & Glaser, R. (1994). Caregivers, mental health, and immune function. In E. Light, G. Niederehe & B.D. Lebowitz (eds), *Stress effects on family caregivers of Alzheimer's patients: Research and interventions* (pp. 64–75). New York: Springer.

Kikendall, K.A. (1994). Self-discrepancy as an important factor in addressing women's emotional reactions to infertility. *Professional Psychology Research and Practice, 25*, 214-220.

Kilbourne, J. (1994). Still killing us softly: Advertising and the obsession with thinness. In P. Fallon, M.A. Katzman & S.C. Wooley (eds), *Feminist perspectives on eating disorders* (pp. 395–418). New York: Guilford Press.

King, A.C., Oka, R.K., & Young, D.R. (1994). Ambulatory blood pressure and heart rate responses to the stress of work and caregiving in older women. *Journals of Gerontology, 49*, M239-M245.

Kipnis, D. (1994). Accounting for the use of behavior technologies in social psychology. *American Psychologist, 49*, 165–172.

Kitzinger, C. (1987). *The social construction of lesbianism*. London: Sage.

Kitzinger, C. (1993). The 'real' lesbian feminist therapist: Who is she? *Feminism and Psychology, 2*, 262–264.

Kitzinger, C., & Perkins, R. (1993). *Changing our minds: Lesbian feminism and psychology.* New York: New York University Press.

Kitzinger, C., & Wilkinson, S. (1993). Theorizing heterosexuality. In S. Wilkinson & C. Kitzinger (eds), *Heterosexuality: A feminism and psychology reader* (pp. 1–32). London: Sage.

Kitzinger, S. (1982). *Birth over 35*. London: Allen & Unwin.

Klebanov, P.K., & Jemmott, J.B. (1992). Effects of expectations and bodily sensations on self-reports of premenstrual symptoms. *Psychology of Women Quarterly, 16*, 289–310.

Klebanov, P.K., & Ruble, D.N. (1994). Toward an understanding of women's experience of menstrual cycle symptoms. In V.J. Adesso, D.M. Reddy & R. Fleming (eds), *Psychological perspectives on women's health* (pp. 183–221). Washington, DC: Taylor & Francis.

Klingenspor, B. (1994). Gender identity and bulimic eating behavior. *Sex Roles, 31*, 407–431.

Klonoff, E.A., & Landrine, H. (1995). The Schedule of Sexist Events: A measure of lifetime and recent sexist discrimination in women's lives. *Psychology of Women Quarterly, 19*, 439–472.

Knodel, J., Saengtienchai, C., & Sittitrai, W. (1995). Living arrangements of the elderly in Thailand: Views of the populace. *Journal of Cross-Cultural Gerontology, 10*, 79–111.

Koch, P.B., Boose, L.A., Cohn, M.D., Mansfield, P.K., Vicary, J.R., & Young, E.W. (1991). Coping strategies of traditionally and nontraditionally employed women at home and at work. *Health Values: Health Behavior, Education and Promotion, 15*, 19–31.

Koff, E., Rierdan, J., & Stubbs, M.L. (1990). Conceptions and misconceptions of the menstrual cycle. *Women and Health, 16*, 119–136.

Kolker, A., & Burke, B.M. (1993). Grieving the wanted child: Ramifications of abortion after prenatal diagnosis of abnormality. *Health Care for Women International, 14*, 513–526.

Koss, M.P. (1990). The women's mental health research agenda: Violence against women. *American Psychologist, 45*, 374–380.

Koster, A., & Garde, K. (1993). Sexual desire and menopausal development: A prospective study of Danish women born in 1936. *Maturitas, 16*, 49–60.

Kraft, P., & Rise, J. (1991). Contraceptive behaviour of Norwegian adolescents. *Health Education Research, 6*, 431–441.

Kulczycki, A., Potts, M., & Rosenfield, A. (1995). Abortion and fertility regulation. *Lancet, 347*, 1663–1668.

Kumar, R. (1994). Postnatal mental illness: A transcultural perspective. *Social Psychiatry and Psychiatric Epidemiology, 29,* 250–264.

Kurdek, L.A. (1993). Nature and prediction of changes in marital quality for first-time parent and nonparent husbands and wives. *Journal of Family Psychology, 6,* 255–265.

Kurdek, L.A. (1994). The nature and correlates of relationship quality in gay, lesbian, and heterosexual cohabiting couples: A test of the individual difference, interdependence, and discrepancy models. In B. Greene & G.M. Herek (eds), *Lesbian and gay psychology: Theory, research and clinical applications, Vol. 1* (pp. 133–155). Thousand Oaks, CA: Sage.

Kutner, N.G., Schechtman, K.B., Ory, M.G., & Baker, D.I. (1994). Older adults' perceptions of their health and functioning in relation to sleep disturbance, falling, and urinary incontinence. *Journal of the American Geriatrics Society, 42,* 757–762.

Laessle, R.G., Tuschl, R.J., Schweiger, U., & Pirke, K.M. (1990). Mood changes and physical complaints during the normal menstrual cycle in healthy young women. *Psychoneuroendocrinology, 15,* 131–138.

Lahelma, E. (1992). Paid employment, unemployment and mental well-being. *Psychiatria Fennica, 23,* 131–144.

Lampman, C., & Dowling-Guyer, S. (1995). Attitudes toward voluntary and involuntary childlessness. *Basic and Applied Social Psychology, 17,* 213–222.

Lancelot, C., & Kaslow, N. (1994). Sex role orientation and disordered eating in women: A review. *Clinical Psychology Review, 14,* 139–157.

Landrine, H. (1995). Introduction: Cultural diversity, contextualism, and feminist psychology. In H. Landrine (ed.), *Bringing cultural diversity to feminist psychology: Theory, research and practice* (pp. 1–20). Washington, DC: American Psychological Association.

Landrine, H., Klonoff, E.A., Gibbs, J., Manning, V., & Lund, M. (1995). Physical and psychiatric correlates of gender discrimination: An application of the Schedule of Sexist Events. *Psychology of Women Quarterly, 19,* 473–492.

Lask, B., & Bryant-Waugh, R. (1992). Early-onset anorexia nervosa and related eating disorders. *Journal of Child Psychology and Psychiatry and Allied Disciplines, 33,* 281–300.

Lauderdale, J.L., & Boyle, J.S. (1994). Infant relinquishment through adoption. *IMAGE Journal of Nursing Scholarship, 26,* 213–217.

Lawrence, M. (1984). *The anorexic experience.* London: Women's Press.

Laws, S. (1992). 'It's just the monthlies, she'll get over it': Menstrual problems and men's attitudes. *Journal of Reproductive and Infant Psychology, 10,* 117–128.

LeBlanc, A.J., Aneshensel, C.S., & Wight, R.G. (1995). Psychotherapy use and depression among AIDS caregivers. *Journal of Community Psychology, 23,* 127–142.

LeClere, F.B., & Kowalewski, B.M. (1994). Disability in the family: The effects on children's well-being. *Journal of Marriage and the Family, 56,* 457–468.

Lee, C. (1991). Women and aerobic exercise: Directions for research development. *Annals of Behavioral Medicine, 13,* 133–140.

Lee, C. (1993). Factors related to the adoption of exercise among older women. *Journal of Behavioral Medicine, 16,* 323–334.

Lee, C. (1997). Health habits and psychological functioning among young, middle-aged and older Australian women. Unpublished manuscript, Research Institute for Gender and Health, University of Newcastle, Australia.

Lee, C. (1998). *Alternatives to cognition: A new look at explaining human social behavior.* Hillsdale, NJ: Lawrence Erlbaum Associates.

Lee, M-L., Lin, H.S., & Chang, M.C. (1995). Living arrangements of the elderly in Taiwan: Qualitative evidence. *Journal of Cross-Cultural Gerontology, 10,* 53–78.

Lee, S. (1993). How abnormal is the desire for slimness? A survey of eating attitudes and behaviour among Chinese undergraduates in Hong Kong. *Psychological Medicine, 23,* 437–451.

Lee, S., Leung, T., Lee, A.M., Yu, H., & Leung, C.M. (1996). Body dissatisfaction among Chinese undergraduates and its implications for eating disorders in Hong Kong. *International Journal of Eating Disorders, 20,* 77–84.

Leibel, R.L., Rosenbaum, M., & Hirsch, J. (1995). Changes in energy expenditure resulting from altered body weight. *New England Journal of Medicine, 332,* 621–628.

Leiblum, S.R. (1990). Sexuality and the midlife woman. *Psychology of Women Quarterly, 14,* 495–508.

Leith, L.M., & Taylor, A.H. (1990). Psychological aspects of exercise: A decade literature review. *Journal of Sport Behavior, 13,* 219–239.

Lennon, M.C. (1987). Is menopause depressing? An investigation of three perspectives. *Sex Roles, 17,* 1–16.

Leonard, R.J. (1996). Complementary activities and multiplex relationships in the life-courses of educated women. *Journal of Family Studies, 2,* 3–14.

Lerner, D.J., & Kannel, W.B. (1986). Patterns of coronary heart disease morbidity and mortality in the sexes: A 26-year follow-up of the Framingham population. *American Heart Journal, 111,* 383–390.

Lerner, J.V., & Galambos, N.L. (1986). Child development and family change: The influences of maternal employment on infants and toddlers. *Advances in Infancy Research, 4,* 39–86.

Leutz, W.N., Capitman, J.A., MacAdam, M., & Abrahams, R. (1992). *Care for frail elders: Developing community solutions.* Westport, CT: Auburn House.

Levey, J., McDermott, S., & Lee, C. (1989). Current issues in the study of bulimia nervosa. *Australian Psychologist, 24,* 171–185.

Levy-Skiff, R. (1994). Individual and contextual correlates of marital change across the transition to parenthood. *Developmental Psychology, 30,* 591–601.

Lewis, M. (1985). Older women and health: An overview. *Women and Health, 10,* 1–16.

Li, G. (1995). The interaction effect of bereavement and sex on the risk of suicide in the elderly: An historical cohort study. *Social Science and Medicine, 40,* 825–828.

Li, P.S., & Currie, D. (1992). Gender differences in work interruptions as unequal effects of marriage and childrearing: Findings from a Canadian national survey. *Journal of Comparative Family Studies, 23,* 217–229.

Liff, S. (1991). Part-time workers: Current contradictions and future opportunities. In M.J. Davidson & J. Earnshaw (eds), *Vulnerable workers: Psychosocial and legal issues* (pp. 261–278). Chichester, UK: Wiley.

Lindell, M.E., & Olsson, H.M. (1993). Swedish students' attitudes toward abortion. *Health Care for Women International, 14,* 281–291.

Lindell, M.E., Olsson, H.M., & Sjöden, P-O. (1995). Choice of contraceptive method for birth control and attitudes toward abortion in Swedish women aged 23–29. *Health Care for Women International, 16,* 75–84.

Lindesay, J. (1990). The Guy's/Age Concern Survey: Physical health and psychiatric disorder in an urban elderly community. *International Journal of Geriatric Psychiatry, 5,* 171–178.

Lindsay, R., & Tohme, J.F. (1990). Estrogen treatment of patients with established postmenopausal osteoporosis. *Obstetrics and Gynecology, 76,* 290–295.

Lindstrom, T.C. (1995). Anxiety and adaptation in bereavement. *Anxiety, Stress and Coping, 8,* 251–261.

Litt, M.D., Tennen, H., Affleck, G., & Klock, S. (1992). Coping and cognitive factors in adaptation to in vitro fertilization failure. *Journal of Behavioral Medicine, 15,* 171–187.

Logue, C., & Moos, R. (1986). Perimenstrual symptoms: Prevalence and risk factors. *Psychosomatic Medicine, 48,* 388–409.

Lovering, K.M. (1995). The bleeding body: Adolescents talk about menstruation. In S. Wilkinson & C. Kitzinger (eds), *Feminism and discourse: Psychological perspectives* (pp. 10–31). London: Sage.

Lovestone, S., & Kumar, R. (1993). Postnatal psychiatric illness: The impact on partners. *British Journal of Psychiatry, 163,* 210–216.

Lubben, J.E. (1988). Gender differences in the relationship of widowhood and psychological well-being among low income elderly. *Women and Health, 14,* 161–189.

Lucas, V.A. (1992). An investigation of the health care preferences of the lesbian population. *Health Care for Women International, 13,* 221–228.

Lundberg, U. (1996). Influence of paid and unpaid work on psychophysiological stress responses of men and women. *Journal of Occupational Health Psychology, 1,* 117–130.

Lundh, W., & Gyllang, C. (1993). Use of the Edinburgh Postnatal Depression Scale in some Swedish child health care centres. *Scandinavian Journal of Caring Sciences, 7,* 149–154.

Lupton, D. (1994). *Medicine as culture: Illness, disease and the body in Western societies.* London: Sage.

Lynxweiler, J., & Gay, D. (1994). Reconsidering race differences in abortion attitudes. *Social Science Quarterly, 75,* 67–84.

Lynxweiler, J., & Wilson, M. (1994). A case study of race differences among late abortion patients. *Women and Health, 21,* 43–56.

MacEwan, I. (1994). Differences in assessment and treatment approaches for homosexual clients. *Drug and Alcohol Review, 13,* 57–62.

MacLennan, A.H. (1988). Current management of the menopause. *Australian Family Physician, 17*(3), 158–169.

MacLennan, A.H., MacLennan, A., O'Neill, S., Kirkgard, Y., Wenzel, S., & Chambers, H.M. (1992). Oestrogen and cyclical progestogen in postmenopausal HRT. *Medical Journal of Australia, 157,* 167–170.

MacSween, M. (1993). *Anorexic bodies: A feminist and sociological perspective on anorexia nervosa.* London: Routledge.

Madden, M.E. (1994). The variety of emotional reactions to miscarriage. *Women and Health, 21,* 85–104.

Maddocks, S., Hahn, P., & Moller, F. (1986). A double-blind placebo-controlled trial of progesterone vaginal suppositories in the treatment of premenstrual syndrome. *American Journal of Obstetrics and Gynecology, 154*, 573–581.

Magaziner, J., Cadigan, D.A., Hebel, J.R., & Parry, R.E. (1988). Health and living arrangements among older women: Does living alone increase the risk of illness? *Journals of Gerontology, 43*, M127-M133.

Magni, E., Zanetti, O., Bianchetti, A., Binetti, G., & Trabucchi, M. (1995). Evaluation of an Italian educational programme for dementia caregivers: Results of a small-scale pilot study. *International Journal of Geriatric Psychiatry, 10*, 569–573.

Maine, D., Karkazis, K., & Bolan, N. (1994). The bad old days are still here: Abortion mortality in developing countries. *Journal of the American Women's Medical Association, 49*, 137–142.

Major, B., & Cozzarelli, C. (1992). Psychosocial predictors of adjustment to abortion. *Journal of Social Issues, 48*, 121–142.

Major, B., Cozzarelli, C., Sciacchiatano, A.M., Cooper, M.L., Testa, M., & Mueller, P.M. (1990). Perceived social support, self-efficacy, and adjustment to abortion. *Journal of Personality and Social Psychology, 59*, 452–463.

Mansfield, P.K., Theisen, S.C., & Boyer, B. (1992). Midlife women and menopause: A challenge for the mental health counselor. *Journal of Mental Health Counseling, 14*, 73–83.

Mansfield, P.K., & Voda, A.M. (1993). From Edith Bunker to the 6:00 news: How and what midlife women learn about menopause. *Women and Therapy, 14*, 89–104.

Mantecon, V.H. (1993). Where are the archetypes? Searching for symbols of women's midlife passage. *Women and Therapy, 14*, 77–88.

Marks, M.N., Wieck, A., Checkley, S.A., & Kumar, R. (1991). Life stress and postpartum psychosis: A preliminary report. *British Journal of Psychiatry, 158*, 45–49.

Markus, H.R., & Kitayama, S. (1991). Culture and the self: Implications for cognition, emotion, and motivation. *Psychological Bulletin, 98*, 224–253.

Marsh, M.S., & Whitehead, M.I. (1992). Management of the menopause. *British Medical Bulletin, 48*, 426–457.

Marshall, H. (1991). The social construction of motherhood: An analysis of childcare and parenting manuals. In A. Phoenix, A. Woollett & E. Lloyd (eds), *Motherhood: Meanings, practices and ideologies* (pp. 66–85). London: Sage.

Marsiglio, W., & Donnelly, D. (1991). Sexual relations in later life: A national study of married persons. *Journals of Gerontology, 46*, S338-S344.

Martin, E. (1988). Medical metaphors of women's bodies: Menstruation and menopause. *International Journal of Health Services, 18*, 237–254.

Martin, M.C., & Kennedy, P.F. (1994). The measurement of social comparison to advertising models: A gender gap revealed. In J.A. Costa (ed.), *Gender issues and consumer behavior* (pp. 104–124). Thousand Oaks, CA: Sage.

Martz, D.M., Handley, K.B., & Eisler, R.M. (1995). The relationship between feminine gender role stress, body image, and eating disorders. *Psychology of Women Quarterly, 19*, 493–508.

Matthews, K.A. (1992). Myths and realities of the menopause. *Psychosomatic Medicine, 54*, 1–9.

Matthews, K.A., Wing, R.R., Kuller, L.H., Meilahn, E.N., Kelsey, S.F., Costello, E.J., & Caggiula, A.W. (1990). Influences of natural menopause on psychological characteristics and symptoms of middle-aged healthy women. *Journal of Consulting and Clinical Psychology, 58*, 345–351.

Mauldin, T., & Meeks, C.B. (1990). Sex differences in children's time use. *Sex Roles, 22*, 537–554.

Maume, D.J., & Mullin, K.R. (1993). Men's participation in child care and women's work attachment. *Social Problems, 40*, 533–546.

Mauthner, N. (1993). Towards a feminist understanding of 'postnatal depression': I. *Feminism and Psychology, 3*, 350–355.

Max, W., Webber, P., & Fox, P. (1995). Alzheimer's disease: The unpaid burden of caring. *Journal of Aging and Health, 7*, 179–199.

Mayekiso, T.V., & Twaise, N. (1993). Assessment of parental involvement in imparting sexual knowledge to adolescents. *South African Journal of Psychology, 23*, 21–23.

McBride, A.B. (1989). Fat is generous, nurturing, warm . . . *Women and Therapy, 8*, 93–103.

McCallum, J., Shadbolt, B., & Wang, D. (1994). Self-rated health and survival: A 7-year follow-up study of Australian elderly. *American Journal of Public Health, 84*, 1100–1105.

McDougall, G.J. (1993). Therapeutic issues with gay and lesbian elders. *Clinical Gerontologist, 14*, 45–57.

McFarlane, J.M., Martin, C., & Williams, T.M. (1988). Mood fluctuations: Women versus men and menstrual versus other cycles. *Psychology of Women Quarterly, 12*, 201–223.

McFarlane, J.M., & Williams, T.M. (1994). Placing premenstrual syndrome in perspective. *Psychology of Women Quarterly, 18*, 339–373.

McHugh, M.C., Koeske, R.D., & Frieze, I.H. (1986). Issues to consider in conducting nonsexist psychological research: A guide for researchers. *American Psychologist, 41*, 879–890.

McIntosh, J.L. (1995). Suicide prevention in the elderly (age 65–99). In M.M. Silverman & R.W. Maris (eds), *Suicide prevention: Toward the year 2000* (pp. 180–192). New York: Guilford Press.

McKinlay, J.B., Crawford, S.L., & Tennstedt, S.L. (1995). The everyday impacts of providing informal care to dependent elders and their consequences for the care recipients. *Journal of Aging and Health, 7*, 497–528.

McKinlay, J.B., McKinlay, S.M., & Brambilla, D. (1987). The relative contributions of endocrine changes and social circumstances to depression in mid-aged women. *Journal of Health and Social Behavior, 28*, 345–363

McLellan, B., & McKelvie, S.J. (1993). Effects of age and gender on perceived facial attractiveness. *Canadian Journal of Behavioural Science, 25*, 135–142.

McMahon, C.A., Ungerer, J.A., Beaurepaire, J., & Tennant, C. (1995). Psychosocial outcomes for parents and children after in vitro fertilization: A review. *Journal of Reproductive and Infant Psychology, 13*, 1–16.

McNaughton, M.E., Patterson, T.L., Smith, T.L., & Grant, I. (1995). The relationship among stress, depression, locus of control, irrational beliefs, social support, and health in Alzheimer's disease caregivers. *Journal of Nervous and Mental Disease, 183*, 78–85.

Mehta, K., Osman, M.M., & Lee, A.E.Y. (1995). Living arrangements of the elderly in Singapore: Cultural norms in transition. *Journal of Cross-Cultural Gerontology*, *10*, 113–143.

Menaghan, E.G., & Parcel, T.L. (1991). Transitions in work and family arrangements: Mothers' employment conditions, children's experiences, and child outcomes. In K.A. Pillemer & K. McCartney (eds), *Parent–child relations throughout life* (pp. 225–251). Hillsdale, NJ: Lawrence Erlbaum Associates.

Mendola, R., Tennen, H., Affleck, G., McCann, L., & Fitzgerald, T. (1990). Appraisal and adaptation among women with impaired fertility. *Cognitive Therapy and Research*, *14*, 79–93.

Meyerowitz, B.E., & Hart, S. (1995). Women and cancer: Have assumptions about women limited our research agenda? In A.L. Stanton & S.J. Gallant (eds), *The psychology of women's health: Progress and challenges in research and application* (pp. 51–84). Washington, DC: American Psychological Association.

Miller, B., McFall, S., & Montgomery, A. (1991). The impact of elder health, caregiver involvement, and global stress on two dimensions of caregiver burden. *Journals of Gerontology*, *46*, S9-S19.

Miller, B., & Montgomery, A. (1990). Family caregivers and limitations in social activities. *Research on Aging*, *12*, 72–93.

Millett, K. (1970). *Sexual politics*. New York: Ballantine Books.

Mischel, H.N., & Fuhr, R. (1988). Maternal employment: Its psychological effects on children and families. In S.M. Dornbusch & M.H. Strober (eds), *Feminism, children, and the new families* (pp. 191–211). New York: Guilford Press.

Mitchell, V., & Helson, R. (1990). Women's prime of life: Is it the 50s? *Psychology of Women Quarterly*, *14*, 451–470.

Modrcin, M.J., & Wyers, N.L. (1990). Lesbian and gay couples: Where they turn when help is needed. *Journal of Gay and Lesbian Psychotherapy*, *1*, 89–104.

Moen, P. (1996). A life course perspective on retirement, gender, and well-being. *Journal of Occupational Health Psychology*, *1*, 131–144.

Moen, P., Dempster-McClain, D., & Williams, R.M. (1992). Successful aging: A life-course perspective on women's multiple roles and health. *American Journal of Sociology*, *97*, 1612–1638.

Moen, P., Robison, J., & Dempster-McClain, D. (1995). Caregiving and women's well-being: A life course approach. *Journal of Health and Social Behavior*, *36*, 259–273.

Monahan, D.J. (1993). Utilization of dementia-specific respite day care for clients and their caregivers in a social model program. *Journal of Gerontological Social Work*, *20*, 57–70.

Monahan, D.J., & Hooker, K. (1995). Health of spouse caregivers of dementia patients: The role of personality and social support. *Social Work*, *40*, 305–314.

Moos, R. (1968). The development of a Menstrual Distress Questionnaire. *Psychosomatic Medicine*, *30*, 853–867.

Morgan, D.L., & March, S.J. (1992). The impact of life events on networks of personal relationships: A comparison of widowhood and caring for a spouse with Alzheimer's disease. *Journal of Social and Personal Relationships*, *9*, 563–584.

Morgan, S.P., & Chen, R. (1992). Predicting childlessness for recent cohorts of American women. *International Journal of Forecasting*, *8*, 477–493.

Morgan, S.P., & Waite, L.J. (1987). Parenthood and the attitudes of young adults. *American Sociological Review, 52*, 541–547.

Morris, E.K. (1988). Contextualism: The world view of behavior analysis. *Journal of Experimental Child Psychology, 46*, 289–323.

Morris, R.G., Woods, R.T., Davies, K.S., & Morris, L.W. (1991). Gender differences in carers of dementia sufferers. *British Journal of Psychiatry, 158* (Suppl. 10), 69–74.

Morrow, K.A., Thoreson, R.W., & Penney, L.L. (1995). Predictors of psychological distress among infertility clinic patients. *Journal of Consulting and Clinical Psychology, 63*, 163–167.

Morse, C.A., Smith, A., Dennerstein, L., Green, A., Hopper, J., & Burger, H. (1994). The treatment-seeking woman at menopause. *Maturitas, 18*, 161–173.

Moss, P., Bolland, G., Foxman, R., & Owen, C. (1986). Marital relations during the transition to parenthood. *Journal of Reproductive and Infant Psychology, 4*, 57–67.

Moss, P., Bolland, G., Foxman, R., & Owen, C. (1987). The division of household work during the transition to parenthood. *Journal of Reproductive and Infant Psychology, 5*, 71–86.

Motenko, A.K. (1989). The frustrations, gratifications, and well-being of dementia caregivers. *Gerontologist, 19*, 166–172.

Moulder, C. (1994). Towards a preliminary framework for understanding pregnancy loss. *Journal of Reproductive and Infant Psychology, 12*, 65–67.

Muehrer, P. (1995). Suicide and sexual orientation: A critical summary of recent research and directions for future research. *Suicide and Life Threatening Behavior, 25* (Suppl.), 72–81.

Mui, A.C. (1995a). Caring for frail elderly parents: A comparison of adult sons and daughters. *Gerontologist, 35*, 86–93.

Mui, A.C. (1995b). Perceived health and functional status among spouse caregivers of frail older persons. *Journal of Aging and Health, 7*, 283–300.

Muller, C. (1986). Health and health care of employed women and homemakers: Family factors. *Women and Health, 11*, 7–26.

Mumford, D.B., Whitehouse, A.M., & Platts, M. (1991). Sociocultural correlates of eating disorders among Asian schoolgirls in Bradford. *British Journal of Psychiatry, 158*, 222–228.

Mutchler, J.E., & Bullers, S. (1994). Gender differences in formal care use in later life. *Research on Aging, 16*, 235–250.

Neugebauer, R., Kline, J., O'Connor, P., Shrout, P., Johnson, J., Skodol, A., Wicks, J., & Susser, M. (1992). Determinants of depressive symptoms in the early weeks after miscarriage. *American Journal of Public Health, 82*, 1332–1339.

Ngo, H-Y. (1992). Employment status of married women in Hong Kong. *Sociological Perspectives, 35*, 475–488.

NHMRC (National Health and Medical Research Council of Australia) (1995). *Long-term effects on women from assisted conception.* Canberra: Author.

Nicholas, L. (1993). Intra-familial communication about contraception: A survey of Black South African freshmen. *International Journal for the Advancement of Counselling, 16*, 291–300.

Nicolson, P. (1989). Counselling women with post natal depression: Implications from recent qualitative research. *Counselling Psychology Quarterly, 2*, 123–132.

Nicolson, P. (1990). A brief report of women's expectations of men's behaviour in the transition to parenthood: Contradictions and conflicts for counselling therapy practice. *Counselling Psychology Quarterly, 3,* 353–361.

Nicolson, P. (1992). Menstrual-cycle research and the construction of female psychology. In J.T.E. Richardson (ed.), *Cognition and the menstrual cycle* (pp. 174–199). New York: Springer.

Nicolson, P. (1993). Motherhood and women's lives. In D. Richardson & V. Robinson (eds), *Thinking feminist: Key concepts in women's studies.* (pp. 201–223). New York: Guilford Press.

Niemela, P., & Lento, R. (1993). The significance of the 50th birthday for women's individuation. *Women and Therapy, 14,* 117–127.

Niven, C.A., & Carroll, D. (1993). *The health psychology of women.* Chur, Switzerland: Harwood.

Nordin, B.E.C. (1986). Calcium. *Journal of Food and Nutrition, 42,* 67–82.

Nuss, W.S., & Zubenko, G.S. (1992). Correlates of persistent depressive symptoms in widows. *American Journal of Psychiatry, 149,* 346–351.

Oakley, A. (1993). *Essays on women, medicine and health.* Hillsdale, NJ: Lawrence Erlbaum Associates.

O'Brien, M. (1991). Never married older women: The life experience. *Social Indicators Research, 24,* 301–315.

O'Brien, S.J., & Vertinsky, P.A. (1991). Unfit survivors: Exercise as a resource for aging women. *Gerontologist, 31,* 347–357.

O'Connor, D.W., Pollitt, P.A., Roth, M., Brook, C.P.B., & Reiss, B.B. (1990). Problems reported by relatives in a community study of dementia. *British Journal of Psychiatry, 156,* 835–841.

Oddens, B.J., Boulet, M.J., Lehert, P. & Visser, A.P. (1992). Has the climacteric been medicalised? A study on the use of medication for climacteric complaints in four countries. *Maturitas, 15,* 171–181.

Oddens, B.J., Boulet, M.J., Lehert, P., & Visser, A.P. (1994). A study on the use of medication for climacteric complaints in Western Europe: II. *Maturitas, 19,* 1–12.

Ogur, B. (1986). Long day's journey into night: Women and prescription drug abuse. *Women and Health, 11,* 99–115.

O'Hara, M.W. (1986). Social support, life events, and depression during pregnancy and the puerperium. *Archives of General Psychiatry, 43,* 569–573.

O'Hara, M.W., Schlechte, J.A., Lewis, D.A., & Varner, M.W. (1991). Controlled prospective study of mood disorders: Psychological, environmental, and hormonal variables. *Journal of Abnormal Psychology, 100,* 63–73.

O'Hara, M.W., Zekoski, E.M., Philipps, L.H., & Wright, E.J. (1990). Controlled prospective study of postpartum mood disorders: Comparison of childbearing and nonchildbearing women. *Journal of Abnormal Psychology, 99,* 3–15.

Oheneba-Sakyi, Y. (1992). Determinants of current contraceptive use among Ghanaian women at the highest risk of pregnancy. *Journal of Biosocial Science, 24,* 463–475.

Olds, J., Schwartz, R.S., Eisen, S.V., & Betcher, R.W. (1993). Part-time employment and marital well-being: A hypothesis and pilot study. *Family Therapy, 20,* 1–16.

Oliver, K.K., & Thelen, M.H. (1996). Children's perceptions of peer influence on eating concerns. *Behavior Therapy, 27,* 25–39.

O'Moore, M.A., & Harrison, R.F. (1991). Anxiety and reproductive failure: Experiences from a Dublin fertility clinic. *Irish Journal of Psychology, 12,* 276–285.

Orzek, A.M. (1988). The lesbian victim of sexual assault: Special considerations for the mental health professional. *Women and Therapy, 8,* 107–117.

Osterbusch, S., Keigher, S., Miller, B., & Linsk, N. (1987). Community care policies and gender justice. *International Journal of Health Services, 17,* 217–232.

Padgett, D. (1988). Aging minority women: Issues in research and health policy. *Women and Health, 14,* 213–225.

Palkovitz, R., & Copes, M. (1988). Changes in attitudes, beliefs and expectations associated with the transition to parenthood. *Marriage and Family Review, 12,* 183–199.

Parkes, C.M. (1992). Bereavement and mental health in the elderly. *Reviews in Clinical Gerontology, 2,* 45–51.

Patterson, C.J. (1994). Children of the lesbian baby boom: Behavioral adjustment, self-concepts, and sex role identity. In B. Greene & G.M. Herek (eds), *Lesbian and gay psychology: Theory, research and clinical applications, Vol. 1* (pp. 156–175). Thousand Oaks, CA: Sage.

Patterson, C.J. (1995). Families of the baby boom: Parents' division of labor and children's adjustment. *Developmental Psychology, 31,* 115–123.

Patterson, D.G. (1995). Alcoholism: Treating the 'second sex'. *Irish Journal of Psychological Medicine, 12,* 46–47.

Paykel, E.S. (1991). Depression in women. *British Journal of Psychiatry, 158,* 22–29.

Peace, S. (1986). The forgotten female: Social policy and older women. In C. Phillipson & A. Walker (eds), *Ageing and social policy: A critical assessment* (pp. 61–86). Brookfield, VT: Gower Press.

Peak, T., Toseland, R.W., & Banks, S.M. (1995). The impact of a spouse-caregiver support group on care recipient health care costs. *Journal of Aging and Health, 7,* 427–449.

Peirce, K. (1990). A feminist theoretical perspective on the socialization of teenage girls through 'Seventeen' magazine. *Sex Roles, 23,* 491–500.

Penrod, J.D., Kane, R.A., Kane, R.L., & Finch, M.D. (1995). Who cares? The size, scope, and composition of the caregiver support system. *Gerontologist, 35,* 489–508.

Perkins, K. (1992). Psychosocial implications of women and retirement. *Social Work, 37,* 526–532.

Perkins, R.E. (1991). Therapy for lesbians? The case against. *Feminism and Psychology, 1,* 325–338.

Perlick, D., & Silverstein, B. (1994). Faces of female discontent: Depression, disordered eating and changing gender roles. In P. Fallon, M.A. Katzman & S.C. Wooley (eds), *Feminist perspectives on eating disorders* (pp. 77–93). New York: Guilford Press.

Perry-Jenkins, M. (1993). Family roles and responsibilities: What has changed and what has remained the same? In J. Frankel (ed.), *The employed mother and the family context* (pp. 245–259). New York: Springer.

Perry-Jenkins, M., & Crouter, A.C. (1990). Men's provider-role attitudes: Implications for household work and marital satisfaction. *Journal of Family Issues, 11,* 136–156.

Peterson, B.E., Doty, R.M., & Winter, D.G. (1993). Authoritarianism and attitudes toward contemporary social issues. *Personality and Social Psychology Bulletin, 19*, 174–184.

Pettingale, K.W., Hussein, M., & Tee, D.E.H. (1994). Changes in immune status following conjugal bereavement. *Stress Medicine, 10*, 145–150.

Pfost, K.S., Lum, C.U., & Stephens, M.J. (1989). Femininity and work plans protect women against postpartum dysphoria. *Sex Roles, 21*, 423–431.

Phares, V. (1992). Where's poppa? The relative lack of attention to the role of fathers in child and adolescent psychopathology. *American Psychologist, 47*, 656–664.

Philipps, L.H., & O'Hara, M.W. (1991). Prospective study of postpartum depression: $4\text{-}\frac{1}{2}$ year follow-up of women and children. *Journal of Abnormal Psychology, 100*, 151–155.

Phoenix, A., & Woollett, A. (1991). Motherhood: Social construction, politics and psychology. In A. Phoenix, A. Woollett & E. Lloyd (eds), *Motherhood: Meanings, practices and ideologies* (pp. 13–27). London: Sage.

Phoenix, A., Woollett, A., & Lloyd, E. (eds). (1991). *Motherhood: Meanings, practices and ideologies*. London: Sage.

Piechowski, L.D. (1992). Mental health and women's multiple roles. *Families in Society, 73*(3), 131–139.

Pleck, J.H. (1977). The work–family role system. *Social Problems, 24*, 417–427.

Pohl, J.M., Given, C.W., Collins, C.E., & Given, B.A. (1994). Social vulnerability and reactions to caregiving in daughters and daughters-in-law caring for disabled aging parents. *Health Care for Women International, 15*, 385–395.

Poole, M.E., & Langan-Fox, J. (1992). Conflict in women's decision-making about multiple roles. *Australian Journal of Marriage and the Family, 13*, 2–18.

Pope, H.G., & Hudson, J.I. (1992). Is childhood sexual abuse a risk factor for bulimia nervosa? *American Journal of Psychiatry, 149*, 455–463.

Popenoe, D. (1993). American family decline, 1960–1990: A review and appraisal. *Journal of Marriage and the Family, 55*, 527–542.

Porcino, J. (1985). Psychological aspects of aging in women. *Women and Health, 10*, 115–122.

Posavac, E.J., & Miller, T.Q. (1990). Some problems caused by not having a conceptual foundation for health research: An illustration from studies of the psychological effects of abortion. *Psychology and Health, 5*, 13–23.

Poston, D.L., & Trent, K. (1982). International variability in childlessness: A descriptive and analytical study. *Journal of Family Issues, 3*, 473–491.

Prettyman, R.J., Cordle, C.J., & Cook, G.D. (1993). A three-month follow-up of psychological morbidity after early miscarriage. *British Journal of Medical Psychology, 66*, 363–372.

Prigerson, H.G., Frank, E., Kasl, S.V., Reynolds, C.F., Anderson, B., Zubenko, G.S., Houck, P.R., George, C.J., & Kupfer, D.J. (1995). Complicated grief and bereavement-related depression as distinct disorders: Preliminary empirical validation in elderly bereaved spouses. *American Journal of Psychiatry, 152*, 22–30.

Prilleltensky, I. (1989). Psychology and the status quo. *American Psychologist, 44*, 795–802.

Prilleltensky, I. (1990). Enhancing the social ethics of psychology: Toward a psychology at the service of social change. *Canadian Psychology, 31*, 310–319.

Proctor, C.D., & Groze, V.K. (1994). Risk factors for suicide among gay, lesbian, and bisexual youths. *Social Work, 39,* 504–513.

Pruchno, R.A., & Potashnik, S.L. (1989). Caregiving spouses: Physical and mental health in perspective. *Journal of the American Geriatrics Society, 37,* 697–705.

Purdy, D., & Frank, E. (1993). Should postpartum mood disorders be given a more prominent or distinct place in the DSM-IV? *Depression, 1,* 59–70.

Purdy, J.K., & Arguello, D. (1992). Hispanic familism in caretaking of older adults: Is it functional? *Journal of Gerontological Social Work, 19,* 29–43.

Quirouette, C., & Gold, D.P. (1992). Spousal characteristics as predictors of well-being in older couples. *International Journal of Aging and Human Development, 34,* 257–269.

Radecki, S.E., & Beckman, L.J. (1994). Contraceptive risk-taking in a medically underserved, low-income population. *Women and Health, 21,* 1–15.

Radford, J. (1993). The lesbian custody project. In P.N. Stern (ed.), *Lesbian health: What are the issues?* (pp. 139–147). Washington, DC: Taylor & Francis.

Rahim, F.A., & Al-Sabiae, A. (1991). Puerperal psychosis in a teaching hospital in Saudi Arabia: Clinical profile and cross-cultural comparison. *Acta Psychiatrica Scandinavica, 84,* 508–511.

Ramoso-Jalbuena, J. (1994). Climacteric Filipino women: A preliminary survey in the Philippines. *Maturitas, 19,* 183–190.

Rankow, E.J. (1995). Lesbian health issues for the primary care provider. *Journal of Family Practice, 40,* 486–493.

Rasmussen, S.J. (1991). Lack of prayer: Ritual restrictions, social experience, and the anthropology of menstruation among the Tuareg. *American Ethnologist, 18,* 751–769.

Ravnikar, V.A. (1992). Hormonal management of osteoporosis. *Clinical Obstetrics and Gynecology, 35,* 913–922.

Reading, A.E., Chang, L.C., & Kerin, J.F. (1989). Psychological state and coping styles across an IVF treatment cycle. *Journal of Reproductive and Infant Psychology, 7,* 95–103.

Reading, J., & Amatea, E.S. (1986). Role deviance or role diversification: Reassessing the psychosocial factors affecting the parenthood choices of career-oriented women. *Journal of Marriage and the Family, 48,* 255–260.

Redei, E., & Freeman, E.W. (1995). Daily plasma estradiol and progesterone levels over the menstrual cycle and their relation to premenstrual symptoms. *Psychoneuroendocrinology, 20,* 259–267.

Reid, P.T., & Comas-Diaz, L. (1990). Gender and ethnicity: Perspectives on dual status. *Sex Roles, 22,* 397–408.

Reifman, A., Biernat, M., & Lang, E.L. (1991). Stress, social support, and health in married professional women with small children. *Psychology of Women Quarterly, 15,* 431–445.

Reitzes, D.C., & Mutran, E.J. (1994). Multiple roles and identities: Factors influencing self-esteem among middle-aged working men and women. *Social Psychology Quarterly, 57,* 313–325.

Remennick, L.I., Amir, D., Elimelech, Y., & Novikov, Y. (1995). Family planning practices and attitudes among former Soviet new immigrant women in Israel. *Social Science and Medicine, 41,* 569–577.

Renzetti, C.M. (1995). Studying partner abuse in lesbian relationships: A case for the feminist participatory research model. In C.T. Tully (ed.), *Lesbian social services: Research issues* (pp. 29–42). New York: Harrington Park Press.

Repetti, R.L., Matthews, K.A., & Waldron, I. (1989). Employment and women's health. *American Psychologist, 44*, 1394–1401.

Research Institute for Gender and Health (1996). *Data book for the baseline survey of the Australian Longitudinal Survey of Women's Health (main cohort).* University of Newcastle, Australia.

Resnick, M.D., Bearinger, L.H., Stark, P., & Blum, R.W. (1994). Patterns of consultation among adolescent minors obtaining an abortion. *American Journal of Orthopsychiatry, 64*, 310–316.

Reviere, R., & Eberstein, I.W. (1992). Work, marital status, and heart disease. *Health Care for Women International, 13*, 393–399.

Rich, A. (1982). *Of women born: Motherhood as experience and institution.* London: Virago.

Richardson, J.T.E. (1992a). Memory and the menstrual cycle. In J.T.E. Richardson (ed.), *Cognition and the menstrual cycle* (pp. 98–131). New York: Springer.

Richardson, J.T.E. (1992b). The menstrual cycle, cognition, and paramenstrual symptomatology. In J.T.E. Richardson (ed.), *Cognition and the menstrual cycle* (pp. 1–38). New York: Springer.

Richman, J.A., Raskin, V.D., & Gaines, C. (1991). Gender roles, social support, and postpartum depressive symptomatology: The benefits of caring. *Journal of Nervous and Mental Disease, 179*, 139–147.

Riddick, C.C., & Daniel, S.N. (1984). The relative contribution of leisure activities and other factors to the mental health of older women. *Journal of Leisure Research, 16*, 136–148.

Riger, S.C. (1992). Epistemological debates, feminist voices: Science, social values and the study of women. *American Psychologist, 47*, 730–740.

Riggs, B.L., & Melton, L.J. (1986). Involutional osteoporosis. *New England Journal of Medicine, 314*, 1676–1686.

Rittenhouse, C. (1991). The emergence of PMS as a social problem. *Social Problems, 38*, 412–421.

Rivera-Tovar, A.D., & Frank, E. (1990). Late luteal phase dysphoric disorder in young women. *American Journal of Psychiatry, 147*, 1634–1636.

Robertson, M.M. (1992). Lesbians as an invisible minority in the health services arena. *Health Care for Women International, 13*, 155–163.

Robinson, G.E., Olmsted, M.P., Garner, D.M., & Gare, D.J. (1988). Transition to parenthood in elderly primiparas. *Journal of Psychosomatic Obstetrics and Gynaecology, 9*, 89–101.

Robinson, G.E., & Stewart, D.E. (1993). Postpartum disorders. In D.E. Stewart & N.L. Stotland (eds), *Psychological aspects of women's health care: The interface between psychiatry and obstetrics and gynecology* (pp. 115–138). Washington, DC: American Psychiatric Press.

Robson, R. (1994). Resisting the family: Repositioning lesbians in legal theory. *Signs, 19*, 975–996.

Rodeheaver, D., & Datan, N. (1988). The challenge of double jeopardy: Toward a mental health agenda for aging women. *American Psychologist, 43*, 648–654.

Rodgers, C.S. (1992). The flexible workplace: What have we learned? *Human Resource Management, 31*, 183–199.

Rodin, J., & Ickovics, J.R. (1990). Women's health: Review and research agenda as we approach the 21st century. *American Psychologist, 45*, 1018–1034.

Rodin, J., & McAvay, G. (1992). Determinants of change in perceived health in a longitudinal study of older adults. *Journals of Gerontology, 47*, P373-P384.

Rodin, J., Silberstein, L., & Striegel-Moore, R. (1984). Women and weight: A normative discontent. *Nebraska Symposium on Motivation, 32*, 267–307.

Rogo, K.O. (1993). Induced abortion in sub-Saharan Africa. *East African Medical Journal, 70*, 386–395.

Rogoff, B., & Chavajay, P. (1995). What's become of research on the cultural basis of cognitive development? *American Psychologist, 50*, 859–877.

Romans, S.E., Walton, V.A., McNoe, B.M., Herbison, G.P. & Mullen, P.E. (1993). Otago women's health survey 30-month follow-up: I. Onset patterns of non-psychotic psychiatric disorder. *British Journal of Psychiatry, 163*, 733–738.

Romans-Clarkson, S.E. (1989). Psychological sequelae of induced abortion. *Australian and New Zealand Journal of Psychiatry, 23*, 555–565.

Root, M.P. (1990). Disordered eating in women of color. *Sex Roles, 22*, 525–536.

Rosenbloom, C.A., & Whittington, F.J. (1993). The effects of bereavement on eating behaviors and nutrient intakes in elderly widowed persons. *Journals of Gerontology, 48*, S223-S229.

Rosenfield, S. (1989). The effects of women's employment: Personal control and sex differences in mental health. *Journal of Health and Social Behavior, 30*, 77–91.

Rosenthal, M.G. (1994). Single mothers in Sweden: Work and welfare in the welfare state. *Social Work, 39*, 270–278.

Rostosky, S.S., & Travis, C.B. (1996). Menopause research and the dominance of the biomedical model 1984–1994. *Psychology of Women Quarterly, 20*, 285–312.

Rothblum, E.D. (1988). Lesbianism as a model of a positive lifestyle for women. *Women and Therapy, 8*, 1–12.

Rothblum, E.D. (1990). Depression among lesbians: An invisible and un-researched phenomenon. *Journal of Gay and Lesbian Psychotherapy, 1*(3) 67–87.

Rothblum, E.D. (1994a). 'I'll die for the revolution but don't ask me not to diet': Feminism and the continuing stigmatization of obesity. In P. Fallon, M.A. Katzman & S.C. Wooley (eds), *Feminist perspectives on eating disorders* (pp. 53–76). New York: Guilford Press.

Rothblum, E.D. (1994b). Lesbians and physical appearance. Which model applies? In B. Greene & G.M. Herek (eds), *Lesbian and gay psychology: Theory, research and clinical applications, Vol. 1* (pp. 84–97). Thousand Oaks, CA: Sage.

Rothblum, E.D. (1994c). Transforming lesbian sexuality. *Psychology of Women Quarterly, 18*, 627–641.

Rowland, R. (1992). *Living laboratories: Woman and reproductive technologies.* Sydney: Pan Macmillan.

Roy, A., Gang, P., Cole, K., Rutsky, M., Reese, L., & Weisbord, J.A. (1993). Use of Edinburgh Postnatal Depression Scale in a North American population. *Progress in Neuro-Psychopharmacology and Biological Psychiatry, 17*, 501–504.

Rubinow, D.R., Hoban, M., Grover, G.N., Galloway, D.S., Roy-Byrne, P., Andersen, R., & Merriam, G.R. (1988). Changes in plasma hormones across the menstrual cycle in patients with menstrually related mood disorders and in control subjects. *American Journal of Obstetrics and Gynecology, 158*, 5–11.

Ruble, D.N. (1977). Premenstrual symptoms: A reinterpretation. *Science, 197*, 291–292.

Ruble, D.N., Fleming, A.S., Hackel, L.S., & Stangor, C. (1988). Changes in the marital relationship during the transition to first time motherhood: Effects of violated expectations concerning division of household labor. *Journal of Personality and Social Psychology, 55*, 78–87.

Ruchala, P.L., & Halstead, L. (1994). The postpartum experience of low-risk women: A time of adjustment and change. *Maternal-Child Nursing Journal, 22*, 83–89.

Russo, N.F., Horn, J.D., & Schwartz, R. (1992). US abortion in context: Selected characteristics and motivations of women seeking abortions. *Journal of Social Issues, 48*, 183–202.

Russo, N.F., Horn, J.D., & Tromp, S. (1993). Childspacing intervals and abortion among Blacks and Whites: A brief report. *Women and Health, 20*, 43–51.

Ryan, C., & Bradford, J. (1993). The national lesbian health care survey: An overview. In L.D. Garnets & D.C. Kimmel (eds), *Psychological perspectives on lesbian and gay male experiences* (pp. 541–556). New York: Columbia University Press.

Ryff, C.D. (1989). In the eye of the beholder: Views of psychological well-being among middle-aged and older adults. *Psychology and Aging, 4*, 195–210.

Sai, F.T. (1993). Political and economic factors influencing contraceptive uptake. *British Medical Bulletin, 49*, 200–209.

Saint-Germain, M.A., Bassford, T.L., & Montano, G. (1993). Surveys and focus groups in health research with older Hispanic women. *Qualitative Health Research, 3*, 341–367.

Sampson, E.E. (1988). The debate on individualism: Indigenous psychologies of the individual and their role in personal and social functioning. *American Psychologist, 43*, 15–22.

Sanchez, L. (1994). Material resources, family structure resources, and husbands' housework participation: A cross-national comparison. *Journal of Family Issues, 15*, 379–402.

Sanik, M.M. (1990). Parents' time use: A 1967–1986 comparison. *Lifestyles, 11*, 299–316.

Sarason, S.B. (1981). An asocial psychology and a misdirected clinical psychology. *American Psychologist, 36*, 827–836.

Savin-Williams, R.C. (1989). Gay and lesbian adolescents. *Marriage and Family Review, 14*, 197–216.

Savin-Williams, R.C. (1994). Verbal and physical abuse as stressors in the lives of lesbian, gay male, and bisexual youths: Associations with school problems, running away, substance abuse, prostitution, and suicide. *Journal of Consulting and Clinical Psychology, 62*, 261–269.

Scalise, R.M. (1989). I riti del sangue in alcune culture del sud. [Blood rituals in some cultures of Southern Italy]. *Psichiatria e Psicoterapia Analitica, 8*, 75–78.

Scarr, S., Phillips, D., & McCartney, K. (1989). Working mothers and their families. *American Psychologist, 44*, 1402–1409.

Scharlach, A.E. (1995). Elder care and the changing workforce. In L.R. Murphy, J.J. Hurrell, S.L. Sauter & G.P. Keita (eds), *Job stress interventions* (pp. 295–307). Washington, DC: American Psychological Association.

Schiller, N.G. (1993). The invisible women: Caregiving and the construction of AIDS health services. *Culture, Medicine and Psychiatry, 17*, 487–512.

Schneider, J.A., O'Leary, A., & Jenkins, S.R. (1995). Gender, sexual orientation, and disordered eating. *Psychology and Health, 10*, 113–128.

Schopf, J., & Rust, B. (1994). Follow-up and family study of postpartum psychoses: I. Overview. *European Archives of Psychiatry & Clinical Neuroscience, 244*, 101–111.

Schulz, R., Visintainer, P., & Williamson, G.M. (1990). Psychiatric and physical morbidity effects of caregiving. *Journals of Gerontology, 45*, P181-P191.

Scritchfield, S.A. (1995). The social construction of infertility: From private matter to social concern. In J. Best (ed.), *Images of issues: Typifying contemporary social problems. Social problems and social issues.* (pp. 131–146). New York: Aldine de Gruyter.

Seccombe, K. (1991). Assessing the costs and benefits of children: Gender comparisons among childfree husbands and wives. *Journal of Marriage and the Family, 53*, 191–202.

Seeman, T.E. (1994). Successful aging: Reconceptualizing the aging process from a more positive perspective. In B. Vellas, J.L. Albarede & P.J. Garry (eds), *Facts and research in gerontology 1994: Epidemiology and aging* (pp. 61–73). New York: Springer.

Segal, S.J. (1993). Trends in population and contraception. *Annals of Medicine, 25*, 51–56.

Segest, E. (1994). Some aspects regarding teenage pregnancy in Denmark. *Medicine and Law, 13*, 381–396.

Seid, R.P. (1994). Too 'close to the bone': The historical context for women's obsession with slenderness. In P. Fallon, M.A. Katzman & S.C. Wooley (eds), *Feminist perspectives on eating disorders* (pp. 3–16). New York: Guilford Press.

Severino, S.K., & Yonkers, K.A. (1993). A literature review of psychotic symptoms associated with the premenstruum. *Psychosomatics, 34*, 299–306.

Sharp, C.W., & Freeman, C.P. (1993). The medical complications of anorexia nervosa. *British Journal of Psychiatry, 162*, 452–462.

Sharpe, P.A. (1995). Older women and health services: Moving from ageism toward empowerment. *Women and Health, 22*, 9–23.

Shaw, E., & Burns, A. (1993). Guilt and the working parent. *Australian Journal of Marriage and the Family, 14*, 30–43.

Shelley, J., & Smith, A. (1992). *The use of HRT in Melbourne: Preliminary findings from the Women's Midlife Health Study.* Melbourne: Health Sharing Women Research Forum Series III.

Shelton, B.A. (1990). The distribution of household tasks: Does wife's employment status make a difference? *Journal of Family Issues, 11*, 115–135.

Shepler, L.T. (1991). Values, gender and the abortion question: A feminist perspective. In N.L. Stotland (ed.), *Psychiatric aspects of abortion* (pp. 75–87). Washington, DC: American Psychiatric Press.

Shisslak, C.M., & Crago, M. (1994). Toward a new model for the prevention of eating disorders. In P. Fallon, M.A. Katzman & S.C. Wooley (eds), *Feminist perspectives on eating disorders* (pp. 419–437). New York: Guilford Press.

Shumaker, S.A., & Smith, T.R. (1995). Women and coronary heart disease: A psychological perspective. In A.L. Stanton & S.J. Gallant (eds), *The psychology of women's health: Progress and challenges in research and application* (pp. 25–49). Washington, DC: American Psychological Association.

Siegal, D.L. (1990). Women's reproductive changes: A marker, not a turning point. *Generations, 14*(3), 31–32.

Siever, M.D. (1994). Sexual orientation and gender as factors in socioculturally acquired vulnerability to body dissatisfaction and eating disorders. *Journal of Consulting and Clinical Psychology, 62,* 252–260.

Silverstein, B., Carpman, S., Perlick, D., & Perdue, L. (1990). Nontraditional sex role aspirations, gender identity conflict, and disordered eating among college women. *Sex Roles, 23,* 687–695.

Silverstein, L.B. (1996). Fathering is a feminist issue. *Psychology of Women Quarterly, 20,* 3–37.

Simonsick, E.M. (1993). Relationship between husband's health status and the mental health of older women. *Journal of Aging and Health, 5,* 319–337.

Sinclair, H.Z., Bond, C.M., & Taylor, R.J. (1993). Hormone replacement therapy: a study of women's knowledge and attitudes. *British Journal of General Practice, 43,* 365–370.

Singhi, P.D., Goyal, L., Pershad, D., Singhi, S., & Walia, B.N.S. (1990). Psychosocial problems in families of disabled children. *British Journal of Medical Psychology, 63,* 173–182.

Sinnott, J.D. (1984). Older men, older women: Are their perceived sex roles similar? *Sex Roles, 10,* 847–856.

Skinner, W.F. (1994). The prevalence and demographic predictors of illicit and licit drug use among lesbians and gay men. *American Journal of Public Health, 84,* 1307–1310.

Slade, P. (1994). Predicting the psychological impact of miscarriage. *Journal of Reproductive and Infant Psychology, 12,* 5–16.

Slade, P., Raval, H., Buck, P., & Lieberman, B.E. (1992). A 3-year follow-up of emotional, marital and sexual functioning in couples who were infertile. *Journal of Reproductive and Infant Psychology, 10,* 233–243.

Slater, R. (1995). *The psychology of growing old: Looking forward.* Buckingham, UK: Open University Press.

Slaven, L., & Lee, C. (1994). Psychological effects of exercise among adult women: The impact of menopausal status. *Psychology and Health, 9,* 297–303.

Slaven, L., & Lee, C. (1997). Mood and symptom reporting among middle-aged Australian women: The relationships between menopausal status, hormone replacement therapy and exercise participation. *Heath Psychology, 16,* 203–208.

Slaven, L., & Lee, C. (1998). A cross-sectional survey of menopausal status, symptoms and psychological distress in a community sample of Australian women. *Journal of Health Psychology, 3,* 117–123.

Small, R., Brown, S., Lumley, J., & Astbury, J. (1994). Missing voices: What women say and do about depression after childbirth. *Journal of Reproductive and Infant Psychology, 12,* 89–103.

Smith, E.L., Smith, K.A., & Gilligan, C. (1990). Exercise, fitness, osteoarthritis, and osteoporosis. In C.J. Bouchard, R.J. Shephard, T. Stephens, J.R. Sutton & B.D. McPherson (eds), *Exercise, fitness, and health: A consensus of current knowledge* (pp. 517–528). Champaign, IL: Human Kinetics Publishers.

Smith, G.B. (1993). Homophobia and attitudes toward gay men and lesbians by psychiatric nurses. *Archives of Psychiatric Nursing, 7,* 377–384.

Smith, H. (1991). Caring for everyone? The implications for women of the changes in community care services. *Feminism and Psychology, 1,* 279–292.

Snyder, B., & Keefe, K. (1985). The unmet needs of family caregivers for frail and disabled adults. *Social Work in Health Care, 10*(3) 1–14.

Sobol, M., & Daly, K. (1992). The adoption alternative for pregnant adolescents: Decision-making, consequences, and policy implications. *Journal of Social Issues, 48,* 143–161.

Social Trends (1995). *Social Trends on CD-ROM – Version 1.0.* London: Central Statistical Office of the UK.

Solomon, S.E. (1993). Women and physical distinction: A review of the literature and suggestions for intervention. *Women and Therapy, 14,* 91–103.

Somers, M.D. (1993). A comparison of voluntarily childfree adults and parents. *Journal of Marriage and the Family, 55,* 643–650.

Sommer, B. (1992). Cognitive performance and the menstrual cycle. In J.T.E. Richardson (ed.), *Cognition and the menstrual cycle* (pp. 39–66). New York: Springer.

Sommers, T., & Shields, L. (1987). *Women take care: The consequences of caregiving in today's society.* Gainesville, FL: Triad.

Sourander, L.B. (1994). Geriatric aspects of estrogen effects and sexuality. *Gerontology, 40* (Suppl. 3), 14–17.

South, S.J., & Spitze, G. (1994). Housework in marital and nonmarital households. *American Sociological Review, 59,* 327–347.

Spangenberg, J.J., & Pieters, H.C. (1991). Factors related to postpartum depression. *South African Journal of Psychology, 21,* 159–165.

Speare, A., & Avery, R. (1993). Who helps whom in older parent-child families. *Journals of Gerontology, 48,* S64-S73.

Speckhard, A., & Rue, V. (1993). Complicated mourning: Dynamics of impacted post abortion grief. *Pre- and Peri-Natal Psychology Journal, 8,* 5–32.

Spence, J.T. (1985). Achievement American style. *American Psychologist, 40,* 1275–1295.

Srebnik, D.S., & Saltzberg, E.A. (1994). Feminist cognitive-behavioral therapy for negative body image. *Women and Therapy, 15,* 117–133.

Stake, J.E., & Lauer, M.L. (1987). The consequences of being overweight: A controlled study of gender differences. *Sex Roles, 17,* 31–47.

Stanford, J.L., Weiss, N.S., Voigt, L.F., Daling, J.R., Habel, L.A., & Rossing, M.A. (1995). Combined estrogen and progestin hormone replacement therapy in relation to risk of breast cancer in middle-aged women. *Journal of the American Medical Association, 274,* 178–179.

Stanton, A.L. (1995). Psychology of women's health: Barriers and pathways to knowledge. In A.L. Stanton & S.J. Gallant (eds), *The psychology of women's health: Progress and challenges in research and application* (pp. 3–21). Washington, DC: American Psychological Association.

Stanton, A.L., & Danoff-Burg, S. (1995). Selected issues in women's reproductive health: Psychological perspectives. In A.L. Stanton & S.J. Gallant (eds), *The psychology of women's health: Progress and challenges in research and application* (pp. 261–305). Washington, DC: American Psychological Association.

Stanton, A.L., & Gallant, S.J. (1995a). Psychology of women's health: Challenges for the future. In A.L. Stanton & S.J. Gallant (eds), *The psychology of women's health: Progress and challenges in research and application* (pp. 567–582). Washington, DC: American Psychological Association.

Stanton, A.L., & Gallant, S.J. (eds). (1995b). *The psychology of women's health: Progress and challenges in research and application.* Washington, DC: American Psychological Association.

Stanton, A.L., Tennen, H., Affleck, G., & Mendola, R. (1992). Coping and adjustment to infertility. *Journal of Social and Clinical Psychology, 11,* 1–13.

Steege, J.F., & Blumenthal, J.A. (1993). The effects of aerobic exercise on premenstrual symptoms in middle-aged women. *Journal of Psychosomatic Research, 37,* 127–133.

Steiner-Adair, C. (1994). The politics of prevention. In P. Fallon, M.A. Katzman & S.C. Wooley (eds), *Feminist perspectives on eating disorders* (pp. 381–394). New York: Guilford Press.

Steinhausen, H.C., Rauss-Mason, C., & Seidel, R. (1991). Follow-up studies of anorexia nervosa: A review of four decades of outcome research. *Psychological Medicine, 21,* 447–454.

Stevens, P.E. (1992). Lesbian health care research: A review of the literature from 1970 to 1990. *Health Care for Women International, 13,* 91–120.

Stevens, P.E. (1994). Lesbians' health-related experiences of care and noncare. *Western Journal of Nursing Research, 16,* 639–659.

Stevens, P.E. (1995). Structural and interpersonal impact of heterosexual assumptions on lesbian health care clients. *Nursing Research, 44,* 25–30.

Stevens, P.E., & Hall, J.M. (1990). Abusive health care interactions experienced by lesbians: A case of institutional violence in the treatment of women. *Response to the Victimization of Women and Children, 13*(3), 23–27.

Stevens, P.E., & Hall, J.M. (1991). A critical historical analysis of the medical construction of lesbianism. *International Journal of Health Services, 21,* 291–307.

Stevenson, J.C. (1990). Pathogenesis, prevention and treatment of osteoporosis. *Obstetrics and Gynecology, 75,* S36-S41.

Stewart, D. E. (1989). Positive changes in the premenstrual period. *Acta Psychiatrica Scandinavica, 79,* 400–405.

Stice, E. (1994). Review of the evidence for a sociocultural model of bulimia nervosa and an exploration of the mechanisms of action. *Clinical Psychology Review, 14,* 633–661.

Stice, E., Schupak-Neuberg, E., Shaw, H.E., & Stein, R.I. (1994). Relation of media exposure to eating disorder symptomatology: An examination of mediating mechanisms. *Journal of Abnormal Psychology, 103,* 836–840.

Stifter, C.A., Coulehan, C.M., & Fish, M. (1993). Linking employment to attachment: The mediating effects of maternal separation anxiety and interactive behavior. *Child Development, 64,* 1451–1460.

Stommel, M., Collins, C.E., & Given, B.A. (1994). The costs of family contributions to the care of persons with dementia. *Gerontologist, 34,* 199–205.

Stone, R., Cafferata, G., & Sangl, J. (1987). Caregivers of the frail elderly: A national profile. *Gerontologist, 27,* 616–626.

Stone, R., & Kemper, P. (1989). Spouses and children of disabled elders: How large a constituency for long-term care reform. *Milbank Memorial Quarterly, 67,* 485–506.

Stotland, N.L. (1991). Psychiatric issues in abortion, and the implications of recent legal changes for psychiatric practice. In N.L. Stotland (ed.), *Psychiatric aspects of abortion* (pp. 1–16). Washington, DC: American Psychiatric Press.

Strassman, B.I. (1992). The function of menstrual taboos among the Dogon: Defense against cuckoldry? *Human Nature, 3,* 89–131.

Strawbridge, W.J., & Wallhagen, M.I. (1991). Impact of family conflict on adult child caregivers. *Gerontologist, 31,* 770–777.

Strawbridge, W.J., & Wallhagen, M.I. (1992). Is all in the family always best? *Journal of Aging Studies, 6,* 81–92.

Strickland, B.R. (1988). Menopause. In E.A. Blechman & K.D. Brownell (eds), *Handbook of behavioral medicine for women* (pp. 41–47). New York: Pergamon.

Strickler, R.C., Borth, R., & Cecutti, A. (1977). The role of oestrogen replacement in the climacteric syndrome. *Psychological Medicine, 7,* 531–539.

Striegel-Moore, R. (1994). A feminist agenda for psychological research on eating disorders. In P. Fallon, M.A. Katzman & S.C. Wooley (eds), *Feminist perspectives on eating disorders* (pp. 438–454). New York: Guilford Press.

Striegel-Moore, R., Silberstein, L.R., & Rodin, J. (1986). Toward an understanding of risk factors for bulimia. *American Psychologist, 41,* 246–263.

Striegel-Moore, R., & Smolak, L. (1996). The role of race in the development of eating disorders. In L. Smolak, M.P. Levine & R. Striegel-Moore (eds), *The developmental psychopathology of eating disorders: Implications for research, prevention, and treatment* (pp. 259–284). Mahwah, NJ: Lawrence Erlbaum.

Stroebe, M.S. (1994). The broken heart phenomenon: An examination of the mortality of bereavement. *Journal of Community and Applied Social Psychology, 4,* 47–61.

Stroebe, M.S., van den Bout, J., & Schut, H. (1994). Myths and misconceptions about bereavement: The opening of a debate. *Omega Journal of Death and Dying, 29,* 187–203.

Szmukler, G.I., Dare, C., & Treasure, J. (1995). *Handbook of eating disorders: Theory, treatment and research.* Chichester, UK: Wiley.

Tang, G.W.K. (1994). The climacteric of Chinese factory workers. *Maturitas, 19,* 177–182.

Tapia Uribe, F.M., LeVine, R.A., & LeVine, S.E. (1993). Maternal education and maternal behaviour in Mexico: Implications for the changing characteristics of Mexican immigrants to the United States. *International Journal of Behavioral Development, 16,* 395–408.

Tasker, F., & Golombok, S. (1995). Adults raised as children in lesbian families. *American Journal of Orthopsychiatry, 65,* 203–215.

Tavecchio, L.W., van Ijzendoorn, M.H., Goossens, F.A., & Vergeer, M.M. (1984). The division of labor in Dutch families with preschool children. *Journal of Marriage and the Family, 46,* 231–242.

Taylor, R., Ford, G., & Dunbar, M. (1995). The effects of caring on health: A community-based longitudinal study. *Social Science and Medicine, 40,* 1407–1415.

Terefe, A., & Larson, C.P. (1993). Modern contraception use in Ethiopia: Does involving husbands make a difference? *American Journal of Public Health, 83,* 1567–1571.

Terry, D.J., McHugh, T.A., & Noller, P. (1991). Role dissatisfaction and the decline in marital quality across the transition to parenthood. *Australian Journal of Psychology, 43,* 129–132.

Thelen, M.H., Powell, A.L., Lawrence, C., & Kuhnert, M.E. (1992). Eating and body image concerns among children. *Journal of Clinical Child Psychology, 21,* 41–46.

Thompson, B.W. (1992). 'A way outa no way': Eating problems among African-American, Latina, and White women. *Gender and Society, 6,* 546–561.

Thompson, B.W. (1994). Food, bodies and growing up female: Childhood lessons about culture, race and class. In P. Fallon, M.A. Katzman & S.C. Wooley (eds), *Feminist perspectives on eating disorders* (pp. 355–378). New York: Guilford Press.

Thompson, D. (1992). Against the dividing of women: Lesbian feminism and heterosexuality. *Feminism and Psychology, 2,* 387–398.

Thompson, L.W., Gallagher-Thompson, D., Futterman, A., Gilewski, M.J., & Peterson, J. (1991). The effects of late-life spousal bereavement over a 30-month interval. *Psychology and Aging, 6,* 434–441.

Thomson, J., & Oswald, I. (1977). Effect of oestrogen on the sleep, mood and anxiety of menopausal women. *British Medical Journal, 2,* 1317–1319.

Thornton, B., Leo, R., & Alberg, K. (1991). Gender role typing, the superwoman ideal, and the potential for eating disorders. *Sex Roles, 25,* 469–484.

Tietze, C., & Henshaw, S.K. (1986). *Induced abortion: A world review, Volume 6.* New York: Alan Guttmacher Institute.

Tiggemann, M., & Rothblum, E.D. (1988). Gender differences in social consequences of perceived overweight in the United States and Australia. *Sex Roles, 18,* 75–86.

Tiggemann, M., Winefield, H.R., Winefield, A.H., & Goldney, R.D. (1994). Gender differences in the psychological correlates of body-weight in young adults. *Psychology and Health, 9,* 345–351.

Timpson, J. (1996). Abortion: The antithesis of womanhood? *Journal of Advanced Nursing, 23,* 776–785.

Tizard, B. (1991). Employed mothers and the care of young children. In A. Phoenix, A. Woollett & E. Lloyd (eds), *Motherhood: Meanings, practices and ideologies* (pp. 178–194). London: Sage.

Tokyo Metropolitan Government (1995). *Living conditions of the elderly.* Tokyo: Author.

Tomlinson, P.S., & Irvin, B. (1993). Qualitative study of women's reports of family adaptation pattern four years following transition to parenthood. *Issues in Mental Health Nursing, 14,* 119–138.

Topo, P., Klaukka, T., Hemminki, E., & Uutela, A. (1991). The use of HRT in 1976–89 by 45–64 year old Finnish women. *Journal of Epidemiology and Community Health, 45,* 277–280.

Toseland, R.W., Labrecque, M.S., Goebel, S.T., & Whitney, M.H. (1992). An evaluation of a group program for spouses of frail elderly veterans. *Gerontologist, 32,* 382–390.

Traustadottir, R. (1991). Mothers who care: Gender, disability and family life. *Journal of Family Issues, 12,* 211–218.

Treneman, A. (1988). Cashing in on the curse. In L. Gamman & M. Marshment (eds), *The female gaze: Women as viewers of popular culture* (pp. 153–165). London: Women's Press.

Trippet, S.E. (1994). Lesbians' mental health concerns. *Health Care for Women International, 15,* 317–323.

Trippet, S.E., & Bain, J. (1990). Preliminary study of lesbian health concerns. *Health Values: Health Behavior, Education and Promotion, 14*(6), 30–36.

Trippet, S.E., & Bain, J. (1992). Reasons American lesbians fail to seek traditional health care. *Health Care for Women International, 13,* 145–153.

Truett, K.R. (1993). Age differences in conservatism. *Personality and Individual Differences, 14,* 405–411.

Tucker, P., & Aron, A. (1993). Passionate love and marital satisfaction at key transition points in the family life cycle. *Journal of Social and Clinical Psychology, 12,* 135–147.

Udoff, L., Langenberg, P., & Adashi, E.Y. (1995). Combined continuous hormone replacement therapy: A critical review. *Obstetrics and Gynecology, 86,* 306–316.

Ulbrich, P.M., Coyle, A.T., & Llabre, M.M. (1990). Involuntary childlessness and marital adjustment: His and hers. *Journal of Sex and Marital Therapy, 16,* 147–158.

Ullrich, H.E. (1992). Menstrual taboos among Havik Brahmin women: A study of ritual change. *Sex Roles, 26,* 19–40.

Ulvik, O.S. (1993). Parenthood by choice. New conditions: New decision making processes. *Tidsskrift for Norsk Psykologforening, 30,* 1069–1080.

Umberson, D., Wortman, C.B., & Kessler, R.C. (1992). Widowhood and depression: Explaining long-term gender differences in vulnerability. *Journal of Health and Social Behavior, 33,* 10–24.

US Bureau of the Census (1987). *Fertility of American women: June 1986.* Current Population Reports, Series P–20, No. 421. Washington, DC: US Government Printing Office.

US Bureau of the Census (1991). *Statistical abstracts of the United States: I* (111th edn). Washington, DC: US Government Printing Office.

US Bureau of the Census (1992a). *Households, families and children: A 30-year perspective.* Current Population Reports, Series P–23, No. 181. Washington, DC: US Government Printing Office.

US Bureau of the Census (1992b). *Sixty-five plus in America.* Current Population Reports, Series P–23, No.178RV. Washington, DC: US Government Printing Office.

US Bureau of the Census (1993). *Primary child care arrangements used by employed mothers for children under 5 years, 1977 to 1991.* Current Population Reports, Series P–23, No. 610. US Government Printing Office.

US Bureau of Labor Statistics (1991). *Employment and earnings, January 1991, 38*(1). Washington, DC: US Government Printing Office.

US National Institutes of Health (1992). *Opportunities for research on women's health.* (NIH pub. No. 92–3457). Washington, DC: US Department of Health and Human Services.

Ussher, J.M. (1992a). The demise of dissent and the rise of cognition in menstrual-cycle research. In J.T.E. Richardson (ed.), *Cognition and the menstrual cycle* (pp. 132–173). New York: Springer.

Ussher, J.M. (1992b). Reproductive rhetoric and the blaming of the body. In P. Nicolson & J. Ussher (eds), *The psychology of women's health and health care* (pp. 31–61). Basingstoke, UK: Macmillan.

Ussher, J.M. (1992c). Research and theory related to female reproduction: Implications for clinical psychology. *British Journal of Clinical Psychology, 31,* 129–151.

Ussher, J.M., & Wilding, J.M. (1992). Interactions between stress and performance during the menstrual cycle in relation to the premenstrual syndrome. *Journal of Reproductive and Infant Psychology, 10,* 83–101.

Valentine, D.P. (1986). Psychological impact of infertility: Identifying issues and needs. *Social Work in Health Care, 11*(4), 61–69.

Van den Akker, O.B.A., Eves, F.F., Service, S., & Lennon, B. (1995). Menstrual cycle symptom reporting in three British ethnic groups. *Social Science and Medicine, 40,* 1417–1423.

Van der Ploeg, H., & Lodder, E. (1993). Longitudinal measurement in the diagnostics of the premenstrual syndrome. *Journal of Psychosomatic Research, 37,* 33–38.

van Every, J. (1995). *Heterosexual women changing the family: Refusing to be a 'wife!'.* London: Taylor & Francis.

Vanselow, W., Dennerstein, L., Greenwood, K.M., & de Lignieres, B. (1996). Effect of progesterone and its 5-alpha and 5-beta metabolites on symptoms of premenstrual syndrome according to route of administration. *Journal of Psychosomatic Obstetrics and Gynecology, 17,* 29–38.

Vartiainen, H.T. (1992). Effects of psychosocial factors, especially work-related stress on female fertility and pregnancy. *Psychiatria Fennica, 23,* 103–121.

Veevers, J.E. (1980). *Childless by choice.* Toronto: Butterworth.

Victor, S.B., & Fish, M.C. (1995). Lesbian mothers and their children: A review for school psychologists. *School Psychology Review, 24,* 456–479.

Wagner, D.L., & Neal, M.B. (1994). Caregiving and work: Consequences, correlates, and workplace responses. *Educational Gerontology, 20,* 645–663.

Waldeck, R. (1988). Der rote Fleck im dunklen Kontinent: I. Das Tabu der Menstruation. [The red spot in the dark continent: I. The taboo of menstruation]. *Zeitschrift für Sexualforschung, 1,* 189–205.

Waldron, I., & Jacobs, J.A. (1989). Effects of multiple roles on women's health: Evidence from a national longitudinal study. *Women and Health, 15,* 3–19.

Walker, A. (1992). Conceptual perspectives on gender and family caregiving. In J. Dwyer & R. Coward (eds), *Gender, families and elder care* (pp. 34–49). Newbury Park, CA: Sage.

Walker, A. (1994). Mood and well-being in consecutive menstrual cycles: Methodological and theoretical implications. *Psychology of Women Quarterly, 18,* 271–290.

Wasser, S.K. (1990). Infertility, abortion, and biotechnology: When it's not nice to fool Mother Nature. *Human Nature, 1,* 3–24.

Wasser, S.K. (1994). Psychosocial stress and infertility – cause or effect? *Human Nature, 5,* 293–306.

Watkins, P.C., Williamson, D.A., & Falkowski, C. (1989). Prospective assessment of late-luteal phase dysphoric disorder. *Journal of Psychopathology and Behavioral Assessment, 11,* 249–259.

Wearing, B. (1984). *The ideology of motherhood.* Sydney: Allen & Unwin.

Webster, M.L., Thompson, J.M.D., Mitchell, E.A., & Werry, J.S. (1994). Postnatal depression in a community cohort. *Australian and New Zealand Journal of Psychiatry, 28*, 42–49.

Weinreib, W.L., & Murphy, B.C. (1988). The birth mother: A feminist perspective for the helping professional. *Women and Therapy, 7*, 23–36.

Welch, M.R., Leege, D.C., & Cavendish, J.C. (1995). Attitudes toward abortion among US Catholics: Another case of symbolic politics? *Social Science Quarterly, 76*, 142–157.

Wells, N., & Freer, C. (1988). Introduction. In N. Wells & C. Freer (eds), *The ageing population: Burden or challenge?* (pp. xiii–xviii). Basingstoke, UK: Macmillan.

Wenger, G.C. (1994). Dementia sufferers living at home. *International Journal of Geriatric Psychiatry, 9*, 721–733.

Wenger, N.K., Speroff, L., & Packard, B. (1993). Cardiovascular health and disease in women. *New England Journal of Medicine, 329*, 247–256.

Westhoff, C., & Rosenfield, A. (1993). The impact of family planning on women's health. *Current Opinion in Obstetrics and Gynaecology, 5*, 793–797.

Wetle, T. (1991). Successful aging: New hope for optimizing mental and physical well-being. *Journal of Geriatric Psychiatry, 24*, 3–12.

Whiffen, V.E. (1991). The comparison of postpartum with non-postpartum depression: A rose by any other name. *Journal of Psychiatry and Neuroscience, 16*, 160–165.

Whiffen, V.E. (1992). Is postpartum depression a distinct diagnosis? *Clinical Psychology Review, 12*, 485–508.

Whiffen, V.E., & Gotlib, I. H. (1993). Comparison of postpartum and non-postpartum depression: Clinical presentation, psychiatric history, and psycho-social functioning. *Journal of Consulting and Clinical Psychology, 61*, 485–494.

Whiteford, L.M., & Gonzalez, L. (1995). Stigma: The hidden burden of infertility. *Social Science and Medicine, 40*, 27–36.

Whitehead, M.I., Campbell, S., Dyer, G., Collins, W.P., Pryse-Davies, J., Ryder, T.A., Rodney, M.I., McQueen, J., & King, R. (1978). Progestogen modification of endometrial histology in menopausal women. *British Medical Journal, 2* (6152), 1643–1644.

White-Means, S.I. (1993). Informal home care for frail Black elderly. *Journal of Applied Gerontology, 12*, 18–33.

Wilbur, J., Dan, A., Hedricks, C., & Holm, K. (1990). The relationship among menopausal status, menopausal symptoms, and physical activity in midlife women. *Family and Community Health, 13*(3), 67–78.

Wiley, M.G. (1991). Gender, work, and stress: The potential impact of role-identity salience and commitment. *Sociological Quarterly, 32*, 495–510.

Wilkinson, S., & Kitzinger, C. (1994). Towards a feminist approach to breast cancer. In S. Wilkinson & C. Kitzinger (eds), *Women and health: Feminist perspectives* (pp. 124–140). London: Taylor & Francis.

Willén, H. (1994). How do couples decide about having their first child? An explorative study. *Göteborg Psychological Reports, 24*(1), 1–40.

Willén, H., & Montgomery, H. (1993). The impact of wish for children and having children on attainment and importance of life values. *Göteborg Psychological Reports, 23*(3), 1–18.

Williams, R., Ming, F., & Vyse, D. (1992). Prevalence of HRT in Perth perimeno-pausal women. Unpublished manuscript, University of Western Australia, Department of Public Health, Perth.

Willis, E. (1984). Abortion: Is the woman a person? In A. Snitow, S. Stansel & S. Thompson (eds), *Powers of desire: The politics of sexuality* (pp. 471–476). London: Virago.

Wilmoth, G.H., deAlteriis, M., & Bussell, D. (1992). Prevalence of psychological risks following legal abortion in the US: Limits of the evidence. *Journal of Social Issues, 48*, 37–66.

Wilson, G.T. (1996). Acceptance and change in the treatment of eating disorders and obesity. *Behavior Therapy, 27*, 417–439.

Wilson, R.A. (1966). *Feminine forever*. Philadelphia: Lippincott.

Wine, J.D. (1985). Women's sexuality. *International Journal of Women's Studies, 8*, 58–63.

Wister, A.V. (1985). Living arrangement choices among the elderly. *Canadian Journal on Aging, 4*, 127–144.

Wolf, N. (1994). Hunger. In P. Fallon, M.A. Katzman & S.C. Wooley (eds), *Feminist perspectives on eating disorders* (pp. 94–111). New York: Guilford Press.

Wolinsky, F.D., & Johnson, R.J. (1992). Widowhood, health status, and the use of health services by older adults: A cross-sectional and prospective approach. *Journals of Gerontology, 47*, S8-S16.

Woo, J., Ho, S.C., Lau, J., Yuen, Y.K., Chiu, H., Lee, C.H., & Chi, I. (1994). The prevalence of depressive symptoms and predisposing factors in an elderly Chinese population. *Acta Psychiatrica Scandinavica, 89*, 8–13.

Wood, K.C., Becker, J.A., & Thompson, J.K. (1996). Body image dissatisfaction in preadolescent children. *Journal of Applied Developmental Psychology, 17*, 85–100.

Wooley, O.W. (1994). . . . And man created 'woman': Representations of women's bodies in Western culture. In P. Fallon, M.A. Katzman & S.C. Wooley (eds), *Feminist perspectives on eating disorders* (pp. 17–52). New York: Guilford Press.

Woollett, A., Dosanjh-Matwala, N., & Hadlow, J. (1991). Reproductive decision making: Asian women's ideas about family size, and the gender and spacing of children. *Journal of Reproductive and Infant Psychology, 9*, 237–252.

World Health Organization (1981). *Research on the menopause*. Geneva: Author.

Wright, K. (1988). The elderly today. I: An economic audit. In N. Wells & C. Freer (eds), *The ageing population: Burden or challenge?* (pp. 33–51). Basingstoke, UK: Macmillan.

Writing Group for the PEPI Trial (1995). Effects of estrogen or estrogen/progestin regimens on heart disease risk factors in postmenopausal women. The Post-menopausal Estrogen/Progestin Interventions (PEPI) Trial. *Journal of the American Medical Association, 273*, 240–241.

Wyche, K.F. (1993). Psychology and African-American women: Findings from applied research. *Applied and Preventive Psychology, 2*, 115–121.

Young, R.F., & Kahana, E. (1993). Gender, recovery from late life heart attack, and medical care. *Women and Health, 20*, 11–31.

Youngblut, J.M., Loveland-Cherry, C.J., & Horan, M. (1991). Maternal employ-ment effects on family and preterm infants at three months. *Nursing Research, 40*, 272–275.

Youngblut, J.M., Loveland-Cherry, C.J., & Horan, M. (1994). Maternal employment effects on families and preterm infants at 18 months. *Nursing Research, 43,* 331–337.

Yu, L.C., Yu, Y., & Mansfield, P.K. (1990). Gender and changes in support of parents in China: Implications for the one-child policy. *Gender and Society, 4,* 83–89.

Zabin, L.S., Astone, N.M., & Emerson, M.R. (1993). Do adolescents want babies? The relationship between attitudes and behavior. *Journal of Research on Adolescence, 3,* 67–86.

Zelkowitz, P., & Milet, T.H. (1995). Postpartum psychiatric disorders: Their relationship to psychological adjustment and marital satisfaction in the spouses. *Journal of Abnormal Psychology, 105,* 281–285.

Zellner, D.A., Harner, D.E., & Adler, R.L. (1989). Effects of eating abnormalities and gender on perceptions of desirable body shape. *Journal of Abnormal Psychology, 98,* 93–96.

Zerbe, K.J., Marsh, S.R., & Coyne, L. (1993). Comorbidity in an inpatient eating disordered population: Clinical characteristics and treatment implications. *Psychiatric Hospital, 24*(1), 3–8.

Zick, C.D., & McCullough, J.L. (1991). Trends in married couples' time use: Evidence from 1977–78 and 1987–88. *Sex Roles, 24,* 459–487.

Ziel, H.K., & Finkle, W.D. (1975). Increased risk of endometrial carcinoma among users of conjugated estrogens. *New England Journal of Medicine, 293,* 1167–1170.

Zipp, A., & Holcomb, C.A. (1992). Living arrangements and nutrient intakes of healthy women aged 65 and older: A study in Manhattan, Kansas. *Journal of Nutrition for the Elderly, 11,* 1–18.

Zisook, S., & Shuchter, S.R. (1991). Early psychological reaction to the stress of widowhood. *Psychiatry, 54,* 320–333.

Zisook, S., & Shuchter, S.R. (1993). Major depression associated with widowhood. *American Journal of Geriatric Psychiatry, 1,* 316–326.

Zisook, S., Shuchter, S.R., Irwin, M., Darko, D.F., Sledge, P., & Resovsky, K. (1994). Bereavement, depression, and immune function. *Psychiatry Research, 52,* 1–10.

Zisook, S., Shuchter, S.R., & Mulvihill, M. (1990). Alcohol, cigarette, and medication use during the first year of widowhood. *Psychiatric Annals, 20,* 318–326.

Zisook, S., Shuchter, S.R., Sledge, P., & Mulvihill, M. (1993). Aging and bereavement. *Journal of Geriatric Psychiatry and Neurology, 6,* 137–143.

Ziv, B., Russ, M.J., Moline, M., Hurt, S., & Zendell, S. (1995). Menstrual cycle influences on mood and behavior in women with borderline personality disorder. *Journal of Personality Disorders, 9,* 68–75.

Zolese, G., & Blacker, C.V. (1992). The psychological complications of therapeutic abortion. *British Journal of Psychiatry, 160,* 742–749.

INDEX